The World of the Roosevelts

Series Editor
David B. Woolner
The Roosevelt Institute
New York City, USA

This longstanding series has published high-quality monographs and edited collections related to the presidencies of Franklin Roosevelt for nearly two decades. Combining economic, political, diplomatic, social, and intellectual history, it constitutes a comprehensive, multi-faceted exploration of a pivotal era in American and global history.

More information about this series at
http://www.palgrave.com/gp/series/14319

Michael Patrick Cullinane

Remembering Theodore Roosevelt

Reminiscences of his Contemporaries

Michael Patrick Cullinane
Department of Humanities
University of Roehampton
London, UK

The World of the Roosevelts
ISBN 978-3-030-69295-7   ISBN 978-3-030-69296-4   (eBook)
https://doi.org/10.1007/978-3-030-69296-4

© The Editor(s) (if applicable) and The Author(s), under exclusive licence to Springer Nature Switzerland AG 2021
This work is subject to copyright. All rights are solely and exclusively licensed by the Publisher, whether the whole or part of the material is concerned, specifically the rights of translation, reprinting, reuse of illustrations, recitation, broadcasting, reproduction on microfilms or in any other physical way, and transmission or information storage and retrieval, electronic adaptation, computer software, or by similar or dissimilar methodology now known or hereafter developed.
The use of general descriptive names, registered names, trademarks, service marks, etc. in this publication does not imply, even in the absence of a specific statement, that such names are exempt from the relevant protective laws and regulations and therefore free for general use.
The publisher, the authors and the editors are safe to assume that the advice and information in this book are believed to be true and accurate at the date of publication. Neither the publisher nor the authors or the editors give a warranty, expressed or implied, with respect to the material contained herein or for any errors or omissions that may have been made. The publisher remains neutral with regard to jurisdictional claims in published maps and institutional affiliations.

Cover illustration: Theodore Roosevelt, sitting on a large stone, at Glacier Point in California. Glacier Point California, ca. 1904. Photograph. Library of Congress, https://www.loc.gov/item/2013650922/

This Palgrave Macmillan imprint is published by the registered company Springer Nature Switzerland AG.
The registered company address is: Gewerbestrasse 11, 6330 Cham, Switzerland

Praise for *Remembering Theodore Roosevelt*

"Thought-provoking, engrossing, and entertaining, this book enriches our understanding of Theodore Roosevelt through first-hand accounts from people—the famous and the forgotten—who knew him. The interviewees' recollections, ably enhanced by Cullinane's useful historical context, provide a deeper, more nuanced picture of the politician and the private man."
—Stacy A. Cordery, *author of Alice Roosevelt Longworth, from White House Princess to Washington Power Broker*

"Fascinated by Theodore, Franklin, or Eleanor Roosevelt? Here is an edition of rare interviews full of news and insights unavailable elsewhere. Highly recommended for fans and scholars alike."
—Kathleen Dalton, *author of Theodore Roosevelt: A Strenuous Life*

"Roosevelt scholars owe Cullinane a debt of gratitude for tracking down the tapes and digitizing them, creating what seemed impossible: a brand new and valuable source to enrich our understanding of Theodore Roosevelt."
—Edward P. Kohn, *author of Heir to the Empire City: New York and the Making of Theodore Roosevelt*

Contents

1	Introduction	1
Part I	Family	23
2	The Other Washington Monument: Alice Roosevelt Longworth	25
3	From Hyde Park to Oyster Bay: Helen Roosevelt Robinson	59
4	The Next Generation: William and Margaret Cowles and Corinne Alsop Cole	75
5	First Lady of the World: Anna Eleanor Roosevelt	123
6	The Scions of Sagamore Hill: Ethel Roosevelt Derby and Eleanor Butler Roosevelt	133

Part II	Neighbors	141
7	A Grande Dame: Georgiana Farr Sibley	143
8	The Worst Friend of the Worst Boy: Barclay H. Farr	155
Part III	Political Disciples	171
9	The Political Backroom: William M. Chadbourne	173
10	That Tammany Boy: Henry Root Stern, Sr.	193
11	Secondhand Memories: Murray T. Quigg	203
12	The Account of a College Man: Karl H. Behr	211
13	When Trumpets Call: Stanley M. Isaacs	225
Part IV	Brothers in Arms	237
14	Roosevelt's Enduring Legacy: Frederick Trubee Davison	239
15	The Last Rough Rider: Jesse Langdon	245
Notes		271
Works Consulted		281
Acknowledgments		285
Index		287

List of Figures

Fig. 2.1	Alice Roosevelt Longworth christening USS Theodore Roosevelt submarine (1959), U.S. Navy	25
Fig. 3.1	Helen Roosevelt Robinson at Campobello (1925), FDR Library	59
Fig. 4.1	Photo portrait of Anna Roosevelt Cowles (date unknown), TR Center, Dickinson State University	75
Fig. 5.1	Eleanor Roosevelt at Val Kill (1947), National Archives and Records Administration	123
Fig. 6.1	Photo portraits of Ethel Roosevelt Derby (1908) and Eleanor Butler Roosevelt (1905), National Park Service and Library of Congress	133
Fig. 7.1	Photo portrait of Georgiana Farr Sibley (1908), Library of Congress	143
Fig. 8.1	Kermit Roosevelt with dog Jack (1902), Library of Congress	155
Fig. 9.1	Photo portrait of William M. Chadbourne (1918), *Leaders of the Twentieth Century*	173
Fig. 10.1	Photo portrait of Captain Henry Root Stern (1918), Library of Congress	193
Fig. 11.1	Photo of Lemuel E. Quigg testifying before the Thompson Committee (1916), Library of Congress	203
Fig. 12.1	Photo of Karl Behr at tennis court (1915), Library of Congress	211
Fig. 13.1	Photo portrait of Stanley M. Isaacs (1922). Edith S. Isaacs, *Love Affair with a City*	225
Fig. 14.1	Photo of Frederick Trubee Davison at Bolling Air Field (1926), Library of Congress	239
Fig. 15.1	Photo of Colonel Roosevelt and the Rough Riders atop San Juan Hill (1898), Library of Congress	245

CHAPTER 1

Introduction

Theodore Roosevelt needs no introduction. The former U.S. president ranks as one of the most recognizable icons in American history. Biographies have scoured every aspect of his life; monuments like Mount Rushmore immortalize him in stone; and popular culture pays tribute in countless ways, from films and fiction to parodies and performance art.

Roosevelt's enduring legacy owes much to one man: Hermann Hagedorn, the long-serving director of the Theodore Roosevelt Memorial Association. For more than four decades, Hagedorn led campaigns to erect monuments, establish foundations, and promote scholarship—anything to keep the former president relevant to successive generations. He also gathered Rooseveltiana for the same purpose, collecting election ephemera, photographs, motion pictures, books, periodicals, newspaper clippings, artwork, and artifacts. Nothing escaped his purview, and the collection he acquired swelled to such an extent that it required a full-time archivist. Even as costs to maintain the collection became prohibitive, Hagedorn continued to accumulate.[1]

It struck me as significant that Hagedorn's first impulse was to collect oral histories. When Roosevelt died in 1919, he scrambled to record the former president's contemporaries. Initially, he intended to write a biography and, as any investigative journalist would, Hagedorn recognized the value of oral history for his research. He equally understood its power for future interpretations of Roosevelt. As sociologist Paul Thompson writes, oral histories, "can be used to change the focus of history itself, and open up new areas of inquiry," and it gives voice to "the people who made and experienced history through their own words."[2] For Hagedorn, no other form of Rooseveltiana compared. Only the memories of Roosevelt's friends and family could preserve his legacy.

Hagedorn never had singular plans. His interest in recording Roosevelt's contemporaries had greater utility than source material for his biography and when he contacted Roosevelt's friends and family, he related a second motive. He wished to make a motion picture about Roosevelt's beloved home, Sagamore Hill at Oyster Bay, Long Island. Hagedorn planned to cast Roosevelt's friends and family as reprisers. The footage he collected would preserve their stories as well as the visual landscape of Roosevelt's life. The idea was ahead of its time. Video testimony would afford vivid portrayals of Roosevelt, his associates, and their surroundings, but when Hagedorn approached participants, he found many unwilling to partake.[3] Friends and family guarded Roosevelt's legacy, especially in the period immediately after his passing. They worried that opportunistic sorts might contrive an unflattering portrait. Former First Lady Edith Roosevelt kept thousands of documents from prying eyes. She rarely gave interviews and Long Island neighbors and friends took their lead from her. They refused to record statements with Hagedorn. Perhaps as daunting to the participants was the novel and unfamiliar motion picture technology.

Still, Hagedorn refused to abandon the project. Luckily for posterity, he found willing participants in the North Dakota Badlands. These included friends of Roosevelt who met the young New Yorker when he ranched out West in the 1880s. Hagedorn scrapped plans for a sweeping biography and film about Sagamore Hill, and settled on a book about Roosevelt's frontier experiences. He assembled a film crew and traveled to Medora, a small town near Roosevelt's Elkhorn ranch on the Little Missouri River. Dozens of friends turned out and told stories, unfazed by the camera. The interviews became the basis for a short, silent film released in 1919 called *Through the Roosevelt Country with Roosevelt's Friends*. As expected, the interviews also provided the necessary research for Hagedorn's 1922 book, *Roosevelt in the Badlands*.[4] The biography and film have become valuable resources for historians and treasured artifacts for North Dakotans who can turn back the clock and see what their state looked like before modern civilization advanced it beyond recognition. For Hagedorn, the most gratifying result of the project was that it legitimized his approach to commemoration. It confirmed the value of oral history.

Hagedorn's expedition to the Badlands predated widespread interest in oral history. The progenitor of the modern oral history movement was the Federal Writers' Project, a 1930's New Deal program that employed writers during the Depression.[5] The project collected thousands of personal testimonies about the Civil War, slavery, the Chicago fire, immigrant life, and the Wild West from a vanishing generation of Americans that could still recall such momentous episodes. The academic community followed suit, led by Professor Allan Nevins of Columbia University who called on historians to use stories "fresh and direct from men once prominent," which contain "information that every obituary column shows to be perishing."[6] Nevins feared that telecommunications would deprive historians of evidence found in correspondence and private papers. Oral histories would, accordingly, become a necessary supplement and, in 1948, Nevins founded the Columbia University Center for Oral History. The Center's staff took statements by longhand transcription at first, and began projects funded by external donors to demonstrate viability. Companies like Ford Motors supported Nevins, as did the oil and timber industries, which led to criticism of the project as a repository for the memories of rich, white businessmen.[7] The Center gradually expanded its focus, and the field of oral history flourished. Recording devices replaced handwriting, hastening the process of collection. By the 1950s, a dozen universities from New York to Los Angeles had founded centers like Columbia's.

Hagedorn met Nevins in the early 1940s, when the Roosevelt Memorial Association sought to divest its library due to the cost. Before donating the archive to Harvard in 1943, the Association proposed bestowing it to Columbia. Much to the chagrin of Nevins and Hagedorn, Columbia passed on the offer. Nevertheless, the men forged a connection based on common interests and undertook several collaborations, not least in the realm of oral history research.[8] When Hagedorn learned that the Columbia Oral History Center had coincidentally gathered statements from several of Roosevelt's political friends, it reignited his impulse to collect testimony.[9] In 1953, the Columbia Center and the Theodore Roosevelt Memorial Association interviewed Barclay Harding Farr, a friend of TR's son Kermit Roosevelt.[10] Harlan "Bud" Phillips, a PhD candidate working with Nevins, joined Hagedorn at Sagamore Hill and recorded Farr's childhood memories. The reminiscences had everything that written correspondence could not: emotions, insecurities, adrenaline, pride, and misgivings. Farr recalls playing tennis with the president, the hijinks of the Roosevelt children, and hosting a Bull Moose campaign reception for the former president. On one occasion, Farr tells how Kermit and his friends—in a prank—consumed all the food in the White House pantry over a holiday weekend, depriving visiting dignitaries. On another instance, they upset Oyster Bay neighbors by setting off fireworks too close to their houses. From these memories an intimate impression emerges.

In typical fashion, Hagedorn made the most of this resource. After he interviewed Farr, he revived plans to write a book about Sagamore Hill. Realizing the undocumented insight neighbors like Farr offered, Hagedorn set about collecting more interviews with Columbia. Timing necessitated quick work. Roosevelt's family and friends were an aging set, many of whom had never shared their memories for posterity. It was Hagedorn's last chance to hear them. By the 1950s, he no longer suffered from a lack of credibility. Having built close relationships with Roosevelt's contemporaries over the decades, Hagedorn took advantage of his reputation to attract prominent figures to the project. For Nevins, the partnership with Hagedorn and the Roosevelt Memorial Association would help expand the Center's archive and build capacity for aspiring historians like Bud Phillips and Louis M. Starr who accompanied Hagedorn on multiple interviews.[11]

Another leading figure in the endeavor was Hagedorn's daughter Mary. Her father encouraged Mary to enroll in Columbia's oral history master's degree program, run by Nevins, Phillips, and Starr. In September 1954, she began learning how to operate a reel-to-reel magnetic tape recorder. The Columbia program put students through their paces by testing their ability to decipher inaudible recordings or drilling them on shorthand dictation.[12] Mary excelled and quickly became her father's assistant. She accompanied him to several interviews with Roosevelt family members, and before long began interviewing them on her own. Without question, she became as vital as her father on the project, even if she often deferred to his boundless knowledge during the interviews.

Female participants particularly took a fondness to Mary, including TR's eldest daughter Alice Roosevelt Longworth, who told Mary to simply ask "straight away ... if you want me to do another [recording], I'll do another. Because, 'Now that I talked to Mary,' I'll say, 'I'm less awkward about it.'"[13] Other participants made it clear that Mary put them at ease during the interview. Whereas her father tended to cross-examine participants, a tactic that stunted conversation and gave the impression that he knew more than they did, Mary gave participants time to ramble without interruption. Perhaps this was a product of her training at Columbia, but regardless of where she learned the technique, Mary made participants comfortable and allowed them to fill silences with their memories.

In total, Mary and Hermann Hagedorn recorded twenty-one interviews between 1954 and 1956. Some of the interviewees spoke to the Hagedorns individually, some in groups of two or three. The participants included TR's daughters, nieces, nephews, in-laws, political comrades, neighbors, and acquaintances. Some, like Alice Roosevelt Longworth, needed to be talked through the process of recording, being somewhat unacquainted with the technology:

Mary Hagedorn:	Now that is, that is on again.
Mrs. Longworth:	It's on again? On us or on what?
Mary Hagedorn:	On us.
Mrs. Longworth:	On us, but I mean if you turned it on, can it still be someone else?
Mary Hagedorn:	If you turned it on and, you see now, we're speaking into it.
Mrs. Longworth:	Yes.
Mary Hagedorn:	And it erases the past one.
Mrs. Longworth:	Oh, it does?
Mary Hagedorn:	As it goes along, and I'll show you.[14]

Mrs. Longworth, and others immediately recognized the significance of the recordings for the historical record:

Mary Hagedorn:	The great advantage about a tape recorder is that you can get the personality of the person which you can't always get in writing.
Mrs. Longworth:	No, you can't get down in paper ... It's very interesting, and extraordinary innovation for getting opinion or to get the person's story, where they mesh and where they're completely different.[15]

Sadly, not all of the recordings survived. Only seven, two-sided reels still exist. The National Park Service (NPS) has maintained the reels since

1963, when the Roosevelt Birthplace at East 20th Street became a government property. Before then, the reels were kept by the Theodore Roosevelt Memorial Association, which maintained a small archive in the Birthplace. The reels stayed behind after the bulk of the collection went to Harvard. No evidence exists to suggest these reels have been accessed or listened to during the Park Service's administration. Interestingly, the cassette tape became the standard format for recordings soon after the NPS took over in the 1960s and, since then, reel-to-reel devices have become obsolete. The NPS does not even maintain a reel-to-reel recorder at the Birthplace, making it impossible to listen to them. According to park rangers, these reels went completely disregarded for decades. In 2019, with the permission of the Park Service, I had the reels digitized by a professional duplication service. To recover the sound, the reels required cleaning and some cyber-wizardry. For the first time, they are available to researchers in a digital format.[16]

In addition to the taped recordings, several transcribed interviews were gathered by the Hagedorns and others, from 1945 to 1970. Half of these transcripts have been available to researchers via special collections at Columbia University, but many of these oral histories were stashed away in the Theodore Roosevelt Birthplace archive, and rarely accessed. Since then, the transcripts have been transferred from the Roosevelt Birthplace to the Sagamore Hill archive. In 2018, they have become accessible to researchers and among their assets include Mary Hagedorn's interview with First Lady Eleanor Roosevelt and a conversation with TR's daughter Ethel Roosevelt Derby and his daughter-in-law Eleanor Butler Roosevelt.

* * *

New sources have the power to change our perception of the past and this motivated Hermann Hagedorn. Throughout the 1930s and 1940s, Franklin Roosevelt eclipsed his cousin in public consciousness and negative portrayals of TR dominated. Hagedorn saw the 1950s as a period ripe for reappraisal, and under his leadership the memorial association funded several public history projects to revive TR's image.[17] The most prominent was the publication of Roosevelt's correspondence. In 1951, a team of academics published the first of eight volumes of Roosevelt's letters and, when complete, these reference books transformed perceived wisdom.[18] The impression of TR as a boisterous demagogue, hasty and juvenile—a depiction one historian has aptly called the crazy Teddy theory—receded as historians of the 1950s examined the letters.[19] These eight volumes even changed the view of some firm adherents to the crazy Teddy theory. Richard Hofstatder, the leading historian of American politics in the mid-century, softened his take on Roosevelt as he read more correspondence.[20] The memorial association also commissioned journalist and Roosevelt contemporary John Callan O'Laughlin to write a hagiography. Although O'Laughlin died in 1949, and the memorial association abandoned the project, it continued to support writers with a favorable view of Roosevelt like biographer Carleton Putnam.[21] The oral history project was conceived in the same vein as the letters and these book projects.

The oral history project achieved its end in two ways. First, the testimony from friends and family humanized TR. Instead of portraying a president, the participants retold stories of the father, the uncle, the exuberant boy, the mannerly and kind friend, the private source of inspiration, and the dutiful husband. Of course, the political episodes that defined Roosevelt's rise to the presidency come out in reminiscences, but these well-worn stories of his public life wither in comparison to the warm portrayal of Roosevelt's personality and private life. Hagedorn had insisted that "a far deeper reservoir of nostalgic memories of Theodore Roosevelt" existed in the minds of those who knew him, "undimmed by the passage of time."[22] Relaying these memories, he believed, would spark a revival.

The second way the oral histories prompted reappraisal was in supporting the so-called "consensus" histories of the 1950s. This short-lived school of thought in American history theorized that consistency existed in politics whereby politicians shared ideas, civic-mindedness, and national values.[23] Consensus historians put Theodore Roosevelt in a class of political actors who led the nation since its inception and promoted a mythologized national experience. They diminished the novelty of his presidency. Instead, TR shared the same goals as Washington, Jefferson, Lincoln, and even Dwight Eisenhower. That might seem convoluted in the twenty-first century, but consensus historians writing in the Cold War context could be forgiven for reducing American history in such a way. The polarization of society and the all-consuming nature of the Cold War encouraged Americans to push aside their differences to fight against a common foe. Consensus historians working in this period created a longue durée of American progress from the colonial era to the Second World War, and Roosevelt took his place in that narrative.[24]

One useful example of how the oral history project fit the consensus interpretation comes from Frederick Trubee Davison. In 1955, Davison recalled a moment during World War II when Theodore Roosevelt's ghost appeared in the offices of the Pentagon. Secretary of War Henry L. Stimson, a contemporary of TR enlisted by FDR to organize the war effort, brought together the nation's top brass in 1944 for a meeting designed to inspire their efforts against the Axis Powers. Stimson read aloud a eulogy to Theodore Roosevelt, and Davison recounts the episode as an "emotional experience" for all those in attendance.[25] Stimson drew a historical line from the 1890s to the 1940s, from Theodore Roosevelt to Franklin Roosevelt, casting all political efforts in-between as the fateful progress toward common national objectives. Similarly, Historian Howard K. Beale constructed a pathway from TR to the Cold War in his 1956 book *Theodore Roosevelt and the Rise of America to World Power*. Beale deemed the 1950s a "desperate state" of existence "that threatens to destroy civilization itself," and explained how American foreign policy "started down this road" with TR's internationalism.[26]

Anachronistic as it might be, we remember the past from our vantage in the present. History comes into relief like a camera adjusting its focus, and in the 1950s the Cold War featured heavily in the thoughts and concerns of the project's participants. That tendency to re-order historical events to fit the present appears in the recollections of Progressive Party activist William Savacool who spent one hour with the Hagedorns discussing the 1912 presidential election. The most thought-provoking exchange came when Savacool offered a counterfactual scenario whereby TR won reelection in 1912:

William Savacool: One of the conversations that I had with Mr. Roosevelt was at his house in Oyster Bay in June, 1916. He was very much concerned because we didn't do something about the situation in Europe at the time. He said, "If we didn't get into this war now, Russia is going to blow up and you'll have Bolshevism, Communism, spreading all over the world."

That was the reason he gave me for not running on a third ticket in 1916, which would elect Woodrow Wilson president again, and he did not agree with Wilson's foreign policy at all. He thought that if we got into the War much sooner it would be over sooner, fewer lives would be lost—and now, as I think back over it, I feel he was right …

Mary Hagedorn:	Do you feel that if Mr. Roosevelt had been President in 1912, he would not only have prevented World War I but there might not have been World War II?
William Savacool:	That is my belief. I know positively that Mr. Roosevelt told the Kaiser before any war, that in case of a war against England that he would be on the side of England. The Kaiser sent over an Ambassador [to Wilson] who *assured* him that we would not go into the War. That's why he struck.[27]

Naturally, hindsight can lead to counterfactual fantasies, and several interviews digress in a similar way as Savacool. Oral histories suffer from misremembering, and every participant falls prey to some degree of obfuscation. As Bertrand Russell once wrote, "When a man tells you that he knows the exact truth about anything, you are safe in inferring that he is an inexact man."[28]

In addition to misremembering, the Cold War had another noticeable influence on the participants.[29] As McCarthyism reached its zenith in the mid-1950s, anti-communism led to a reinvigorated commitment to American democracy and nationalism. Hagedorn tethered Roosevelt's legacy to such concepts and, not surprisingly, some of the oral history dialogue reflects the surge in nationalism and exceptionalism. New York politician Ezra Prentice told Mary Hagedorn that Roosevelt could be likened to a god, and that his supporters "thought Roosevelt was infallible ... as though it were a religious belief."[30] Alice Roosevelt Longworth relates how the threat of communism required a fearless leader, namely a man like her father. Karl H. Behr hopes his children will read more about Roosevelt to be prepared for the international strife and to lead a more patriotic life. Marie Bissell thought her steadfast patriotism had its roots in an "upbringing and education" in the early twentieth century, of which Roosevelt stood out like a role model.

Other participants avoided proleptic forecasting. Samuel McCune Lindsay, a Roosevelt-appointee to the Philippine Executive, recalls his work as an educator in the American colony. He restricted conversation to factual recollections and avoids casting Roosevelt as an unblemished idol or imagining how he would fare as a cold warrior. Consequently, the Hagedorns seem to lose interest. At one juncture Lindsay abruptly turns to a moment when TR asked him and others in his company: "Do you gentlemen know whom I would select if I had the power to name my successor?" This seemed a chance to glean an insight into one of Roosevelt's most important decisions as president and should have jolted the Hagedorns out of their seat. Lindsay reported that Roosevelt plainly announced: "It would be Elihu Root whom I consider the best qualified man I know but probably you couldn't elect him dog catcher, because he is chiefly known as a corporation lawyer, and has never ridden in the cab of a locomotive. My choice will be Taft."[31] Then, almost as soon as Lindsay completed the story, the interview moved on to a tedious reminiscence of TR's reading habits. The Hagedorns, disappointingly, did not press Lindsay to elaborate.

Indeed, many of the interviews leave readers with more questions. Several detail important political relationships that would prompt historical reconsideration if we believe the testimony. The 1916 Republican presidential nominee Charles Evans Hughes and New York Republican Party boss Thomas Collier Platt—often mooted as political foes—appear as key collaborators in some accounts. A friendly relationship between Platt and Hughes would certainly change the way we think about New York politics in the Progressive Era. And some interviews produce new perspectives on the Roosevelt family. Of particular interest will be Elliott Roosevelt (TR's brother and father to First Lady Eleanor Roosevelt) and James "Tadd" Roosevelt (FDR's nephew). Elliott and Tadd have been presented as family deviants, outcast for their waywardness. Historians cite Elliott's alcoholism and substance abuse, while Tadd's marriage to a prostitute came as such a shock that his father disowned him. FDR, according to many biographies, blamed Tadd for his father taking ill and dying.[32] The oral histories add new contours to the lives of Elliott and Tadd, and perhaps change our take on the family dynamics. Alice Roosevelt Longworth, for one, tells the Hagedorns of her affection for Elliott. In her recollection, Elliott had debilitating epilepsy, a condition which provoked his abuse of alcohol and opium. Elliott's poor physical health preceded his addiction, she attests. For Tadd, Oyster Bay and Hyde Park relatives reference him as a sensitive man who separated from his wife within a year of their marriage. He moved to Florida where he became a mechanic. Tadd was a recluse, rather than an outcast, and he occasionally met his sister Helen Roosevelt Robinson in New York. These stories refute the harsh opinion of historians like William J. Mann who argues that "no room was made for their idiosyncrasies."[33] In the reminiscences it becomes evident that the Roosevelts grappled with Tadd's eccentricities and Elliott's illness.

The testimonies of the Roosevelt family also relate an unyielding devotion to their relatives, despite considerable differences among disagreeable characters. As relations frayed between the Oyster Bay and Hyde Park clans, often over politics as much as personality, family relations soured. Those Roosevelts interviewed for the oral history project nevertheless concede a constant "devotion" to their family. In fact, the word "devotion" comes up in nearly every account as if it had special meaning for the Roosevelts. Corinne Robinson Alsop uses the word frequently in her interview, fearing that her recollections of Eleanor will unfairly depict the former first lady. She impulsively tells Mary Hagedorn several times how much she adores Eleanor before taking shots at her character. Mrs. Longworth, who had an infamously strained relationship with Eleanor and Franklin, tells how much affection she has for them, and only then does she relate the unpleasant stories.[34] The abuse of alcohol, which claimed the lives of many Roosevelt family members, gets ample attention. So do infidelities. The Cowleses tell of Mrs. Longworth's love affair with Senator William Borah and how her only child Paulina derived from that relationship rather than her marriage. Mrs. Longworth tells of her nephew Theodore Douglas Robinson's habitual rendezvouses with prostitutes. Nieces and nephews remark on Edith Roosevelt's stern and cold demeanor. Yet for each charge levied, the speakers reiterate their love, affection, and admiration.

Heed two things when reading these interviews. First, the Roosevelt family is like almost any other. Although certainly wealthier and more famous than most, the Roosevelts have black sheep and high achievers. Mrs. Longworth remarked in one of her interviews that "when you go into them, almost all families are odd."[35] Second, readers should consider the partiality of the Roosevelts. Mrs. Longworth made reference to her father's "posterity letters" in one interview. TR wrote these "to inoculate against the future," she said, and readers can assume that participants like Mrs. Longworth had fully considered that the oral history transcripts would find their way into archives and eventually pass by the desks of researchers.[36] In some cases, participants asked archivists to seal transcripts, knowing that their reminiscences would become part of the historical record. The recordings and transcripts contain a mix of candid description as well as cagey restraint. We can assume the recordings afford the best view into the participants' opinions. Unlike the typescript testimonies that went through two rounds of edits (one from the Hagedorns, and another from the participants), the recordings remain unedited.

This book has not reproduced all the oral histories the Hagedorns collected. In total, they exceed more than 200,000 words. Instead, I have made strategic omissions. Several accounts have been omitted entirely, including some never before heard recordings, with good reason. Some overlapped considerably with others and repetition dilutes the potency of these accounts. For instance, only two of Roosevelt's neighbors—Barclay Farr and Georgiana Farr Sibley—feature in the book, and yet four more contributed to the project (Marie Bissell, Marian Knight Garrison, Helen Sargant Hitchcock, and Augusta Munn Tilney). Mrs. Garrison and Mrs. Tilney interviewed together and made similar observations as the Farrs, particularly about Stewart Robinson's death, the exuberant spirit of the Roosevelt family, and the awkward childhood of Eleanor Roosevelt. Tilney calls Eleanor "a living freak," which is a harsh missive echoed in some of the testimony made by Eleanor's cousins.[37] Tilney also recalls a supernatural moment when TR's sister Corinne met an apparition of her deceased brother Elliott:

> Mrs. Robinson told me herself that she was up at Herkimer [New York] and that she was walking through the woods. Suddenly, she saw the figure she identified as her brother Elliott, walking ahead of her. She never could catch up to him, and this shadowy figure she followed to the front door. When they arrived there the figure vanished through the door. The door was then opened and she was handed a cable of a telegram or a message saying her brother Elliott had died … She told me this herself.[38]

The neighbors reveal humorous stories of Alice Roosevelt Longworth's rocky relationship with her father. When TR instructed his daughter to call on Senator John Kean when she visited Washington, Mrs. Longworth protested, but TR demanded that she leave calling cards, at least. "I will, but you'll be sorry," she told her father. Mrs. Garrison reported that Mrs. Longworth "left three cards: a knave and two old maid cards!"[39]

Outside of a few exceptional revelations, the neighbors share overlapping impressions with other participants.[40] Among the other interviews, common portrayals of Roosevelt make reference to the president's gracious hosting or the abundant attention he gave his children. It certainly does seem remarkable that a sitting president could devote so much time to his friends and family, as well as the country's demands. The participants also tell of Roosevelt's personal talents, some of which seem like fantastical parlor tricks like his ability to read and talk at the same time, his memory of people and events, or his general exuberance. In some omitted interviews, participants make unsubstantiated statements or concede that they could not recall aspects of the past. Some participants were simply less interesting. The interviews with William Savacool, Samuel McCune Linsey, and Ezra Prentice mentioned in this introduction do not appear elsewhere. The few germane aspects of their interviews did not justify adding dozens of pages to the book. Judgment on what to edit and omit followed the same rationale as the academic letters project in the 1950s. The goal of the editing team sifting through 150,000 letters was "to make easily accessible all the available [material] that seem[ed] necessary to reveal" the subject of study.[41] I took the same approach with the oral histories. No doubt other researchers will see value in recordings and transcripts I have excluded, however, as much as 70% of the oral histories have been reproduced in this book.

One aspect of the project warrants further comment: the immense role of women in Theodore Roosevelt's life and legacy. Hermann Hagedorn summed it up best, calling the testimony "perfectly extraordinary," because it described a "group of brilliant, able, powerful, effective women!" Hagedorn referred specifically to four women—Anna Roosevelt Cowles, Corinne Roosevelt Robinson, Eleanor Roosevelt, and Sara Delano Roosevelt—but equally wished to recognize "a half dozen other women who figure in the story [and] are all important women in themselves, quite apart from their connections with TR."[42] And the Roosevelt women are anything but monolithic. TR's eldest sister Anna Roosevelt Cowles comes across as charming, businesslike and, as a potential presidential candidate had the laws disqualifying women for high office not existed or had she desired to run (she did not). TR's youngest sister Corinne Roosevelt Robinson seems a syrupy, sensitive poet, as indomitable as her brother. Despite their many differences, Mrs. Cowles and Mrs. Robinson agreed that women should not get the right to vote, a curiosity for two politically active women, and while this seems implausible, the oral history interviews explain how Victorian ideas about women allowed TR's sisters to find political agency through traditional gender roles and their class. Of equivalent interest, TR's eldest daughter broke all the era's gender roles it seems, while his youngest daughter Ethel conformed to them. One hope in publishing the oral histories is that the Roosevelt women come to the fore, as Betty Boyd Caroli accomplished in her landmark book. This book also observes what "made them 'special' and, at the same time, show what they shared with other families facing similar challenges outside the public eye."[43]

Much more awaits the reader. Family life at Sagamore Hill—what the Roosevelts ate, how they played, who helped raise the children, and why they loved Long Island—is available in abundance. The political landscape of New York in the Gilded Age and Progressive Era emerges from city and state politicos that held office for decades after TR's death. The Wilson-Roosevelt rivalry that dominated national politics helps to reconstruct an image of the World War I period and the sharp divergences in domestic and foreign policies between Republicans and Democrats. We can even travel along with the Rough Riders as they battle up San Juan Heights to glory.

Hermann Hagedorn regarded oral history as a resource that sparks reconsideration. In 1957, at his 75th birthday party, he reportedly pushed aside his birthday cake to explain how he would make Roosevelt's 100th birthday a pivotal moment.[44] Hagedorn traipsed through the corridors of Congress, petitioning for a government-sponsored celebration and his efforts eventually led to a presidential commission, ostensibly led by President Eisenhower. But all the while, Hagedorn lurked as the figurehead, the maestro of Roosevelt's legacy conducting the celebrations. He organized events across the country, and even internationally.[45] And his efforts did prompt reimagination. In history books, comics, radio shows, films and television, even theater productions, popular depictions of Theodore Roosevelt emphasized his patriotism, nationalism, heroism, and dedication to the environment. By 1958, the year Roosevelt would have turned 100, Hagedorn had successfully reignited public interest in his hero.

Oddly, the oral histories played a negligible part in the revival. Hagedorn made little use of them and the recordings remained locked away for decades. This book affords those with an interest in Roosevelt an opportunity to learn more from his family and friends. I determined to publish the collection in the hope that readers will find the interviews an additional source, akin to the published letters. The interviews present a colorful portrait of the Roosevelts and their times. Most importantly, it puts history in the words of those who lived it.

A Note on the Sources

The typescripts produced by the Hagedorns include edits to make them read more fluidly, and in some cases the Hagedorns reordered the answers supplied by participants. "You'll find that quite a bit has been done to rearrange the material since the original transcript was made," Mary Hagedorn wrote to Corinne Robinson Alsop, "Dad and I jumped around quite a bit in our questions, which did not make for good continuity!"[46] After the Hagedorns edited the transcripts, they sent them to participants for their approval, and in many cases the participants edited them again before lodging the interview with Columbia or the Theodore Roosevelt Association. Marie Bissell asked that a story she told be omitted from the final transcript, and this type of editing may have occurred in other testimonies. The administrative files of the project indicate that, in several cases, participants self-selected what the final transcript would emphasize or omit. The Hagedorns obliged participants wishing to make edits, but they also kept a master copy in their personal files.[47] Retrieving these files has led me to several archives, all of which are listed in the works consulted. The surviving audio recordings also prove that the Hagedorns made many minor adulterations to the transcripts, and some substantial revisions or omissions.

Oral history purists will balk at any editing as an unnecessary alteration that leaves too much an imprimatur of the interviewer or interviewee. While I agree, the Hagedorns would not have collected these testimonies without concessions like this because participants had deep apprehensions about recording in the first place. Corinne Robinson Alsop, for instance, limited access to her testimony for decades. Only the Hagedorns could access her transcript, until such a time as Mrs. Alsop unsealed the file. Mrs. Alsop also forbade transcripts going to Columbia, unless by special permission. She worried about her opinions being misconstrued. Likewise, Alice Roosevelt Longworth restricted access to her audio recordings and asked Mary Hagedorn if Allan Nevins would honor her request to keep them private. Unperturbed by what others inferred from her commentary, Mrs. Longworth instead complained of her diction, believing it unintelligible.

This book presents an honest reproduction, if not a perfect recreation of the interviews.[48] Each chapter explains what modifications have been made to original recordings or transcripts, and brackets any edits made to the original. Naturally, given the age of the recordings, some audio remains inaudible. Participants repeat words, as we do in speech, or make corrections. In these cases, the Hagedorns, or I, have edited the testimony to convey what the speaker had intended. If researchers seek the originals, they are now easy to locate. Following this note on sources, I have included a glossary of the interviews. The list will point a determined researcher to the original source material. Who knows, perhaps a keener ear can decipher Hermann Hagedorn's baritone mumbling or Alice Roosevelt

Longworth's ramblings. What I can be confident about is that the material included in this book accurately reflects the testimony.

Oral history researchers make the point of investigating participants, as much as their testimony, and each chapter in this volume begins with an introduction of the speakers, their relationship to Roosevelt, and the key moments in the interview. The introductions also explain where testimony makes a contribution to historiographical debates surrounding Roosevelt's life and times.

Glossary of Interviews

Corinne Robinson Alsop

Theodore Roosevelt's niece
Interview: 23 November 1954, Avon, Connecticut, by Hermann and Mary Hagedorn
Transcript (Sagamore Hill NPS Archives)
Interview: 9 December 1954, Avon, Connecticut, by Mary Hagedorn
Transcript (Sagamore Hill NPS Archives)
Interview: 28 December 1954, with William Sheffield Cowles and Margaret Krech Cowles, Farmington, Connecticut, by Herman and Mary Hagedorn
Transcript (Sagamore Hill NPS Archives); Recording, 64 mins. (Theodore Roosevelt Birthplace)

Karl Howell Behr

Professional tennis player, banker, Roosevelt Non-partisan League
Memoirs: 1945, dictated to his daughter Sally Behr Pettit
Transcript (Columbia University Center for Oral History)

Marie Truesdale Bissell

Neighbor of Anna Roosevelt Cowles
Interview: November 1954, Farmington, Connecticut, by Mary Hagedorn

Transcript (Sagamore Hill NPS Archives); Recording, 25 mins. (Theodore Roosevelt Birthplace)

William Merriam Chadbourne

New York City Republican politician and lawyer; Fiorello LaGuardia's campaign manager
Interview: 8 May 1955, by Mary Hagedorn
Transcript (Columbia University Center for Oral History); Recording, 60 mins. (Theodore Roosevelt Birthplace)

Margaret Krech Cowles

Theodore Roosevelt's niece (by marriage)
Interview: 22 November 1954, with William Sheffield Cowles Farmington, Connecticut, by Hermann and Mary Hagedorn
Transcript (Columbia University Center for Oral History and Sagamore Hill NPS Archives)
Interview: 28 December 1954, with William Sheffield Cowles and Corinne Robinson Alsop, Farmington, Connecticut, by Herman and Mary Hagedorn
Transcript (Sagamore Hill NPS Archives); Recording, 64 mins. (Theodore Roosevelt Birthplace)

William Sheffield Cowles

Theodore Roosevelt's nephew
Interview: 22 November 1954, with Margaret Krech Cowles, Farmington, Connecticut, by Hermann and Mary Hagedorn
Transcript (Columbia University Center for Oral History and Sagamore Hill NPS Archives)
Interview: 28 December 1954, with Corinne Robinson Alsop and Margaret Krech Cowles, Farmington, Connecticut, by Herman and Mary Hagedorn
Transcript (Sagamore Hill NPS Archives); Recording, 64 mins. (Theodore Roosevelt Birthplace)

Frederick Trubee Davison

Friend of Theodore Roosevelt's youngest son Quentin Roosevelt
Interview: 30 March 1955, New York City, by Hermann and Mary Hagedorn
Transcript (Columbia University Center for Oral History)

Ethel Roosevelt Derby

Theodore Roosevelt's daughter
Interview: n.d. [likely 1955], with Eleanor Butler Roosevelt, by Hermann and Mary Hagedorn
Transcript (Sagamore Hill NPS Archives)

Barclay H. Farr

Neighbor of Corinne Roosevelt Robinson, friend of Theodore Roosevelt's son, Kermit Roosevelt
Interview: 5 May 1953, Sagamore Hill, New York, by Hermann Hagedorn and Harlan Phillips
Transcript (Columbia University Center for Oral History)

Marian Knight Garrison

Neighbor of Corinne Roosevelt Robinson; suffragist
Interview: 25 April 1955, with Augusta Munn Tilney, Orange, New Jersey, by Mary Hagedorn
Transcript (Sagamore Hill NPS Archives)

Helen Sargant Hitchcock

Neighbor of Corinne Roosevelt Robinson
Interview: 25 August 1956, by Mary Hagedorn
Recording, 32 mins. (Theodore Roosevelt Birthplace)

Stanley Myer Isaacs

New York City politician
Interview: 1955, by Mary Hagedorn
Transcript (Columbia University Center for Oral History)

Jesse Langdon

Rough Rider, inventor
Interview: 10 July 1970, Lafayeteville, New York, by Douglas Scott
Transcript (Columbia University Center for Oral History)

Samuel McCune Lindsay

Sociologist, Commissioner for Education (Puerto Rico)
Interview: April 1955, Winter Park, Florida
Transcript (Columbia University Center for Oral History)

Alice Roosevelt Longworth

Theodore Roosevelt's daughter
Interview: 9 November 1954, Washington, D.C., by Herman and Mary Hagedorn
  Transcript (Columbia University Center for Oral History)
Interview: 2 October 1955, Washington, D.C., by Mary Hagedorn
  Recording, 93 mins. (Theodore Roosevelt Birthplace)
Interview: 2 January 1956, Washington, D.C., by Mary Hagedorn
Partial transcript (Sagamore Hill NPS Archives); Recording, 60 mins. (Theodore Roosevelt Birthplace)

Philip J. McCook

New York Supreme Court justice
Interview: 29 March 1955, New York City, by Mary Hagedorn
Recording, 33 mins. (Theodore Roosevelt Birthplace)

Ezra Parmalee Prentice

New York politician
Interview: 28 June 1956, by Mary Hagedorn
Transcript (Columbia University Center for Oral History); Recording, 9 mins. (Theodore Roosevelt Birthplace)

Helen Roosevelt Robinson

Theodore Roosevelt's niece (by marriage); Franklin Roosevelt's cousin
Interview: 17 November 1955, by Mary Hagedorn
Transcript (Columbia University Center for Oral History or Sagamore Hill NPS Archives)

Anna Eleanor Roosevelt

Theodore Roosevelt's niece; First Lady of the United States
Interview: 18 January 1955, New York City, by Hermann and Mary Hagedorn
Transcript (Sagamore Hill NPS Archives)

Eleanor Butler Roosevelt

Theodore Roosevelt's daughter-in-law (married to Theodore Roosevelt, Jr.)
Interview: n.d. [likely 1955], with Ethel Roosevelt Derby, by Hermann and Mary Hagedorn
Transcript (Sagamore Hill NPS Archives)

Murray T. Quigg

Newspaper editor; son of Republican Party boss Lemuel Quigg
Interview: February 1950, by Owen Bombard
Transcript (Columbia University Center for Oral History)

William Savacool

Progressive Party leader
Interview: 8 December 1955, Durham, New Hampshire, by Mary Hagedorn
Transcript (Columbia University Center for Oral History); Recording, 48 mins. (Theodore Roosevelt Birthplace)

Georgiana Farr Sibley

Neighbor of Corinne Roosevelt Robinson, friend of Ethel Roosevelt Derby
Interview: 10 August 1955, Theodore Roosevelt Birthplace, New York City, by Hermann and Mary Hagedorn
Transcript (Sagamore Hill NPS Archives); Recording, 30 mins. (Theodore Roosevelt Birthplace)

Henry Root Stern

Lawyer and Long Island neighbor of Theodore Roosevelt
Interview: January 1954, by Hermann Hagedorn and Louis M. Starr
Transcript (Columbia University Center for Oral History)

Augusta Munn Tilney

Neighbor of Corinne Roosevelt Robinson; daughter of Charles Munn
Interview: 25 April 1955, with Marian Knight Garrison, Orange, New Jersey, by Mary Hagedorn
 Transcript (Sagamore Hill NPS Archives)

PART I

Family

CHAPTER 2

The Other Washington Monument: Alice Roosevelt Longworth

Fig. 2.1 Alice Roosevelt Longworth christening USS Theodore Roosevelt submarine (1959), U.S. Navy

To describe Alice Roosevelt Longworth as a celebrity seems a disservice. She had a silvery tongue that cut two ways: at once she had the eloquence and persuasiveness of a great orator, venerating those she respected, while also spewing the venom of a pestilent critic, casting aspersions on those she disagreed with. TR once complained that he could either "be President of the United States—or—I can attend to Alice." He could not do both.[1] Never irascible, she had a penchant for making her opinions known in clever and sardonic ways. She clashed frequently with her cousins Franklin and Eleanor Roosevelt. When Franklin took the United States off the gold standard in 1933, she protested by attending a White House reception dripping in gold jewelry: gold pendant, gold necklace, gold watch, gold hair combs, and gold earrings.[2] Her witticisms have become legendary. She called President Warren G. Harding "a decaying Roman emperor," President Calvin Coolidge a "precise little object," and 1944 Republican presidential nominee Thomas Dewey "the bridegroom on the wedding cake."[3] Her sobriquets tended to stick, and it made her a mainstay of the capital's social scene, so much so that she earned a nickname of her own: "the other Washington monument."

Mrs. Longworth's intrigue goes beyond these yarns. She hailed from one of the most influential political families and fraternized with the capital's power brokers. Her opinions held their greatest sway in the early twentieth century when she lived in the White House and in the 1920s when her husband, Ohio congressman Nick Longworth, became speaker of the House. She hosted parties in their Washington home that brought together presidents, congressmen, cabinet officers, journalists, and lobbyists. Late night poker parties in her smoke-filled parlor doubled as strategic planning sessions for the Republican Party. Her vehement opposition to President Woodrow Wilson and the Treaty of Versailles prompted a series of gatherings at her residence designed to keep the United States out of the League of Nations. For her leadership of this network of intransigent senators—the so-called "irreconcilables"—she earned another nickname: The Colonel of the Battalion of Death.

During her husband's tenure as speaker, Mrs. Longworth offered her thoughts on a range of policies from naval disarmament to the budget and taxation, and her influence extended beyond the House to the more deliberative chamber, the Senate. There, she had a powerful ally in Idaho's William Borah, chair of the Senate Committee on Foreign Relations. Throughout the 1920s, she carried on a romantic affair with Borah.

It began with political like-mindedness and a common advocacy of an anti-interventionist foreign policy. At some point during the considerable time they spent together, their intellectual attraction evolved into romance. Reliable accounts, including one of the oral histories contained in this book, confirm Borah as the father of Paulina Longworth, her only child.

Nick Longworth died in 1931, and Borah died in 1940. In their absence, Mrs. Longworth maintained her place as the capital's conservative high priest. An implacable anti-New Dealer, FDR banned her from the White House after repeated slights. Mrs. Longworth persisted to promote laissez-faire economics despite a growing consensus in favor of social welfare and government regulation. International relations interested her even more. She helped organize the Washington chapter of the America First Committee and opposed American intervention in World War II. During the Cold War, Mrs. Longworth instinctively gravitated to anti-communist politicians and, somewhat quixotically for a stalwart isolationist, called for a muscular U.S. foreign policy that would ensure the Soviet Union's containment. During Dwight Eisenhower's presidency she struck up a friendship with Vice President Richard Nixon, one she maintained throughout his presidency and until the Watergate scandal forced him to resign. The Kennedy's—John and Robert—developed a fond rapport with Alice, and her Washington salon reemerged as a hive of political activity in the 1960s. She lived through twenty presidential administrations and died in 1980 at the age of ninety-six, weeks after the inauguration of Ronald Reagan and the revival of her beloved Republican Party.

The recordings and transcripts taken of Mrs. Longworth reveal a privileged upbringing. She had servants, butlers, drivers, and maids, which left her ample time for the pleasures of reading, socializing, and attending Congress to sit in the viewing gallery. Even the timbre of her voice and old-world accent reveal her pedigree. As Daniel Prebutt, the museum curator at the Roosevelt Birthplace said, "some of those accents just don't exist anymore. It's one thing to hear them in the old movies, quite another to hear them in regular conversation."[4] And Mrs. Longworth's conversations with the Hagedorns cover a range of personal experiences. She explores political episodes, perhaps the most intriguing being the role she played in thwarting the ratification of the Treaty of Versailles, as well as her time in the White House. While she spends roughly four hours with her interviewers, Mrs. Longworth offers only a flash into her personal life. She comes across as enigmatic and evasive in many of the recordings. Hermann and Mary Hagedorn complained when interviewing Alice that she failed to remember much of her childhood and young adulthood. More likely, she was reluctant to share her memories. In her 1933 autobiography, she omits reference to her mother Alice Hathaway Lee who died days after giving birth. Likewise, she neglects to mention her father's death in 1919.[5] These were conscious decisions designed to obscure the past or repress painful memories. Her family complained that she never responded to letters, and her love letters to Bill Borah cloaked their affair in coded language.[6] She avoided a paper trail, fearing the pen of journalists and historians. She emphasized the lesson in an interview with Michael Teague in the 1970s: "What do you want? Revelations? With the tape on?" Alice asked, "Well, you are not going to have them, you lovely creature, showing your canine teeth with pleasure."[7]

Like her conversations with Teague, Mrs. Longworth dodged the Hagedorns' enquiries, often by changing the subject or droning on about something less interesting. A great deal of her conversation dwells on social gatherings as a foil for the intimate questions the Hagedorns ask. When Mary Hagedorn asks about her coming of age, Mrs. Longworth says, "And to go back to food, let me see about more food." Mary Hagedorn pleads with her, "Oh, don't." Or, when Mrs. Longworth begins to disparage the welfare state, she pauses, considers whether to delve any deeper into the topic, and says, "Now we've got to get back to Auntie Bye." At times, the Hagedorns treat Mrs. Longworth as a hostile witness. They interrupt her to avoid extraneous tangents as well as to keep her comprehensible.

Michael Teague concluded from his interviews with Mrs. Longworth that she "rarely referred to matters of great personal concern, except obliquely."[8] On the contrary, she shares many candid stories about others. For example, she divulges that her friend Pauline Sabin Davis had a "terrific" affair with Polish diplomat Jan Ciechanowski. And we also hear about intimate family histories, including her perspective on her aunts, cousins, and later generations. She makes clear her affection for some, like her cousin Joseph Alsop whose weekly column *Matter of Fact*, written with his brother Stewart ran in the *Washington Post*, and her father's oldest sister Auntie Bye (Anna Roosevelt Cowles). Others, like her aunt Corinne Roosevelt Robinson get referred to as soppy and overly sensitive, emotional traits Mrs. Longworth had little respect for. Her stepmother, TR's second wife Edith, comes across as cold and stern. Mrs. Longworth even proposes another recording that would be purposely indiscreet about her family. It obviously never happened.

Global communism looms large in Mrs. Longworth's reminiscences. She met with the Hagedorns in 1954 and 1955. China had "gone red" in

1949; McCarthyism had plunged the U.S. into a second communist witch hunt, even if it had largely run its course by 1955; France lost Vietnam at Diem Bien Phu; the Korean War had ended in stalemate. Mrs. Longworth relates her disappointment with American foreign policy during these early years of the Cold War. The leadership of the United States, she insists, lacks direction and thrust. She blames successive administrations on the failure to repel communist expansion in the developing world and her disapproval extends to the architects of the Red Scare, particularly Joseph McCarthy who she describes as "a pretty stupid man." She credits McCarthy with raising the issue of communist infiltration in government agencies, but disapproves of his tactics and manner, whereas another cold warrior earned her respect. She called Richard Nixon "a very able man," and believed he would emerge as a leading figure in the fight against communism. Regardless of which cold warrior she preferred, the anti-communist context saturates Mrs. Longworth's memories of her father and his policies.

The surviving audio recordings offer a unique variation on all previous published interviews. Her conversation with Mary Hagedorn (the first and second sections of this chapter) proceeds naturally, as if Mrs. Longworth forgot that the microphone was on. She replies in unscripted and carefree dialogue. We hear her as she spoke, and how her thoughts meander through Washington gossip. Her dialogue includes much mumbling and truncated remarks. As Teague observed, "she never spoke in a monologue for any length of time" and so Mary Hagedorn attempts to draw out the best stories.[9]

By contemporary standards, the recordings are of poor quality. Background noises like cars and sirens intersect Mrs. Longworth's dialogue. Phones ring and sometimes there are knocks to furniture that drown out the audio, if only momentarily. The chief impediment, however, is Mrs. Longworth. Her old-world accent and rapid pace of speaking make it difficult to follow, and she admits as much. When recalling another recording she made, she tells Mary Hagedorn that the transcriptionist "couldn't make head or tails of me" and when they asked her to listen to the recording and decipher her own words, she said, "I couldn't make head or tails of *it*." Extracting her words verbatim is nearly impossible. Mrs. Longworth mutters, and occasionally strays from the microphone. Consequently, portions of the interview do not appear in this chapter. Inaudible content is omitted and, in some cases, repeated words are condensed to make the transcript clearer. In addition, the chapter excludes some of the Hagedorns questions and digressions. These edits do not detract from the thrust of Mrs. Longworth's testimony. Not every recollection yields a significant insight. If readers want the full account on the food at Sagamore Hill, Mrs. Longworth's childhood chores and her relationship with servants, or would simply like to hear her voice, they should consult the surviving recordings and archived transcripts. One final confession: there is every possibility that minor errors have crept into the transcriptions because of Mrs. Longworth's diction or quality of the tape. It took weeks to identify some of the people she mentions, and no matter how close my ear got to the speakers, I could not make out every syllable. It's likely the Hagedorns also made edits to their transcripts, but they had the opportunity to contact Mrs. Longworth to ask for clarification. In fact, she approved all the transcripts before Columbia archived them. The recordings, however, were never vetted by her.

* * *

9 November 1954

You said boldly yesterday that if your Auntie Bye [Anna Roosevelt Cowles, TR's older sister] had been a man, she would have been the member of the family who was the president. Now why?

Because she had such determination and knew just where she was going. She had power of organization. You felt that she could organize things. She would have been in the organization—whether she would have been the Mark Hanna behind it, I don't know, or whether she would have been eventually the candidate as well as the Mark Hanna. She had that quality, for me. I don't know whether it is a valid quality or not.

Was she interested in political life?

She was interested in political life, she was interested in politics and in literature, in people—she had an *extraordinary* gift with people. She was amazing. Here in Washington, she had this little house on N Street and [on] Tuesday ... every kind of person in the world would come into that house. And on Sundays she was always at home; and you never saw just *one group*—every sort of person turned up there. She was amazing with people.

What was the attraction? I felt it myself, but what was it in your mind?

Well, I think it was because she was so much interested in them. I think it was a sincere interest. And she would take pains and trouble about them. She was not setting herself up as a *saloniste*, but she really liked people. She enjoyed them enormously.

Of course, your father loved people.

And Father had that same thing. They both loved people. Of course, Auntie Bye was able to have the sort of person that she wanted; but Father wasn't—because as you know, Mother [Edith Roosevelt] was, so to speak, anti-fashionable. Auntie Bye was *not*. She enjoyed people of *every* sort, whether they were fashionable or whether they were unfashionable. There was no self-consciousness. She didn't have the self-consciousness that was apparently in my family—my own immediate family. With my family there was something just a little *shady* about being fashionable. There was always that quality; they looked down on it, which I suppose was protective.

Isn't that amusing!

Oh, I suppose so. I can only think so. And it must have come in through Mother, through her rather hard life, do you see, with the drunken father [Charles Carow], and all of the little friends having a little more than they had. Something of that sort must have come in there. I don't know. I've tried to analyze that. When Mother was on some holiday, Father had the most *lovely* time! All of the rather gay friends whom he'd known in the old days like Ralph Ellis, who was a classmate of his, and Betsy Ellis who was the much younger wife of Ralph Ellis; and they all had *lovely* parties and had *such* fun—and then the moment when Mother came back *those* parties stopped immediately. There were no more of those.

Have you ever heard much from Mrs. Cowles about the life at Sagamore Hill while she was running it?

Oh, yes. I even *remember* it! When I was a *very* small child I remember when she was there, and the Fergusons and all sorts of people. It was a pleasant, very friendly life. It was a general feeling of ease and an open house and warmth that it never had from our Mother. She *did* not have warmth about those things. There was always something a *little* [Puritan]—the Jonathan Edwards stock came out in it, I suppose.

There was an old lady in Oyster Bay who remembered the parties that your Auntie Bye used to give up there, and she said they were so infinitely gay and so much gayer than anything that happened later.

Yes. I don't think it was prejudice on my part; I think it was so, that Auntie Bye did give that kind of party. Auntie Corinne [Roosevelt Robinson, TR's younger sister] did it, too—how they did it! They all had that quality; only Mother had such strength of character that she kept that out of the house, except where Father could rise above it, rise *beneath* it.

Where did that quality of social gayety come from in the family?

It came undoubtedly from—at least I say undoubtedly—from my Southern grandmother [Martha Bulloch Roosevelt, better known as "Mittie"], though she was very vague, but I imagine had that ease and gayety that one associates very often with attractive Southerners.

Your father never said very much about his mother.

Oh, but look at his letters! The frightful sentimentality of those letters!

Those early letters, yes. But still, in his autobiography, for instance, he says very little about her in comparison with what he says about his father ... And I always felt that his mother didn't mean a fraction to him what his father meant.

Well, of course, Auntie Bye seems, even at a very tender age, to have managed the household, you know. She was making them be on time for engagements when they were abroad—that comes through some of the things, doesn't it? ... She more or less brought up the other children.

In what way did Mrs. Cowles's power express itself?

I don't know. I'm helpless, helpless about it. She had power over *me* ... Always Auntie Bye meant more to me than anyone. I mean, I was *happier* with her. You see, we were always there when I was three, but we went on living there in the winter, apparently, until we went to Washington. I was still there in the blizzard of [18]88. We were at 689 Madison [Avenue], then, so I was put in the window and told, "Remember this."

It was very easy, because I was four years old. It's a bookshop, now. I go in there every now and then and smell the old kitchen. I do that [illustrating with a sniff]. It's very sentimental.

Did [Mrs. Cowles] tell you many things about Theodore Roosevelt, Sr.?

Well, they worshipped him as though he were a sort of benevolent Norse god, you know. They felt he was the most *wo*nderful man, the goodest man—that was all that I would get about that. Then I saw a lot of pictures of him, a bearded object. I could feel what they felt about him. They adored him! ... In Father's journals, of course, his father's death was the most *frightful* blow to him. For a year or so, I think every month he marked down the day—one month from the death of his father, two months, three months; then it finally drifted away, as those things do. Do you see? That, I should say, was probably the greatest grief that he had, perhaps until the death of my mother, and that, of course, drifted away rapidly, too. But the fire at the death of his father didn't drift away. And, of course, Auntie Bye did talk about my own mother [Alice Hathaway Lee] to me. She was the only person who did. You see, none of the others ever mentioned her. But she did.

What did she tell you about her?

Oh, she said how pretty she was and how attractive she was and how fond Auntie Bye was of her, and things of that sort. You know, making a picture of a very attractive young creature.

That certainly showed great sensitivity to the needs of a child.

Yes, she was the only one who ever said that. The other story was that Mother had told the children, Ted and all of them that if my mother had lived my father couldn't have stood it because he was so bored by her. Then they told me that ... I'm just lucky to be rather tough, to be able to lift an eyebrow and continue to be affectionate, though—like that, shrugging my shoulders.

Didn't your Auntie Corinne ever talk about your mother?

Not that I remember. She talked about *Mother*—my stepmother, whom I always think of as Mother—and she did say they were horrified when Father became engaged to her. They didn't want it at all because they knew her too well and they knew they were going to have a very difficult time—with *her*, that she would come between them and Father. And then Auntie Corinne also said that unless they did just what Mother wanted them to, she would say to Father, "Theodore, I think this winter we've seen a great deal of Douglas and Corinne [the Robinsons] and I don't think we'll ask them down for a little while—yet. We may ask them later." And she knew perfectly well that Father would say, "Very well, very well, Edie, we'll have them later." I don't think he would have if Mother had done this in a rather rude way; but she would have done it quietly, do you see. If it had gone on long enough, then he would have put his foot down, but he wouldn't in the beginning. He did occasionally put his foot down rather firmly. I remember when she became too much like that; I can't think of any special instance at the moment, but he'd stop her if she was being *very* disagreeable about people.

Auntie Bye was never disagreeable about people, but she used to be awfully funny. She was humorous, she was witty. And she was awfully *funny* about people. She could say funny things about them that made you laugh.

It's so difficult to remember. Now [William] Sheffield [Cowles, Jr.] might remember, or [Margaret] Bobbie Cowles; Helen Roosevelt [Robinson] might. If I had ever kept a journal, I would have probably put things down. And Eleanor Roosevelt: I think Eleanor [and] Franklin would probably, though, remember rather fine things—you know, that Auntie Bye had encouraged her to be contented and bear her lot—I don't know what it would be, but you know—that kind of thing, instead of the gayety. [Eleanor] *may* remember the gayety. Auntie Bye used to have these parties for children, for all of us. So did Auntie Corinne. We had much more fun—*I* did—at the parties. There were enough of my younger brothers and sisters close together to have their friends so that they were able to do it; but I was on my own, and just to have *my* friends, I couldn't cope with it. It was no fun. And I always felt it was a slight imposition on the family for me to have these people who, perhaps, were a bore for them. I never did at Sagamore at all. I never had any friends there. The White House was big enough so that I did have people down—there was so much going on of interest in the way of entertainment and of being there, that that was simple. But the other children had a great many Fourth of July parties and all sorts of things. All my gay young parties of my youth were with Auntie Corinne and Auntie Bye. I never had any good times except with them—*young* good times …

Mrs. Cowles's engagement was entirely a surprise to everybody, wasn't it?

A great surprise to everyone. No one could quite understand. Uncle Will [William Sheffield Cowles, Sr.] couldn't have been nicer, but was not in the least what one would have thought Auntie Bye would marry—if she ever married.

He'd been married before, hadn't he?

Had he? Oh, yes, he had, but he had an unfortunate marriage … I think there had been a divorce, yes. It's amazing how people in the Service seem to marry one another. I never knew until the other day that one of Mrs. [Miriam Ham] Radford's other husbands [Earl Winfield Spencer] was also a husband of the Duchess of Windsor [Wallis Simpson] … You found people in the Service do an awful lot of shifting around as they go from post to post—in the Navy, especially.

How large a part did Mrs. Cowles's Washington house play in the Roosevelt administration?

Oh, it was an overflow place. Lots of the people would go there. It was an overflow from the White House. The people who came on always were there, too. She would help the family out by having them at lunch, dinner, all that sort of thing—you know. And people here or there all flocked there because they wanted to see her—and, of course, she was the sister of the president. I suppose that figured to a certain extent.

I was wondering whether your father met people there whom he didn't want to meet in the White House, occasionally, and so forth.

Well, we all used to go there for Sunday evening tea, and the only difference between Sunday evening high tea and dinner was that you had chocolate and whipped cream as well as champagne! It was delightful! I don't know how many people he would meet there; after I was married, he would meet [House Speaker] Uncle Joe Cannon at my house. He didn't want to see him at the White House; so, when he wanted to see him, he met him there. As a rule, he hardly ever wanted to see people without having it known; but he did Cannon, for some reason. It was at the beginning of that Insurgent fight, more towards the end of the administration. I was married in 1906, so it would have been probably have been the next year—1907—when the Insurgent thing was under way. You know, [Kansas Congressman Victor] Murdock, [Massachusetts Congressman] Gussie Gardner, and all that kind [who would become the progressive branch of the Republican Party].

I think he was kidding Joe Cannon with the thought that he might be the candidate in 1908, which rather amused me. That was one of those funny "the hand is quicker than the eye" business that your father enjoyed occasionally.

I don't know whether Uncle Joe Cannon was taken in by it or not. But he *liked* it. He enjoyed it.

It helped their relations.

Yes, it helped. It was all very friendly, very *easing*.

It sounds as though Mrs. Cowles was a very good judge of character. Did she have any feeling that [William Howard] Taft might be a disappointment in not carrying out Theodore Roosevelt's policies?

No, I have no recollection of anything of that sort. I don't think she ever saw the Tafts particularly. I think she would have found them rather boring, which they were. They were not very interesting or attractive, you know, *engaging* people, especially Mrs. [Helen "Nellie"] Taft who was difficult. She would have seen more the—no, she would have seen anyone. She probably did see the Tafts, but they didn't figure at all, as I remember.

I can't remember when Auntie Bye left [Washington, DC]. She must have stayed on a little while after Father left. I don't know whether she was there during the Taft time or not. She began, you know, to have very bad arthritis very soon after that, and became gradually more and more crippled by it. Then she lived in Farmington, [Connecticut].

Did I ever tell you of that extraordinary dinner party at [Mrs. Cowles Farmington house] ... there was Mrs. Cowles at one end of this long table and the Admiral [William Sheffield Cowles, Sr.] way off at the other end of the room, at the other end of the table ... And those two were quipping across the vast distance, your aunt deaf as a post and crippled so she could hardly feed herself—and the life of the party!

That was the extraordinary thing! She was fabulous. When she found she couldn't move at all and was almost stone deaf, except for this hearing thing, she was still the most interested—and interesting—person that you could talk to. She would have me get tea, and then Hopkinson—who was the old butler that she had—Hopkinson would come in and we'd all leave the room. Hopkinson's job then was to simply move her feet. You could hear her say, "Oh Hopkinson! Hopkinson! Oh, Hopkinson!" and you knew that it was anguish, it was torment to have to move them to give her a little change of position. But it never bothered her; I mean, she never bothered people with it. She never let it interfere with her seeing people.

Now you'll hear much more about her from Bobbie who I'm sure will be able to give you stories. Corinne [Robinson] Alsop has a resentment about her and feels that she had to discipline her, that she interfered with Corinne; Corinne had altercations with her.

Auntie Bye always had a few young men. They were known as Joe-Bobs ... One was Bob Ferguson; then he married Isabella [Greenway]. [Mrs. Cowles] didn't quite like that but was nice about it. The other was Joe Alsop who became the successor to Bob Ferguson; then he married Corinne and that was *extremely* displeasing ... Yes, Corinne will tell you that. There's a great deal of truth in that. She always had attractive young men around. Not that she wished to *marry* them—there was no gigolo sense of that sort at all. They enjoyed themselves enormously and then they, not unnaturally, fell in love and got married, but it wasn't entirely pleasing to her. The two Fergusons lived in the coachman's cottage when Auntie Bye owned some property in Oyster Bay ...

There is one thing I would like to ask. There was a certain time—I think before the vice-presidency—when Mr. Roosevelt was writing to Mrs. Cowles, who was in England, and talking about "the conquest of Canada." At one time he wrote, "It seems to me that if England were wise she would fight now ..."

Fight what? Us?

And then later, "If it weren't wrong I should say that personally I would rather welcome a foreign war!" I was wondering what Mrs. Cowles's reactions, living in England among the English, would be to that? I wondered whether you ever knew ...

No! I never even knew it until this moment. I think that is perfectly fascinating.

That's in the collection of letters to Mrs. Cowles.

I think Father had the feeling the whole continent should belong to the United States ...

Well, of course, during all those early years your father was crazy for a war that he could take part in.

Oh, he *longed* to have a war. *How* he wanted a war! Do you suppose that was because his father had not fought?

That was part of it, I think.

I suppose it was, don't you think so? ... The Southern side all fought, do you see; but the Northern side didn't. His father bought a substitute, which was considered reasonable in those days, and didn't spare himself going out with the Allotment Commission with things for the troops. He had discomfort and danger but just didn't fight—didn't think of it. I could always make Father *furious* by saying, "Look at Lincoln, after all, writing that letter to Grant when he said couldn't Grant take his son Robert on his staff—that Robert had now finished Harvard—and he'd like him to *see* a little bit of the war." That was *very* hard on Father about his hero Lincoln! We were teasing him.

Well, certainly in later years that didn't come out quite as strongly ...

You mean about the war with England? Oh, no, because he had had a little blood-letting, so to speak, in the Spanish War. He had *had* that.

Way back, I know, in the Badlands times, in the later [18]80s, he had a sense that he had to make a career. He had to justify himself—and a war seemed to promise the obvious way of doing it.

Then, you know, he liked the Nibelungenlied, the fighters. He loved that. He *loved* it! We were brought up on the Nibelungenlied, so we all had that feeling for fighters. And "Harald, Harald, gracious giver, Jesu rest thy soul forever"—all of those; "Saddle my horse!" and how he jumps over the cliff—that one. All of those rather stern, melancholy ballads.

Your father himself was brought up possibly on too many heroic ballads as a child.

I think he may have been, and I think he did it to Ted, too. He did it to all of us. We all shouted "The Saga of King Olaf"—all of that—at the top of our lungs. We were all brought up on those things. I think Father brought himself up on those. They filled some want of some sort.

But apparently his father was not yearning for warfare ...

Not in the least, you see. That, I think, turned Father to it, from his own father having been perfectly content to go out with allotments ...

Of course, he did it because of his wife, I suppose.

That was the way it would appear. I wonder if there is any trace of that, because one would think it *might* be that ... When you think of [Martha's] two brothers fighting ...

To think of her brothers as possibly fighting her own husband would send her into a tailspin, I suppose.

Yes, it would have been a perfectly awful thing ... And think how near that is! Not a 100 years ago—a brief ninety. And all the feeling in the South still, and people talk about one world! It's so pathetic. They think they can have a united Europe, when we're hardly even a United States yet! ... They were all that kind of thing that Richard Harding Davis thought was so elegant—you know, he'd like to have been one of them but wasn't quite. Wrote stories about them, of that era. And Uncle Ellie [Elliott Roosevelt] must have been the same, because I remember him when I was a child. I was lugged along on walks practically with my feet not touching the ground. I remember Uncle Ellie being there—and I liked Uncle Ellie. But that's just as a *very* small child.

What was the cause of [Elliott's] downfall?

We always were told that it was epilepsy. Eleanor [Roosevelt, FDR's wife] having said, in her book, that he was a drunkard ...

Of course, he must have been.

Oh, he was a drunkard, yes. But he became a drunkard because he was an epileptic. That's what we understood. Now, how much of that is so, I don't know; but I'm inclined to think so, because he was not sent to college. He did not go to college. He went on a trip to India—big game hunting—and I think they kept him occupied because he wasn't able to go to college and they were compensating for that by sending him around the world and giving him treats. He may not have been an epileptic, but in the family, we understood that. You know he became a frightful drunkard.[10]

* * *

October 1955

[Recording begins with Mrs. Longworth discussing her cousin Stewart Alsop's family]

There's Joe [Alsop], Ian [Alsop] and then comes Elizabeth [Winthrop Alsop] and there is little Stewart [Alsop, Jr]. Little Elizabeth came over and conversed because I complimented her on a valentine that she showed us that she'd made. And suddenly as I was talking, as I'm talking now, she said, "As I'm talking, as I'm talking now." She did an imitation of me, which was so superb—she's 6 years old—I laughed until I cried!

I said, "You're a minx! You're a baggage. And up to now, I thought she was a dear little quiet prim child who sat one foot slightly advanced, the other slightly behind that foot with a little ribbon in your hair, your little hands folded in your lap. And you're a wicked child."

We became the kind of friends that never have been; we laughed until we cried and then I got her to do more imitations of me. Just the way I had said to her, I said something, "I thought you're a prim little child," and she said, "I thought you're a prim little child," right after me. It was a gift: imitation, and gaiety. And apparently according to her mother [Patricia Barnard Hankey] she had never done this with people before. She's rather shy.

Then when I left, Corinne [Alsop, Mrs. Longworth's niece and TR's granddaughter] was going back next day. She loves those four children and she's not there at their birthdays and when she is there at any moment, she has what's called an "altogether birthday party" and she takes them out shopping and they have a list, and [she gets] what they want as a present. Each one makes a list and puts down the present or the substitute things. So, she was taking them the next day on the "altogether birthday," and as I left the child says "Are you coming? I hope you're coming I wished that you'd come." I'd never been so flattered. I simply beamed. I looked like the cat with cream on its whiskers. And it was such fun, suddenly I was being sent with another generation. Isn't it fantastic? I think it was Corinne [Alsop], Stewart [Alsop] and now this fourth generation [Stewart's children]. And I went back another day and I never had a better time ... Four generations of hilarity—sheer hilarity.

But I suppose your ability to imitate...

Yes, I am. I speak in a way that is absurd and I know it. And there are a handful of words like "uh-uh-ah" that amuse the child. I've never heard anything as funny as she was. She really was gay! She was a baggage. We had a very good time. She's an engaging child ...

Last year [my nephew] Joe Alsop and [Baltimore journalist] Frank Kent had a seventieth birthday party for me. And I said, "No you can't have a party," and then they said, "we should have a party."

I said, "that's alright, but there must be no speeches. I hate speeches—no speeches, no presents, and no eulogies, tributes, or that sort of thing."

So, they said, "very well." Then Joe said [at the party], "Mrs. L. has told us not to make a [speech], but," he said, "My co-partner Mr. Kent is now going to make a friendly speech which is a combination of affection and venom." It is *the* most—I think sometime I'll put it on the tape recorder. He made it spontaneously, but he added so much of him! I'll read it to [the tape recorder] sometime ... This speech, I can read it and show where it is funny that you described about this party in which a great many people hated and disliked one other intensely and most of them, sometimes liked me, but a great many of them only liked me very infrequently. And certainly, they dislike one another intensely. In fact, when [diplomat William Christian] "Bill" Bullitt came in, he said [something unkind about Joe Alsop]. I cannot stand middle-aged men and elderly men fighting so with one another—he and Joe are on such bad terms, you see? So, he came in the first 6 people he saw when he came in, he didn't speak to them and they didn't speak to him.

Every time John Hollister who is an old friend of mine, who took the first congressional district when Nick [Longworth] represented it—in Cincinnati—and when Nick died, he went to Congress and I visited for years, every time he looked up and saw Felix Frankfurter he gagged. It was marvelous!

Pat Nixon suddenly said to someone, "Is that Justice Frank-fur-ter?" And they said, "Yes." She marched [out].

It was awfully funny, and there are a lot of people that weren't particular friends of mine, but Joe was paying off some debts by having them. Made me feel guilty as hell because they were people I shouldn't have had in the house ... they're too boring ... And things like that, and then suddenly the Bonnets [George and Odette] who is, you know, the French Ambassador, I like them well enough I would say they're my friends, but Joe said, "There must be some drama." That's like Joe, so he invited the Bonnets; he didn't get the Makins; he wanted an ambassador or two. The Makins are very old friends: [British Ambassador to the U.S. Sir] Roger Makin and Alice Makin was the daughter of Ike [Dwight F.] Davis [the former secretary of war] and Helen [Brooks] Davis's predecessor Pauline [Sabin] Davis who is a big friend of mine who's one of the gayest and most amusing people in the world. And Pauline [Sabin] Davis resents—I'm sure she resents so many things; poor Pauline, she's very ill now—but Helen [Brooks] Davis had an affair with [Polish Ambassador] Jan Ciechanowski, a terrific affair, and Helen Davis wouldn't have the Ciechanowskis, never had them in the house. In other words, she resented the fact that her husband, her third husband had the horns put on him, by his first wife by Jan Ciechanowski; it was confused and deceived like that. It was a real affair if I may say, a good old bang-up, old fashion love affair! And Helen resented it! Bloody nonsense. Anyway, Joe didn't have him at his party and I think I was trying to get him ...

When [Frank Kent] mentioned how the people there disliked one another ... He said "Lots of people they mightn't have come to the same rooms with some of the people they could've had." Who knows [if] they rather have had [Wisconsin Senator] Joe McCarthy instead of the Wigglesworths but then nobody else would come [laughs]. I really do know the Wigglesworths; I've only seen McCarthy once or twice. Do you want to know the first time I ever met him; did I ever tell you when I first met McCarthy?

No!

Let's do that now, shall we?

Yes!

Well, this lady, Miss Kay [Katherine Graham of the *Washington Post*], she's supposed to be a Washington hostess, and she'd asked me to dinner many times, very kindly, and I hadn't accepted, and finally she asked me and I didn't answer, and then she telephoned her secretary who telephoned, and I said "yes."

And the next day someone again telephoned and said "Are you really coming here to dinner Mrs. Longworth?"

I said "Yes, I'm really coming," and there's someone else on the telephone and I said "Yes I am coming to dinner!"

And, in fact, I'm going to be in New York but I was coming back that day. And I went to New York and the train was late. This was just five years ago, in [19]50, and the train was late and I got in and discovered that this lady [Miss Kay] was ill or away or something. And a note was there saying she was ill and then a message saying "Senator McCarthy will call for you at quarter past seven." And there was a little box on the table, too, from the florists and I opened it and inside there was white orchid, kind of turned rather brown around the edges where it had atrophied, and a card on which written in rather sloppy handwriting, "Joe McCarthy."

I said, "This serves me right." An elderly lady addicted to politics, they asked her to dinner, and they immediately think who should provide a suitable escort as I believe they do in these circles. I've never been escorted to dinner, but served me right, and it happened to me. It isn't his fault. These things are so foolish. So, instead, leaving a message, which I left, saying, "Tell Senator McCarthy my mother's waiting on a train journey coming up." And dinner was at eight. Why he was sent for me at quarter past seven, I don't know. I popped my head over the banister and said, "Oh, Senator McCarthy how very kind of you to come for me, thank you so much for this lovely orchid and how very considerate of Miss Kay to send you, but my mother's here, and I am going to be there anyway for dinner at eight. And he was standing there giving only the impression of wearing an opera cape, an opera hat fold, looking like that you see, and then I went down to the dinner in due time and it was ridiculous, and I sat between Joe McCarthy and Bob Hope.

In other words, Mr. McCarthy left and went to the party by himself.

And went by himself to the party and I came up in due time. So, I talked to him and said "I was always delighted to see a young man in the business of politics and this-that-and-the-other," and he said "Could I bring a friend of mine to see you?"

And I said, "You can, anytime. I'd love to see her." It was Jean Kerr [one of McCarthy's research staffers] and it took a long time for [Kerr] to make up her mind and marry [McCarthy].

That was that. I never saw Senator McCarthy again; it was three weeks before he made the speech that started the whole thing ["Enemies from Within" speech that began the Red Scare]. Wasn't it fascinating? I saw him a couple of times after that, and well, I hardly know him. Still, I was very strongly for what he was doing. I only deplored some of the profanities, but surely, he did more to alert this county to the communist infiltration than anyone. Only he began at the wrong end.

He alerted the communists so they could hide! Didn't he?

No, they couldn't hide; he really was getting them out. He's an abominable creature, and he's not a very bright man. He's a pretty stupid man I'm afraid, for instance, when he came back to the special session of the censure, he had thirteen members attack him at that committee and then when the censure was passed, then he attacked Eisenhower, escaped marvelously out from the procedure to vote against him to come right back and say that Eisenhower had one or two [communists on the White House staff]. Then when the army case was crumbling practically, he was finished, then he brought in the name of [Fred] Fisher.

That! Was the thing that convinced me that there was something funny.

Oh well it was stupid; the whole thing was stupid ... it was really an ugly situation. I mean there was nothing innocent about it [McCarthy suggested in a live broadcast of the Army hearings that Fisher should be fired for being a communist to which Army counsel Joseph Welch famously retorted, "have you no sense of decency?"]. Because it had all been explained that he had belonged to something, and he belonged to a guild or whatever it was.

The [National] Lawyers' Guild.

Lawyers' Guild, yes Lawyers' Guild—and therefore had to come down [from representing the Army] and that was all there was to it. There was two of them, it was stupid! The Lawyers Guild didn't hurt anybody. [McCarthy] started to moan, and put his head in his hands, you see? And the Army case was gone! Of course, they all wanted to get rid of that. Incredibly stupid! Indecent. The dreadful man [McCarthy] should never have been there … they should have found intelligent and higher competent people to run against him … And about Dick Nixon: he has a very high intelligence; a very able man and I like him very much.

Nixon?

A great friend of mine, yes … I think he'll weather it alright because he's a strong character.

[The discussion strays to other parts of the government where communists were discovered and Mrs. Longworth alludes to clandestine techniques that communists might use to infiltrate society.]

The Russians were training with the Chinese to take over Vietnam?

Oh yes. And they release the armies and now they got what they want there. They say there's a chance of holding them there, but I don't know.

We need someone so much like your father.

At least he was willing to fight! I mean war is a horrible thing, it's a crime and you've got to fight.

In other words, if the choice between peace and righteousness I choose …

And he did that in his third term speech [to Congress] someone told me, a man the other day. "Excellent!" I said, "it's perfect." National honor is not involved anymore.

The UN will do it. In other words, the UN will make up its mind and tell us to do police action, but never go too far [referring to the Korean War]. Shocking. I have no confidence in what Eisenhower is doing … There was always the emphasis of having like-minded nations join together and when the nations we did not consider like-minded became more like-minded then they should be allowed in. But there has never been a question of taking Russia, as Russia behaves … I should be inclined to think that if—at that time Russia, a good many people we all suspected what they were doing, in fact they put on a show of what they were doing, what they've been doing for a long time—that there would have been no question of taking them back into the League.

They were not like-minded, they certainly didn't agree with us, and they put obstacles in the way in the formation of the United Nations. To go back to Wilson, that was the question, in those days we used to talk about national honor and vital interest, about which we don't talk about national honor and vital interest very much now. At least, I don't think we talk about it very much. And anything that conflicted with our vital honor and national interest we would not sacrifice our right to make decisions on those principles.

Listen, this is branching away from Russia and branching away from us and coming back to Father and Wilson, the League. And then of course, there's that terrific antagonism between my father and Wilson.

And the feeling that he was a theorist who never gets ...

Yes. Since you go in to any organization to agree, except blindfolded, anything this organization decided without our having a chance to express ourselves or decide not to join in activities or enterprises of the League.

Now, when you're speaking of like-minded nations, were you speaking of the United Nations or of the League?

No, I'm speaking then of the League. I'm speaking of Father's Nobel Peace Prize speech where you see what his idea of a League of Nations was.

And then, was the difficulty with Russia, in connection with the League of Nations, at that particular time, was she also acting up?

Oh, no. We were sending expeditions to Archangel and I can't remember if that came before the Versailles conference or not. I'm sure she was pretty well on the rocks you see then. Even before the Revolution, or during the Revolution. I say during the revolution—just after the revolution. It could have been the winter of 1919. The revolution is in [19]17. Kerensky had already gone out ...

Because I suppose if [the peace treaty] had been conceived as your father had originally conceived it ...

If [a nation] behaves bad, how are you going to get a de-nationalized international force to cope with them? Who will put force behind the decision? Who's going to do that? Are they not going to [have] still some connection with the nations in which they belong? I don't see how they are going to do it. If you did have a big League, which was in agreement on certain policies, and other nation's outside it violated what you decided were the principles of a League of Nations [how would you discipline it]? In father's speech, he's always allowing for attacking the wrongdoers. It's all a lovely, rather simple thing. I don't know if they took into consideration what the complications would be.

Because the idea of a complete supra-nationalism is something that has to be educated over eons, I suppose.

I should think so. But I don't believe that you'll find the people through all the countries wanting the United Nations or One World—One World, rather, not the United Nations. They love the idea of the United Nations, apparently. But the idea of a One World, you see, that's not a popular idea. I mean a popular idea in the sense that it's considered and thought about by the peoples of the world. They put the interest in this new millennia campaign ... I'm just as fuzzy as anyone can be when you ask a question like that about the League of Nations and United Nations, and Father, and I immediately tell you to go back and read Father's Nobel Prize speech.

Well, I think that is absolutely what I should do.

Well, you'll see there are differences. Not plunging yourself in advance to something without knowing what the circumstances were.

It would be a great danger of getting into entangling alliances.

Well, it would. I mean whether it would be a benefit to this country and possibly to other countries, but *never* in advance ... he said a good deal about that. He said that about [the Treaty of] Portsmouth [that the United States had a] definite job to do, but after that they felt he should take part in everything and he didn't believe in that. All of that comes in what he said that his point of view, different from the Wilson thing, of course different from what we're doing now ...

Well, you didn't feel that Wilson had the experience internationally or enough with people. He was more of a student, more of a scholar. Rather more than a person who knew how to deal with human nature.

Alright. I don't know if you have followed our discussion all wrong. That what [Wilson] was doing: he didn't want a war and Father wanted war, altogether it was very repugnant to him. He felt that [Wilson] wasn't quite a scholar he was supposed to be, that he claimed to be. He said he's antipathetic to people who had long experience in public affairs.

Did you hear Mr. Dulles ... were you at the Theodore Roosevelt [Association] dinner when Mr. Dulles received a medal?

No, I don't think—it was a year ago, wasn't it?

I think that was 2 years ago. Because he spoke of Mr. Roosevelt's saving the world from three possible developments in the World War. Because he stood on his principles and was perfectly honest about what the United States would do and gave contrary to Mr. Wilson's "keeping us out of war" as a campaign slogan and without standing firm on what would the United States would do ...

Probably encouraged the Germans too, with our shifts [in policy]. I think my father thought that if we had been in an organization or Union of Nations, or if we had a treaty saying that we would act if Germany moved, or made an illegitimate move, that then they wouldn't have come in, but that if they doubted us, nothing wouldn't [stop them]. England also kept them in suspense, so to speak. They thought that England would come in, so they didn't move then.

Well, Mr. Dulles mentioned Mr. Wilson's lack of frankness as to what America would do. Also, Franklin Roosevelt's pledging that we would not send our men overseas, I believe that's in 1940, and then also Acheson's drawing a circle which excluded Korea and our interests, and said "Now, those were the places we were not frank and honest and so the enemy moved."

Oh, it was an invitation.

It was a most exciting speech that Mr. Dulles made and his main thesis was that peace has to be fought for harder even than war and that your father fought for peace with honesty and with principles, and that is why he was respected, and why war did not have to come, in contrast to the use of platitudes and slogans to get re-elected, without being frank and, in other words, deceiving the enemy.

Deceiving? Yes. Deceiving the people, deceiving the enemy. Both, you see. Yes. Potential enemy ... Isn't that good. [Dulles] makes such good speeches sometimes and always seems to act up to them ... there is all this business about agonizing reappraisal and massive retaliation. Nobody is doing any massive retaliation, yet. All we do is send someone to hand the thing to the enemy. By handing it to them so they don't even have to lose the life of one man. And they always say we can attack; too bad we don't do it, of course. We evacuate for them, we destroy the fortifications, leave everything to the Chinese in Formosa. But things are different ...

Oh, it's ghastly business, the whole thing.

They were getting our news and radio reports, someone said, as well from other places. What the Chinese communists wanted they got, while not having to fire a shot.

Well, if they move on Formosa, though, then we are more or less pledged to come to the rescue, aren't we?

Yes, but they won't get Formosa that way. They'll get it through a conference. They'll say that Formosa is too strategic, of being another China, it would help them more. All these big busted wars, a big business head is up there the other day, passing the treaty. Wouldn't be very nice [for business]. [China] won't attack—they probably won't—and will get what they want anyway. They'll not attack and start a war they don't particularly want. If we give up Qimei and Matsu [islands], then they have the immediate approaches. They can threaten as much they want. We are threatened from the Russians. [Formosa] can make the line there [in the Taiwan Strait] and leaves it very troublesome for the Chinese communists to have those lands in nationalist's hands. We should do what we want. We say strategically, of course, if we see an amassing of troops the implication is that it seems to threaten an invasion, we could act—that is the strategic thinking. That came in; I can't remember the exact wording of it. But it does not mean anything. It's indefinite. It's a hint.

It's amazing that these people who are so boorish in their diplomacy can be so amazingly clever in their strategy.

Yes. But we take it. They can train us if they want to. We don't care. Here, we sit back if we don't do anything else. There is a limpness. They say, "Be careful. We must not start a war." Took a risk in going to Korea; we took a calculated risk and we were gone and prepared against hot pursuit.

I wonder if that was coming, this finagling.

I don't know if it's just cowardice or communists, what it was. The people who thought we shouldn't have gone beyond the Yalu [River], they said to release troops from southern Asia and then Vietnam was lost and China was gone. France wouldn't fight, wouldn't go on. We wouldn't do anything; we said we'd do something. They said it was overblown, a blockade; we helped them out there. Get the troops out and evacuate it for them, so to speak. They didn't have to go on fighting. We've done everything, in the world, to help them.

To help the Russians, you mean.

And the Chinese. And it's something they learned about: how to get a cease-fire. It's alright. They can have a cease-fire. Not very much firing is going on anyway ...

But, you were starting to speak about ...

Auntie Bye?

I imagine she could be caustic at times because her own son said that if she did not feel that a person was worthy, she could annihilate him in another person's mind in two sentences, and that other person will never feel the same about him.

Isn't that interesting? I can rather imagine. I've never asked those questions. I felt the same way, there was too much agreement. She never annihilated anyone in front of me. She was very neutral in annihilating people. I've never remembered her being caustic with me. Never. And she is one of the only people that ever spoke to me about my own mother. She did that. But that may have been, more or less, disciplining my family, you see. And slightly disciplining them. So, they didn't. And it was such a great pleasure to be with her. It was fun. It was gay.

I love what you said about someone, quite early on in your life, mentioning that she was not at all beautiful and then you suddenly ...

Well, I didn't see what's missing. I know a man that liked her very much, the Spanish ambassador [Juan Riaño y Gayangos] who was a great friend of all of ours. And they met early on, way on thirty years ago, so to speak. I mean, it was well known at the time [but] we had no idea. Just talking about her at the beginning and, of course, I thought her illness a wretched thing, but she was very energetic. She walked a great deal, she rowed and when she used to be at Sagamore she had a cottage and a stable. Near Gracewood. And I remember the Ferguson brothers, two brothers Hector and Bob Ferguson lived in that cottage for a while, and I remember Auntie Bye's horses must have been kept over there. And I can see a very scrappy little stable with two horses, and I remember their names were Fancy and Frolic. Fancy and Frolic and Auntie Bye would go driving off with the groom sitting behind in the rumble seat, you see.

And she would be driving?

Oh yes, she drove through everything. We would just take some amount of clothes that you put on the horses, and then you rowed and you rowed. You would do things, so to speak, that "gentleman" did.

Oh yes. And I understand that in Washington, she used to go walking with the First Lady with her sister-in-law, practically every day.

With Mother? Well, I suppose they didn't take walks. They wandered up and down S Street to go shopping, or something like that. I don't think they ever took real walks. I don't remember them taking walks. Nothing like with Father, for instance.

Well, I guess his were pretty strenuous for any woman.

Well, he used to take us all out. I think that Mother went then, when we were children. We'd come back having forded Rock Creek in a state of dishevelment of wet and mud. But those were little walks and she did go with Father and used to take them to the express wagon and drag his youngest child around the express wagon, in the zoo part of the park, in those days. But I don't remember Auntie Bye in those walks, but we did take Auntie Bye, for instance, Auntie Bye gave us a holiday, two-weeks holiday in Bennington [Vermont]. We all took long walks in the country, Mother, Auntie Bye and all the children. Good long, sturdy walks ... Corinne [Robinson Alsop] and I have been talking about Auntie Corinne [Mrs. Robinson] about various—did she mention [editor and philanthropist] Mr. [Charles Allen] Munn?

Yes, that's been something that has made us both a little curious because [Mrs. Robinson's friend] Mrs. [Helen Sargeant] Hitchcock, who is devoted to Mrs. Robinson, said that she sort of drifted away from Mrs. Robinson because of feeling that there was un-wisdom with regard to her friendship with Mr. Munn.

That, of course, would be a nice prim—it was just like having a cozy follower. He adored her, and it was a cozy thing ... I always felt that it was innocuous like Corinne. Most people don't believe it was, but I think so.

I gathered that and I don't believe that Mrs. Hitchcock had anything to base her judgment on with just the feeling that there was—there were tongues wagging and wasn't it too bad.

Mr. Charlie Munn was around from the very beginning. When I was a child, he was around. And then until Father died, he was still around, although very aged. But I don't think it was more than, not really hardly romantic.

Well, I've always been curious about the poems [Mrs. Robinson wrote] and the stories back of them.

Because it's all personal, I'm sure most of it's personal. I must get it out for [my daughter] Paulina [Longworth Sturm] some time, and look at them trying to find the background. There used to be laughs and jeers. There were too many little words. That's probably her voice, very, very intense. Mother said if you didn't read it that way, they wouldn't be nearly as bad if you read it in a more casual way it's very nicely put: masterpiece poetry. It didn't rhyme, but it had to be called poetry ...

But it was very sweet.

Yes. Like syrup. That's Auntie Corinne. She wept all the way up the aisle on her wedding, she wept all the way down.

Well, according to her daughter, she wept for six months before the wedding.

After six months. She wept a good deal, and cried easily, anyway.

Mrs. Alsop said that in the course of one of her fits of weeping before she was married, Auntie Bye said, "Well, after all you've taken that on and you cannot break an engagement."

Oh, Auntie Bye. Just to get it out of the way. Yes, tidy it up.

It would seem absolutely horrible. I mean breaking an engagement was as bad as divorce.

Oh, just about so. Black. Oh, and dreadful and she was such fun.

Well, apparently according to Mrs. Alsop, [her mother and father] became very devoted.

Oh, very devoted. Corinne [Alsop] doesn't believe that [her father] had affairs with other ladies, I think he did. I don't really know; I said "I met him with a few ladies."

"Oh no," she said.

I think she's wrong about that because he behaved too brutally and we didn't speak. I suppose we encountered gentlemen that took prostitutes. We don't speak and he never mentioned it. I never told anyone, and he knew I wouldn't tell. And he was with some man and a couple of very gay Lillian Russell type ladies, so to speak.

Well, she was certainly most attractive.

Auntie Corinne? Oh, she was a darling. Such a darling. Oh, so gay and all these ridiculous rhymes that she wrote?

Well, she had such bubbling fun in her diary and yet after her son died, apparently she never got over it.

No, I don't think she did. She didn't have the quality Mother had—cast iron about things, you see. Auntie Bye would have had that. But Auntie Corinne, no. [Stewart's death] was with her all the time.

Because apparently, he was quite different from the other children, very special in her eyes.

I wonder if he was? Might have been, yes. He was the youngest, and he was a different color ... they all others were dark and looked like Uncle Douglas a little bit, he was a little different because Stewart was blond. That's possible.

Well, apparently, he and Mrs. Alsop were very, very devoted. They were devoted friends as well as being brother and sister.

Oh, listen, Mo[nroe]'s was a fantastic character and it was ruined by drink.

Apparently, [Monroe] never got along with his father at all.

Not together, he didn't. Lucky, he was patient about it. And, of course, on the Robinson's side there was some fabulous sets of family: the old Henderson who cut the couch in two and made two chaise lounge and spit to the husband, married late in life, oh all of that ... when you go into them almost all families are odd.

Well, it was certainly individual.

Joe Alsop is the person for you to get hold of on family things. Oh, Joe, I am sure will give you much. Do you know Corinne [Alsop] is a class act, but Joe is an artist. Joe would give you; he would just feed things to you. Joe and I have always had been [planning that] we would do a thing together on all the members of the family: about everything and everyone. And if Joe and I did something like that we would have no inhibitions. No, "you wouldn't say it." There was nothing we wouldn't admit, anything. That would be fun. We could do a nice bit on that. When he comes back, I'm going to find out if we can have an hour or an afternoon dedicated to conversation which, he is a superb conversationalist. And that one night we were here, he and Isaiah Berlin and myself and we spent hours talking and he said with three people together, each of whom has all its own voice is the most terrific music in the world. We gave each other time and we didn't interrupt. We were scrupulous, sat there and were scrupulous ... What we really ought to do indiscreet things. We want to be indiscreet and we will, you know, stir it up ...

Well, I tell you we can always turn off the tape.

It really wouldn't be nice. [Mrs. Longworth moves away from microphone and her voice becomes inaudible]

The things that are what?

Things that are fun: about Eleanor and Franklin and all of them.

* * *

2 January 1956

In September [1901] we were in the White House, from then on ... the relatively few brief years, not very many, as you see, from the time our father left the White House, it was only ten years until he died. Then it went on much the same way that it had gone on when they didn't have a young family, and in rather straightened circumstances.

There was always a watchfulness about bills, of course. That's the impression I have about it—that there was a great deal of watchfulness. There was a good deal of talk of the economy. Now, I remember—I may have done this in my book [*Crowded Hours*] I don't remember—but when we got to Albany, and Father had a larger salary than he'd ever had before, and then they took me in, as I was then fourteen or fifteen. It was [18]99, so I was just under fifteen. I remember I was taken into the family councils that they had more money, and they were to save some of it. And we discussed things like that. And as I say, then when he was vice president, he was still in his [Washington accommodation]. The Bellamy Storers [an Ohio family related to Nick Longworth] rented to him for a very nominal sum. They had a fairly good-sized house. And then there was discussion then about my coming out. And I think I read in [Father's autobiography] that they didn't want me to come out, they wanted me to study. But that I don't remember. I never knew where he got that ... I was always going to come out then. And of course, I was rather mean to the family, because by that time I was bored by anything, except coming out with my own friends, seeing my own friends in New York, Boston, and Philadelphia, so to speak. And then branched out to Chicago and St. Louis, which was practically an adventure. Sounds so ridiculous to think the first time I'm in Chicago, I thought I was practically going out to the frontier. It was exciting. It was an excitement to see the look of it. And when you came over the ferry and then took the train to go out to the west. This is me that doesn't belong in this [place].

Oh, that's wonderful. I know that's a part of it.

And to go back to food, let me see about more food.

Oh, don't.

Oh, yes, and always at dinner, always, there was wine. And invariably wine. It was just as natural to have wine as to have bread. We had sherry, and madeira and perhaps claret. And it was there and you had it. You took it or you didn't take it, but it was always something there. And there were two bottles. I should say, in those big coaster things you had bottles on the table. But I never remember when there wasn't wine. There wasn't wine at lunch ... after a drive I'd have a drink of something. I think I also remember, as far as I was concerned, they advised me, they said they thought it would be a very good plan if I didn't drink champagne and things at parties, because my spirits were very high anyway and people would think if I drank things, that it was because I'd had too much to drink. That's a funny way of putting it. Instead of saying they think it "tight" [slang for drunk] as we would say nowadays, they would think I had too much to drink. And so, I didn't ever drink things at balls and that sort of thing when I was young. Didn't want to particularly.

That was a great deal of character, I would say, when everybody else was.

I didn't want to. No, no, the others didn't. They just thought it was better not. I don't think girls ever did take very much. I mean, they may have had a glass of wine at dinner, but not champagne, not at a party. I think they were rather scrupulous about not taking things, not drinking, which was rather good with champagne. Of course, champagne was supposed to be a gay drink ... And, of course, then there were no cocktails. In fact, we never had cocktails at the house until after prohibition. And that was after Father died. And then Mother, out of defiance, had cocktails of a *dubious* quality. It was unbelievable. They were the most horrible thing, made of ghastly, noxious things. But she did it entirely out of disapproval of prohibition. She thought it was perfectly awful, and so she gave everybody cocktails. My father gave them—or I was told often to remind him to offer them all—whiskey and soda, because he never had whiskeys and sodas. After dinner, well, there were certain men there who obviously would want something, to give them whiskey and soda. The only drink that he took, except for drinking in meals, would be eggnogs made with—I don't know whether they were made with sherry or one of the American whiskeys—eggnog, and then he loved mint juleps. And mint juleps after tennis and things of that sort, when they'd been playing tennis. But they weren't a regular thing and the eggnogs were just delicious. I call them eggnogs, but I think [there] may be another name for them. It was milk with something in it, and there was nutmeg on top of it ...

And you just loved to be in that place?

We all loved Sagamore, yes. I mean, I loved it until I was thirteen and fourteen. And as soon as I was about that age, I began not to care for it. But the other children, I think, kept on loving it. They all went back whenever they could. I didn't feel that way about it. In the pond, we used to dig around there and catch little turtles and snakes, things like that. We had such good times ... It really was country then ... We really had good, very, simple, old-fashioned country existence, where it was just the country then. Enormous amounts of long walks. Whenever I go back there now, and get to East Norwich, soon after East Norwich, I'll know every puddle as far; I'll know every inch of it on foot.

Yes. I remember reading in your book about the terrific walks that you took of twelve miles.

That was when I was older, when I was about fourteen.

Here in Washington?

No, there [Sagamore]. I did it here, too, but I did it there. Actually, I walked over to Center Island [directly across from Cove Neck and Oyster Bay Harbor]. And I think I walked back, to Center Island and back, which is a long walk, with a couple of cousins, that sort of thing. Having been rather feeble, I suppose I had to assert myself, prove that I could do those things.

You mean you were delicate as a child?

Oh, frightfully, yes, because I had braces in each leg up to the knee until I was twelve or something like that.

I didn't realize that. I knew that Kermit wore a brace.

No, I wore braces. I had braces on each of my boots had braces on them. And my legs were stretched every night. Now, that's in my book, too. Now, the one leg was stretched five minutes, the other seven and a half so the tendons matched. It is supposed that I'd had infantile paralysis. I think I probably did, because I have a lateral curvature of the spine, and the kind of things you have from a relatively light attack of infantile. So, the sides of the feet were put out like that. And when I was getting over that and because of that, I had to walk. I wouldn't do any games. I didn't like games. I hated games. I hated all of those things, the other things rather violently.

Did you go on the obstacle walk?

Oh, yes, we did those things. We were told to separate, and you'd meet on the other side of the hill or something. Did those around Albany, too.

I feel as if Ethel would remember all sorts of little things. She was much more ... introspective, and she lived to talk to Father about this and that. I didn't. I was always busy concealing—not busy about it, I just concealed.

I was very much interested to read some of the letters that your father wrote to Kermit at the time, when, around 1904, when he wasn't, apparently, at all sure that he was going to win the election ... saying, well, the thing that meant the most in his life anyway was Sagamore Hill and his family ...

Yes, well, also putting yourself on record, vaccinating against what might happen, vaccinating against defeat.

That's an interesting point.

Oh, yes, vaccinating against it, and the posterity of it. A lot of people think they were posterity letters. We called them his posterity letters. Posterity, that's what we called them, very nice posterity letter, written for the biographies. I'm teasing, of course.

That was unconscious, though. I mean, or was that conscious?

Fairly conscious. We were always fairly conscious. Oh, yes. That's a matter of record. And he did love Sagamore. But he wouldn't have liked to have been licked in 1912, I mean in 1904. And, of course, in 1912, he knew he was going to be beaten. We were all pretty sure of that, really. I wish he hadn't run.

Well, Mr. Savacool—who ... worked ... with the Bull Moose campaign—said in retrospect that he felt that if Mr. Roosevelt had not agreed to run ... the whole course of history would've been changed and there would've been neither World War I, nor World War II.

Oh, no, all of those things, yes. And it would've all been changed if he hadn't put Taft in, and hadn't gone out against him then for what he called a third term. Because the moment he sent the [Great White] Fleet round the world to show that we were strong—strong and civil—all of that "speak softly and carry a big stick"—moments after that, Taft did nothing, absolutely nothing.

You mean he relied on Mr. Roosevelt's show of strength to carry through.

Oh, he dropped everything. He dropped everything. He didn't have any idea of the outside world and he made faces to Japan, and waved sticks, and we were uncivil, and didn't keep our guard up. And then came the big war. So many people have felt that if Germany had been sure that we would go in to a war, it would have not attacked. I don't know. There probably would have been a war, but most likely Germany would be the most powerful European country, Eurasian country. So, there might've been a war anyway. It would have been different, no doubt about that.

CHAPTER 3

From Hyde Park to Oyster Bay: Helen Roosevelt Robinson

Fig. 3.1 Helen Roosevelt Robinson at Campobello (1925), FDR Library

Helen Roosevelt Robinson, like her cousin First Lady Eleanor Roosevelt, was born into and married into the Roosevelt family. Eleanor hailed from the Long Island clan otherwise known as the Oyster Bay Roosevelts; she was Theodore Roosevelt's niece. Eleanor married Franklin Delano Roosevelt from the upstate set, better known as the Hyde Park Roosevelts. Conversely, Helen came from the Hyde Park side, and married TR's nephew Theodore Douglas Robinson from the Oyster Bay side. These cross-family matrimonies might seem strange to some, but Roosevelt cousins have a history of getting hitched. It does make the genealogy somewhat complicated, particularly when it comes to the names that appear in the family tree. To make matters more trying, Helen's father's middle name was Roosevelt, making him James Roosevelt Roosevelt. Thankfully, everyone called him Rosy. The family had multiple Robinsons, Cowleses, Halls, Alsops, Jeffries, Derbys, Bullochs, Havermeyers, and du Ponts in the bloodline, as well. First names equally complicate matters. President Theodore Roosevelt's father was Theodore, Sr. and his son Theodore, referred to as Ted, was Theodore, Jr. Ted married an Eleanor, not his famous cousin, however. Children are regularly named after descendants, so there are multiple Theodores, Kermits, Archibalds, Corinnes, Ediths, Elliotts, Saras, and Jameses.

Navigating the labyrinthine family tree pays dividends. With an awareness of its branches comes an understanding of the vast networks to which the Roosevelts belonged, and how the success of individual family members supported others, even over generations. Tracing their American ancestry back to seventeenth-century Dutch immigrants makes the Roosevelts one of the earliest European families to settle in New York. The first Roosevelt Knickerbockers joined local New York government as aldermen, mayors, and bishops. It is no coincidence that later Roosevelts include two presidents, several congressmen, ambassadors or diplomats, and five assistant secretaries of the Navy. Many more have become local officials, elected or appointed, and several have distinguished military service records. This call to public service endures as a tradition and prerogative of a wealthy and connected family.

So often the Roosevelt men have eclipsed the Roosevelt women, likely because the men rose to high office. TR's great-granddaughter Anna Curtenius Roosevelt wondered "why everyone seemed so interested in the Roosevelt men. It was the women," she insisted, "who performed most remarkably while the men fought their wars and died young."[1] Biographers who marveled at TR's ability to overcome asthma and a frail childhood, should have paid due respect to the ailing health of Mrs. Cowles. Her story of perseverance impresses as much as her brother's. Likewise, TR's younger sister Corinne Roosevelt Robinson warrants further attention. Her grief at losing a teenaged son prompted a successful career as a poet, and she also played an active part in Republican politics after TR's death, becoming the first woman to nominate a presidential candidate at a Republican National Convention in 1920, putting Leonard Wood's name into contention. The Roosevelt women, as Helen Roosevelt Robinson recalls, were instrumental in furthering the political futures of the men, and not merely by hosting or entertaining. They served on important boards and societies. When wars raged, many Roosevelt women took to the front, not in combat roles, but in hospitals and surgeries with the Red Cross. Before 1920, they did not vote, and some Roosevelt women did not believe in universal suffrage, but they influenced the Roosevelt men as much as any political handler.[2]

Helen's bloodline demonstrates the aristocratic network of the Roosevelt family. Her mother descended from the wealthy New York Astors, a family line that made Helen wildly affluent before marriage. In high society, Helen even ranked ahead of her cousin Alice Roosevelt as the "most interesting of the Roosevelt debutantes" because of her wealth.[3] When Helen's mother died in 1893, Mrs. Cowles supported Rosy and took over as Helen's surrogate mother. Helen traveled widely before marrying, spending much of her teenage years in London. She married Theodore Douglas Robinson in 1904 and had five children, one who died shortly after birth. During her husband's time as assistant secretary of the Navy (1924–1929), she entertained Coolidge administration officials and cavorted with her cousin Alice Roosevelt Longworth in the capital. After her husband returned to New York and state politics, Helen focused on charitable work. She had an active membership in the Girl Scouts, the Daughters of the American Revolution, and became a benefactor for local New York historical societies. Her charitable work, while less notable than her cousin Eleanor's, brought Helen much personal happiness, especially after her husband died unexpectedly in 1934. And while politics often divided the family, as Helen attests, she seemed to remain above the fray as a friend to both Oyster Bay and Hyde Park Roosevelts. She died in 1962, three months before Eleanor.

The Hagedorns, fascinated by TR's sisters, ask Helen to concentrate her memories on these prominent Roosevelt women, a somewhat disappointing approach because they limited Helen's reminiscences about TR's wife Edith Roosevelt and her cousin Eleanor. That criticism aside, stories about other family members do successfully come to the fore, such as her recollections of TR's mother Martha "Mittie" Bulloch Roosevelt and Martha's sister Annie who married into another esteemed New York family, the Gracies.[4] The central takeaway from Helen Roosevelt Robinson's testimony is the importance of the Roosevelt women. Each woman made a vital contribution to American politics and society. Mary Hagedorn made this point during the interview, interjecting to say, "This is a fascinating American study in women's lives—interrelated as they are, yet individually so vital."

Like the other transcriptions, Helen Roosevelt Robinson edited hers before donating to them to the archives.[5] They are reproduced here with minor edits for style and readability. Some interview questions have been omitted for the same reason.

* * *

I'd like to begin by explaining a little bit as to why Auntie Bye [Mrs. Cowles] came over to England to be with us, because the relationship goes back a long way between her and my father. The two branches of the Roosevelt family—the Democratic and the Republican branch—were very intimate and always stayed very intimate; Auntie Bye had been a friend of my father's (James Roosevelt, known to his friends as "Rosy" Roosevelt, and half-brother to Franklin Delano Roosevelt) ever since they were quite, quite young. She was also my mother's [Helen Astor Roosevelt's] bridesmaid. After I was born, she became my godmother and was at my christening. The relationship was very, very close. I am on the Democratic side. I'm putting it politically so as to divide it, do you see?

My father and Auntie Bye were fifth cousins, but in spite of that remote cousinship they were exactly like very intimate first cousins. The relationship between the two branches of the family—you know they branched off about five generations back—had always been very close; my grandfather was godfather to Elliott Roosevelt, TR's brother, so that there was a very close relationship and friendship.

My mother died in England in 1893, just at the time when my father was appointed First Secretary to the Embassy. People thought it was rather queer, I think, that Auntie Bye should come out and be with us and live with us. But she, in her usual big-hearted way, when she heard of my mother's death, had very soon cabled to him, asking whether he would like to have her come to London, thinking that it might be just for a couple of months, something of that kind. She knew that he was in a very sad state and a good deal at a loss, as he had two children to bring up and also had no hostess for his house in London. He cabled back and said it would help him enormously. So, it was arranged that she should come out, which she did.

After she arrived, she started immediately—it has always amused me since—by getting rid of my very pretty French governess whom I had had for three or four years, because she felt that my father, as a widower, should not have a very pretty young French woman around the house. She was able to find an English governess who was not very old—I think was not more than thirty-nine or forty—but had perfectly white hair, which made everything proper as regards my father.

Auntie Bye naturally made a tremendous difference to me. I was a motherless child and very lonely. The fact that she immediately made friends in England—masses of friends—meant that she provided friends for me, too, so that everything became very happy in the house. I had quantities of little English friends, due to her. She made a wonderful hostess for my father. She was so extraordinary, so full of life, and immediately caught on to the English ways and English people. My father had to entertain a great deal and there were a great many very interesting people buzzing around the house all the time. She ran everything in the most absolutely superb fashion.

It was a curious embassy, in a way. Auntie Bye was a tremendous help to the Ambassadress—the Ambassador was Thomas F. Bayard who had been Secretary of State. Mrs. Bayard was a rather quiet, slightly timid person in one way; I don't think she knew very much as to how to start about her business. Auntie Bye was a tremendous help to her, not only because she was so wonderful in herself, but because there was a great dearth of women in the Embassy. My father was the First Secretary. The Second Secretary was Larz Anderson, who was unmarried. The Third Secretary was David Wells—I think was his name; I don't remember him very well as he was rather a nonentity—but he also was unmarried. The Naval attaché, whom Auntie Bye afterwards married, was also unmarried. The only other married woman whom I recollect at all, and I'm sure I'm right, was Mrs. [Genevieve] Ludlow, the wife of General [William] Ludlow, who was the military attaché. None of the secretaries had any wives; so, Auntie Bye really became the "right hand man" of Mrs. Bayard, who turned to her for everything. I think she ran all of Mrs. Bayard's entertainments, told her just how many feathers to put on her head when she was presented, what kind of gloves to wear and everything. Auntie Bye always seemed to know just what to do and Mrs. Bayard depended on her tremendously. She had her there for every entertainment that she gave in the Embassy and relied upon her absolutely.

She knew [what was in style] instinctively. Things were different in England from what they were over here, but she grasped everything immediately and she knew just what should be done and what the English expected of the Ambassadress. She just ran it all in perfectly extraordinary way.

She made, as I say, an enormous number of English friends and was very often dashing off to the country for weekends with all her new-made friends who adored her. She had friends down in Devonshire and Cornwall and all remote parts of England, and a great many in Scotland through the Fergusons, the Munro-Fergusons. Young Robert Ferguson was later one of the Rough Riders and an intimate friend of the family and all his family were living in Scotland, so she used to go there a great deal to stay in all their different wonderful old houses and castles. Through them she got to know other people in Scotland; and so did I through her, so that we made a great many visits there. We had thought that her visit to us was only going to last, probably, for a couple of months; but she stayed all that winter. I think she went home that summer, for a while, but came right back again in the fall and just made up her mind that she was going to stay with us as long as my father wanted her, and as long as I needed her—which I did very badly.

One or two summers she was with us part of the time, too. I remember her in the houses that we took in the suburbs near London. She came back and forth to this country and back again to us in England for two years.

Then there began to be this romance between her and the Naval attaché, Lt. Commander Cowles as he was then. We saw this coming and my father realized that something might come of it although, of course, by that time Auntie Bye was, I think, nearly forty and Commander Cowles was quite a bit older. He was divorced. There was trouble in getting the divorce papers through, but the two eventually became engaged—much to the surprise of her family over here, and a good deal to my father's surprise, too, because although Commander Cowles was a darling, he was not a ball of fire by any means. He was rather stout and calm and quiet. He simply adored her. I've never seen such adoration! But I think it was a surprise that she married anybody quite so—quiet, calm and peaceful and, well, I don't think I can put it in any other way, but a perfect darling.

I don't think she was in love with him, really. The extraordinary part about both Auntie Bye and my mother-in-law, Mrs. Douglas Robinson, is that I don't think that either of them were ever really in love with any man, including their husbands. But I think Auntie Bye began to feel that her position in London at that time was drawing to an end as regards being my father's hostess, and I think she felt that it would be very pleasant to be still a part of the Embassy and to continue living in London near Father and me, but not any longer a part of our household. I was growing up and he was no longer as sad as he had been two years before, so that I think it all appealed to her very much. The result of it was that she announced her engagement to her family over here and was married from our house.

Judging from the letter Mrs. Cowles wrote to her brother when he was president, there was great affection and regard for her husband.

Oh, there was. There was. Great affection and regard—and sometime after she was married, that grew into love. I don't think she was in love with him when she married him. It turned out to be a very happy marriage. And the fact that he was very much the opposite of what she was—she was such a terrific person and he was so different, so quiet—she felt the security of being married to somebody like that and I think she much preferred it to being married to a more—exciting type of man.

Also, she probably had great respect for the character of someone like him.

Oh, yes, she did. Very definitely. But he was not a glamourous person in any sense of the word. He was a dear, humdrum sort of person—but a dear ... He was absolutely loyal. [Theodore] Roosevelt was fond of him, was really very fond of him as time went on. I think TR depended on him, and there was real affection and admiration, too. Admiral Cowles, as he was afterwards, was such a steady sort of man. He was a rock to Auntie Bye. There was a steadiness about him which appealed very much, I think to TR. He always knew just where his brother-in-law stood. There was complete loyalty, and that means a great deal.

[M]y point of view was so very young ... I was only fourteen and one doesn't remember as much as one should of those days ... I know that when we were still [in London], TR wrote Auntie Bye at least once a week. She got letters all the time from him, a steady flow of letters, and wrote him very, very steadily. I hope that those letters from her can be found. I think that she was able to tell him a good deal about the situation in England and help him a good deal on that. I'm quite sure of it. She was in constant touch with the interesting people in England on account of my father. My father was a very intimate friend of Sir Edward Grey who was one of the great men of England. He was Under Secretary of State for Foreign Affairs at that time and was constantly at our house. I happen to mention him because I perhaps remember him better than some others; he was exceedingly good looking. He was a wonderful looking person, and I used to be allowed to come down sometimes before dinner parties or something of that kind, and I always thought that Sir Edward Grey was the most entrancing person. There were people of that kind around the house a great deal whom Auntie Bye was in touch with, and I'm quite sure that she could write back to her brother on the interesting people of the day. It was with Lord [Edward] Grey of Fallodon, as he was later known, that TR has that wonderful time in England when they took the bird walk together, you know.[6]

Could you give me a little bit of a verbal picture of Mrs. Cowles as you knew her when she was in England?

She was always a very fascinating person. No good looks, whatever; she was really plain. Even her figure was very bad, owing to the fact that when she was a child, she had had trouble with her back, so that she was rather dumpy looking; but when her face was animated it was extraordinary. She gave out a light and an animation which was very, very rare. It was contagious—very much so. She and my mother-in-law both had a great quality of making other people appear at their best. They brought out the best in everybody, and that is a great quality ... What they both did was to bring out the best in people who otherwise might not have showed it through shyness and through reserve. You know the English are a curiously stiff sort of people; they're not relaxed the way we are and they don't give forth the way we do. You have to go after them and get at them. Auntie Bye did that, I know. She was able to break down that extraordinary English reserve, and that's why she had so many English friends. She was able to get behind all that.

That's wonderful, for an American in those days, before America had a very big place in the world picture.

It was very unusual, I think. But it was a great quality which brought about the intimacy with many people.

I'm still thinking a little of Admiral Cowles. There was one curious thing about it. She always said he was "a dear old bear" and she always called him "Bearo"—entirely—never anything but Bearo. She never allowed him to call her by any of the family pet-names, Bamie and Bye. That was never allowed. He always had to call her Anna. And he always did! And he was the only person that ever called her Anna. [Bamie originated] from "bambino." Someone when she was a baby started calling her bambino and it got to "Bamie."

And what about "Bye?"

I don't know how it got to "Bye," but it did. TR called her Bye most of the time, "Bysie" and Bye; and all the children—all the next generation—called her "Auntie Bye," but Bearo was never allowed to call her anything but Anna!

Our English days are now practically over. She was married and stayed over there for about a year, then came back here. Everything else is known about her. The Spanish War came along and the Admiral had to be in the war; then much to the surprise of *everybody*, she produced a baby at the age of forty-two ... which was a miracle on account of her bad back.[7] From then on, I think she was more known—you all know more about her. I think I've told you almost all I can about Auntie Bye, except I do want to say that her courage in later days, which everybody ought to have told you, was something absolutely extraordinary. Later on, there was rheumatic trouble of some kind or other and she became more lame and more crippled ... She had been dropped as a baby and that was the original cause of her bad back ... I think the whole [arthritis] condition was related to it. Her feet got into a terrible state, some sort of poisoning, and she couldn't walk, she could hardly use her hands, and she was completely in a wheel-chair towards the end. The effort of getting up and dressing was very painful; but, needless to say, she always would get up and have herself dressed and put into her wheel-chair and come down for meals, though it was agony. She went through great agony, and her courage was perfectly amazing. Most people would have given up long, long before. I've never seen any woman, I don't think, suffer such pain—and I knew it when other people didn't know it—and yet [to] be able to stick it out as she did and continue to be attractive and interesting and fascinating up to the day that she died.

It's characteristic that in all that I've told you I haven't mentioned her deafness. In other words, I forget about it. Of course, I always knew from the time she came to us that she was deaf, and it was a great handicap. But it made so little impression that I haven't even mentioned it to you. And that's typical. She was very deaf but she never allowed it to be a handicap. Therefore, one wasn't conscious of it; and therefore I, on looking back, haven't been conscious of it ... she never had a hearing aid when she was with us ... She never studied [lip reading]; she may have sensed it a little in a certain way, but she never took any lessons in it, or anything of that kind that I know of.

Because she must have been able to sense what other people were saying, in order to be the life of the parties she gave, as she was.

She was able to grasp a few words here and there. If she didn't get a whole sentence, she got enough to be able to carry on by herself. She was very clever about it. But it wasn't something that one was very conscious of. She was able, somehow, to surmount it entirely—and it just amuses me now to think that I forgot to mention it.

We always kept in very close contact. From then on [after departing London] I not only saw her often, but I began to see a great deal of my mother-in-law [Mrs. Corinne Roosevelt Robinson] who, up to that time, I hadn't known at all. Her son began to be interested in me and I began to adore my mother-in-law. I could tell you a little about my mother-in-law, if you like?

Oh, yes.

There were great differences in my affection for them both. My mother-in-law was, in a way, a somewhat softer character than Auntie Bye. That doesn't sound very nice, but I don't mean it that way. Mother-in-law was tremendously loving and demonstrative. To me she was, in a way—because I married her son partly—more like a real mother, I having lost my mother when I was twelve. She always seemed more like a real mother than Auntie Bye did, although Auntie Bye certainly was a very devoted mother to me when I was little. But as time went on, I think I became quite naturally, more dependent, perhaps, on my mother-in-law, and she came more into my life, at that time too, on account of my marriage. She was just like my own mother. I adored her as if she *were* my mother, exactly. We had a marvelous relationship.

She and Auntie Bye had a great deal in common. Of course, the thing they had most in common was the adoration of their brother. And, curiously enough, although they both worshipped him, and wanted to be with him every possible minute, I don't think there was ever one bit of jealousy between them about him. I've never noticed it in all my years with both of them. They were absorbed in him. Perhaps that's one reason why they weren't in love with their husbands. Everything went into their brother, everything, but I never knew any jealousy. Their whole lives were bound up in their brother. I've never seen a relationship between brother and sisters anywhere—or ever heard of any—that was as close and as absolutely adoring as that ... The one idea of both of them was to do what they could for him. When he was in New York in the old days, Auntie Bye's house was always his headquarters. Later on, when Auntie Bye's house was given up and she moved to Farmington, my mother-in-law's house was always his headquarters for all of his political work. No, it was just give, give, give. They wanted to give everything they possibly could to further *his* interests ... *Absolutely* selfless giving. Completely.

And sentimental, too, as well?

With my mother-in-law it was a little on the sentimental side. It became such an *absorbing* interest that it grew a little bit sentimental. But it was never sentimental with Auntie Bye. That was the difference in them.

Mrs. Longworth is inclined to be sarcastic, but never an iota with regard to Auntie Bye.

She was perfectly devoted to her. Perfectly devoted. The only person I ever knew Auntie Bye to be a little bit afraid of was Aunt Edith Roosevelt, Mrs. Theodore Roosevelt. Both Auntie Bye and my mother-in-law were a little bit afraid of her, which always amused me because they weren't afraid of anybody, ever; except that there was a little feeling about her. In other words, they were watching their p's and q's a little bit when they were with her. Alice Longworth, I think, would know just what I mean ... There was no estrangement of any kind, but just that little feeling of watching their step a little bit. It was quite amusing and interesting.

Aunt Edith was a wonderful person. Oh, I think she was one of the most *marvelous* people that ever was. She was a great person, a *very* great person. She could be sarcastic at times but she was anything but insipid. She was a very strong, determined person—and well, there's the well-known story about "Theodore go bleed in the bathroom."[8] That's one of the most *typical* things of her ... And I think she was almost the only person who really, in a way, dominated him. He definitely paid a great deal of attention to what she thought and what her opinions were ....

She was a wonderful balance-wheel ... But I don't want to go off on a tangent, since this talk is really about Mrs. Robinson and Mrs. Cowles.

Well, of course, I think my mother-in-law was one of the most remarkable people who ever lived. She had that same great love of people her brother had and made everybody at home in her house. She entertained enormously.

As regards her poetry, that was brought out, I think, entirely by the death of her youngest son, which was a terrible shock to her. Up to that time she had always rhymed and jingled and, you know, written odds and ends of rhymes and poetry; but what really brought out that side of her, the deep side, which turned into her poetry was the death of her son.

He fell out of a window at Harvard when he was a Junior, and I was in Boston at the time. I was with him all that evening at a party in Boston. We left the party, my husband and I, at 2 o'clock in the morning. Stewart had had supper with me and had been with me practically all evening. He went back to his room in college and was found the next morning on the sidewalk. Nobody knows whether he flung open the window for air and lost his balance or what happened. But it was as sudden as that, and we had to call up my mother-in-law and tell her about it in the morning when he was found. It was a terrific shock to her.

But it did bring out all her poetic side and, from then on, she wrote some lovely, lovely things. I think it helped her very much. It was an outlet for her.

She was completely devoted to her children. She also was not in love with her husband from the time she married him, though I think she was extremely fond of him afterwards, but her real devotion was her children—and her brother. After her husband was dead her brother absorbed her life, I think, completely, although it wasn't very long afterwards that he died. But even after his death she felt it was her job to keep him before the public and particularly the children. She made a tremendous point of speaking on him wherever she could, especially in schools. Her devotion took that shape after his death. She really made a career of it, almost, before she herself died ... She had a great deal to do with the founding and arranging of Theodore Roosevelt [Birthplace]. She was absorbed in all that. By that time her children were married. That became her life, entirely.

I'd love to know if you know of any feeling that either of the two sisters had regarding the vice-presidency or about the Progressive Party.

They were both absorbed and ardent Progressives, of course. They felt that [TR] was absolutely right on that ... I think they were always doing everything they could to *further* his policies, and I know that they always thought he was right. I'm perfectly sure of that. And, as I said, their houses were always open for any people whom he wanted to have. I remember that my mother-in-law had everybody whom he ever wanted to see, there at her house. I remember the thrill I had sitting next to Booker Washington, for instance, at her house at lunch. That was at the time when people thought it was a little peculiar for him to back up Booker Washington the way he did and have him as a real friend. In that way his sisters were always helping him. But I don't know that I could say definitely about his policies, except that they backed him up on everything. And my mother-in-law worked politically all through the Progressive Party period. She started speaking at that time.

TR said so many things that influenced my life. One day when I was eighteen and we were sitting around the breakfast table at Auntie Bye's house in Washington; somebody started discussing a book of the day, a very important book which had just come out. He turned to me suddenly and said, "Have you read it?"

I answered in a debutante's flip sort of way, "No, I haven't. I haven't had time."

He glared at me, snapped his teeth and said, "You can always find time for anything you *want* to do."

That has influenced me so much. I've never forgotten it.

Do you remember anything that Mrs. Cowles or your mother-in-law might have said about Mr. Roosevelt, Sr.'s attitude toward things that might have brought out the best in his son, his influence on his son?

[Mrs. Cowles and Mrs. Robinson] talked a great deal about their father [Theodore Roosevelt, Sr.], always, with the most *tremendous* admiration. I never knew him but always felt that he was a most remarkable person, a very extraordinary person ... He was the only man I have ever heard of who, on each one of his children's birthdays, by way of a present, gave himself to them for the whole day. That day was set aside. He spent the entire day doing just what they wanted. They thought the world of him. He must have been a great person ... They just gave me the impression that he was the most extraordinary *father* that there ever had been, because of his devotion to his children and to his high ideals, which he handed on to them. His devotion, I think, was very rare. Most fathers don't pay too much attention or give too much time to their children. I think he made a great point of giving a great deal of *time* to his children, to bring them up in the right way. Yet he was a busy man, too. He was on all sorts of boards and charities; he founded the New York Orthopedic Hospital; he founded the Newsboys' Lodging House and did so much for the newsboys in connection with the Children's Aid Society. He was on every kind of civic thing and was a very busy man. But his children simply worshipped him.

They cared for him far more, I think, than for their mother [Martha Bulloch Roosevelt] ... She does seem a nebulous figure. She was beautiful and very Southern in her ways. She never cared whether she was three hours late for a meal or half an hour. She was perfectly vague and perfectly beautiful and always wore lovely white muslin clothes, but I don't think she entered into their lives at all in the way their father did. It was a "pretty little Mother" attitude. They adored her but I don't think she really had the effect upon their lives that their father had, at all.

He must have been largely responsible for their spontaneity, their love of people, their complete—in the finest sense of the word—uninhibitedness.

Yes, I think they got all that from him ... I don't think that their mother had that characteristic at all. Their Aunt Gracie—their Aunt Annie Gracie, who was [Martha] Roosevelt's sister—entered tremendously into their lives and, I think, was more of a mother to them than their own mother. They saw a great deal of their Aunt Annie and their Uncle, Mr. [James King] Gracie, all the time. So did the next generation, too—my husband also was almost brought up by Aunt Annie and Uncle Gracie, like an extra set of parents. They all adored [Aunt Annie], and they spoke of her a great deal more, really, than of their mother. She was the beloved aunt. Everything was Aunt Annie ...

What an extraordinary American saga it is!

I do hope that the story of these two women can be told, because although, in a way, they're a sidelight on their brother, still they were pretty important to him, too. And they were such extraordinary people in themselves!

Yes, they were extraordinary American people! I was so interested that Mrs. Cowles did not believe in woman's suffrage.

No, she didn't at all. She was not interested in it ... I think she did feel that women in the home, doing what they could in the home, were very important and could perhaps do more that way. She just wasn't attuned to the thought of women voting and taking any active part in politics.

Her brother [TR] didn't have any vital feeling one way or the other, I understand, but he said it wouldn't do as much harm as some people thought it might ...

But I don't think he ever was definitively *for* it, was he? I don't think he was.

I don't believe so. He knew, I think, too, in his own home, what a positive influence the women in his family were.

Yes, he did, very much ... Well, nobody could have had in their family three more dynamic women than those three, even though Aunt Edith didn't on the surface, perhaps, appear as dynamic as Auntie Bye, certainly; but nevertheless, it was there ... I'm very grateful that I've known all these three women.

CHAPTER 4

The Next Generation: William and Margaret Cowles and Corinne Alsop Cole

Fig. 4.1 Photo portrait of Anna Roosevelt Cowles (date unknown), TR Center, Dickinson State University

Not long after the death of Theodore Roosevelt, an ugly division emerged between the Oyster Bay and Hyde Park Roosevelts. In 1920, Franklin Roosevelt ran for vice president as a Democrat, and TR's eldest children Alice and Ted attacked Franklin as duplicitous, claiming he used the popularity of his name to attain high office. A two decade-long feud ensued. When Ted ran for governor of New York in 1926, Eleanor and Franklin returned the animosity. They viciously campaigned against their cousin, who lost. It seemed as if the divide among TR's progeny would continue, but when the United States joined the Allies in World War II, Ted and Franklin pulled together. By 1945 when the Axis waved the white flag, both men had died giving their all to the struggle. Ted perished on the beaches of Normandy; Franklin shortly after, spent himself in the prolonged negotiations for a new global order.

Historians have made much of the rivalry, but most members of the Roosevelt family shared goodwill and mutual respect.[1] "Devotion" is a term that appears in many testimonials. More often than not, family members shared a common commitment to those bearing the same name. TR's sisters Corinne and Anna had an abiding reverence for their Hyde Park cousins, including Franklin's mother Sara and half brother Rosy. TR's nieces and nephews—the next generation of Roosevelts—also maintained a close relationship. Corinne Robinson Alsop, TR's niece, frequently visited the White House during Franklin's administration and acted as a conduit between "hissing cousins" Alice Roosevelt Longworth and First Lady Eleanor.[2] The testimony of William Sheffield Cowles ("Shef") and Margaret Krech Cowles ("Bobbie"), provides a discerning account of the various Roosevelt rivalries, love affairs, illegitimate children, alcoholism, repression, and bereavement. Their stories include vivid impressions of the big personalities, the gatherings and vacations, and the legendary tales all families tell, but with a distinctly Rooseveltian flavor. Of course, the politics of the Democratic and Republican parties make their memories of national significance. What prevails through these trials is a "devotion" for the family, even when individual Roosevelts failed to see eye-to-eye.

Shef was Theodore Roosevelt's nephew and the only child of William Sheffield Cowles (the Admiral) and Anna Roosevelt Cowles (Bye), TR's older sister. His accounts provide an excellent insight into the interconnected branches of the family. Shef served as Franklin's personal aide during World War I when Franklin was assistant secretary of the Navy. They returned home from Paris together, after the Treaty of Versailles negotiations, and Shef recalls the trip as one in which Franklin convinced him of the virtues of the League of Nations. Subsequently, his cousin Alice Roosevelt Longworth—a staunch opponent of the League—convinced him otherwise. After the war ended, Shef attended Yale University, took a job in banking, and married Margaret Alwyn Krech, better known to friends as Bobbie (Shef called her Mags). The couple moved into a small cottage at his mother's Oldgate estate in Connecticut, and had two children.

Anna Roosevelt Cowles died in 1931, before Franklin became president, but time enough for her to revel in his success as governor of New York. Bobbie took over as matriarch of Oldgate and managed the Cowleses' busy social life. Shef joined the Navy when the U.S. declared war on the Axis Powers and rose to the rank of captain. He returned to banking after the war, then turned his attention to public service in 1949, winning election to the Connecticut State Assembly. He would serve in the state legislature until 1956, including a term as speaker of the house.[3] In retirement, Shef signed on to a number of corporate and charitable boards, and even served one term as mayor of Farmington. Bobbie died in 1982 and Shef in 1986.

Corinne Robinson Alsop, her mother's namesake and niece of Theodore Roosevelt, joined Shef and Bobbie for part of their interviews with the Hagedorns. Although Mrs. Alsop grew up in Orange, New Jersey, she remained close with the Cowles throughout her life. That intimacy derived, in part, from proximity. In 1909, Corinne married Joseph Alsop, the sire of a prominent Connecticut family. She moved within ten miles of the Cowles and would live nearby for the remainder of her life. Joe and Corinne Alsop—even more than Shef and Bobbie—became a powerful couple in Connecticut politics. They each took to public office: Joe served in the State Assembly and Senate, and ran in 1912 as a Progressive Party candidate for Congress while Corinne won election to the Connecticut State Assembly, serving two non-consecutive terms from 1924 to 1927 and 1931 to 1933. She also led the state Republican Party and had considerable influence at the national level. Her reminiscences offer vibrant portraits of Franklin and Eleanor. In her youth, Mrs. Alsop attended Allenswood Academy in London, the same boarding school as her cousin Eleanor and had overlapping social networks. She also provides an insight into the personalities at Oyster Bay, including her grandmother, Edith Roosevelt, and the curious death of her brother Stewart at Harvard University.

So much emerges from these recollections, but again, some of the most fascinating discussion revolves around the Roosevelt women. TR's sisters Anna and Corinne, and FDR's mother Sara had vast influence, as did the women of the next generation, Corinne, Bobbie, and Eleanor. Each played a vital part in leading their family, and in national, state, and local politics. It should come as no surprise that their children—the following generation—had an equal measure of influence, and that contemporary Roosevelts do as well. The family operates as a network, dedicated to the clan as well as the American public through civic-minded service.

The desire to serve did not compel all Roosevelts, however. The Cowleses and Mrs. Alsop talk about the family's black sheep, specifically TR's prodigal brother Elliott and James "Tadd" Roosevelt, "Rosy's" son. Elliott had a severe alcohol and drug addiction and Tadd's marriage led to his father disowning him. These reminiscences contextualize Tadd's peculiarities and Elliott's dependency, explaining how alcoholism gripped many of the Roosevelt men and how wealth allowed for eccentricities. Their stories tell of a troubled and sick Elliott, more complex in spirit than often credited, and a portrait of Tadd, who visited the family more frequently than originally thought.

Some of these yarns give the Cowleses and Mrs. Alsop pause for further consideration. Particularly Corinne Alsop expresses a feeling that her comments will come across as unkind, believing that fellow family members would not appreciate her frankness. At one point she asks the Hagedorns to "seal" the transcripts, although makes no mention of how long she expected them to remain private. Delicate matters such as Alice Longworth's affair with Senator Borah, and the likelihood that Paulina Longworth was Borah's daughter, were edited out of the Hagedorn's transcripts. The recordings retain the original testimony, and where possible this chapter utilizes the original comments made by the participants.

Bobbie and Shef Cowles met Mary and Hermann Hagedorn twice in 1954, and spent at least three hours reminiscing. For some of that time, Corinne Alsop joined them, but she also recorded two interviews without them. Because this collection includes three subjects, the transcription includes designations for speakers, using names they conversed with (Shef, Bobbie, and Corinne). The five hours of testimony makes this the lengthiest of all the collections in the oral history project. Where audio was available, the chapter uses that dialogue rather than the Hagedorn's edits.

Not surprisingly, overlap exists in the retelling of old stories. For the sake of brevity, several pages of testimony have been omitted. In some cases, the trio tells stories about hired help or offer exhaustive descriptions of medical conditions that seem peripheral to the broader impressions about the family.

* * *

22 November 1954

What I was going to ask, first of all, was if you could give us the basic framework of Mrs. Cowles' life. She was born in 1854—or '55?

Shef: She was seventy-seven years old when she died in 1931, so that would make it 1854 when she was born [she was actually born in January 1855]. The later part of her life I think I can give you better information about.

Bobbie: What age was she when she was dropped and got her back injury?

Shef: I think she was very small when she was dropped.[4] A certain injury to her spine resulted from it, and it was that that motivated her father, Theodore Roosevelt [Sr.] to start the Orthopedic Hospital. I inherited that interest, vicariously, by being taken on the Board in 1931. I became the president of the Board of Trustees in 1938 and remained so until it became merged with the Presbyterian Hospital, and am still chairman of the board of the Orthopedic Committee of the Presbyterian Hospital today. That continuing family interest was aroused through my grandfather starting the Orthopedic Hospital on account of the injury to Mother's back when she was small.

Bobbie: I remember her telling how he used to walk the floor with her for hours at night when she was in great pain. All her life she always wore a pad of lamb's wool on that part of her back.

Shef: It's the reason why the Orthopedic Hospital has one of the three pictures of Mr. Theodore Roosevelt, my mother's father. One of them hangs in our dining room, one belongs to Mrs. Douglas Robinson who has inherited that picture from Aunt Corinne's family ... And the third is hanging in the Orthopedic Hospital and was moved up to the Presbyterian Hospital when the Orthopedic merged with the Presbyterian and is hanging up on the fifth floor of the Presbyterian Hospital. It is due to the fact that he originally founded the Hospital...

Bobbie: Well, then, that injury of Mother-in-law's forced her, all through her early youth, to have long periods of lying down. When she went to school in Paris, until Mlle. Souvestre, who was apparently the most marvelous teacher, Mother-in-law always claims that her facility with words is due to the hour and a half to two hours she was supposed to lie down every day. Mlle. Souvestre would give her a basic thought and, as she was lying there, she'd have to express it in as many ways in French as she could think of, and then at the end of the time come to Mlle. Souvestre and tell her what she thought was the perfect way of describing it. She said it made her word conscious, to try to use economy and the *correct* word. She always said, like Corinne, that she never had any education, you know; but Mlle. Souvestre gave her the one really stimulating thing that she had.

Of course, it was too early for any of them to go to college—the women of that generation.

Bobbie: They didn't very much, did they? There *were* colleges, of course, but it was considered a very strange thing for a woman to do, wasn't it?

I marvel that neither Alice nor Ethel ever considered going to college, apparently. As far as I can see, there was never any thought of it.

Shef: No, never a thought of it even in that generation ... In my mother's and Aunt Corinne's day and age, I suppose, it was absolutely unheard of...

Since your mother was so frail, how was she able to take command of the family as she did.

Shef: I feel that she overcame that. I feel that she became a very strong woman, at the age of about twenty-five, or so.

Bobbie: I think it was just that weakness in the back and they gradually overcame it...

Sheffield: Well, I know that before she got arthritis—I was twelve years old when she got it—she was the most active woman imaginable through my youth. I was always perfectly amazed at the amount of activity that she managed to pack into a day. I was always greatly impressed as a child, because we never could go anywhere—no matter what, train or boat, or where you were—that people didn't flock up recognizing her, and surround her. It happened everywhere. She had the most enormous circle of acquaintances! Now part of that must have come through her brother's having been in the White House by that time. I was always amazed at her memory. She had a remarkable memory and she always remembered them and all about them; very often she'd remark that she'd known them too early, she'd known them before they became famous, and it embarrassed them to know that she knew them at that time ... She was very cool on the suffrage question.

Bobbie: She thought you'd just double the unintelligent vote. I think that was her feeling on that ... I think she felt that that was what a woman was for, that she should be working behind the scenes and let the other fellow do it. I think she had that very strongly ... I've always rather believed that Mother-in-law's judgment was very sound and that Uncle Theodore counted a good deal on her reactions to things.

Shef: Yes. I think he consulted her a good deal ... Of course, Alice, I imagine, is really a very good source of information about Mother because Mother had a great deal to do with Alice. Alice was with Mother a good deal. And Mrs. Franklin Roosevelt was with Mother a good deal at the time. My mother was a spinster then and was a natural depository for odd children who had lost their parents, so she had a good deal to do with both of those, both Eleanor Roosevelt and Alice Roosevelt—and Helen Robinson, Helen Robinson perhaps even more so ... And when Mother was sharing a house with Cousin Rosy Roosevelt, [his daughter] Helen Roosevelt Robinson, was directly under Mother's care for a number of years. I don't know what happened to the camp they had in the Adirondacks; I imagine that was also a joint proposition between Cousin Rosy and my mother, but I know that Helen Roosevelt got engaged to Teddy Robinson up at that camp ... it was at that camp that Helen Robinson's brother became of age, James ["Tadd"] Roosevelt. James Roosevelt became of age at that camp and told Mother and his father that he had to go down to New York to settle certain matters of business. He left for New York and on his trip to New York married a girl named Dutch Zadie [also known as Sadie Messinger who was reportedly a prostitute]. My cousin James Roosevelt Roosevelt, cousin Rosy, then told James his son that he never wanted to see him again and James was no longer ever to come back into the family household.

It was not for years after that that Mother saw James. At the time, very little was known of James. Mother talked to a Mr. Brown who was of the same real estate office that my uncle Douglas Robinson was in. It was Brown, Wheelock & Co. Mother saw Mr. Brown and Mr. Brown told Mother that he thought that Mother ought to get in touch with James Roosevelt. He thought that James Roosevelt was very lonely and knew nothing about his family—that she ought to get in contact with him. So, she wrote him a letter and asked him to come up here. This was about 1922, shortly after my wife and I were married. [By this time Tadd and Sadie were no longer living together, but remained married]. James Roosevelt came up to the Hartford station. I was sent to meet him and was to hold an envelope with a black edging so he would recognize me. I failed to meet him and came back, saying that I didn't think he'd caught the train. But James Roosevelt appeared in three quarters of an hour, just in time for lunch, looking very dusty. He'd walked most of the way out. He said he didn't expect to be met so had started walking when somebody picked him up and gave him a ride out. Mother had a talk with him in the front room. At that time the family thought that he probably was a drunkard, they thought that he probably was still married to this Dutch Zadie, they thought that he was everything that he shouldn't be. Actually, none of that was the case. He parted with Dutch Zadie after a very short marriage of less than a year's duration [1901 or 1902 by this account], he stopped drinking, he was most careful of himself—he never drank or smoked or spent any money at all, but spent the life of a hermit. He lived on the second floor of a house in Kew Gardens [Queens, NY] ... His only method of transportation was a bicycle. He complained a good deal over the fact that it was most

	difficult for him to get into New York City because the bridges were becoming so dangerous for bicycles. The idea of buying an automobile probably didn't occur to him.
Bobbie:	Oh, he had a car. He used to go to Florida and he had a trailer all fixed up on it and he adored working on it. He would have been happy as a garage mechanic. That was what he enjoyed more than anything.
Shef:	He not only would have been happy as a garage mechanic, but when he was in Florida, he *was* a garage mechanic. That's exactly what he did in Florida. He had a small boat down there but he also worked in a garage, but complained to Mother that he had to give up working in a garage because lying on the cement floors gave him arthritis.
Bobbie:	And he was living on the income of his income.
Shef:	By that time, having not spent any of this same Astor money that Helen got, he became extraordinarily well off ... He's still alive ... Helen sees him very occasionally ... Mother corresponded with Helen about him and said, "Helen, you must see your brother, James."

So, Helen asked James to come to 750 Park Avenue, which was where Helen and Teddy [Douglas Robinson] were living at that time. And then James came and asked Helen if he could take her to lunch. Helen said she would be delighted. He said that he ordinarily lunched in New York at a place called Boston's Beanery, if that suited Helen, and Helen said, "Yes, it would be fine." Helen said, "I've got a car outside."

And he said, "Well, that's fine because I've got a bicycle and I'll just leave my bicycle here—it's easier than walking. And tell me about both your children!"

She said, "I've got four!"

He said, "Oh, I've followed the newspapers very carefully and noticed that you had two, but I didn't know about the two others."

He knew about Douglas and he knew about Alida, but he didn't know about the two intervening daughters. He was rather shocked with Helen. He thought she was too modern and too fast and not the sort of person, really, to have as a sister.

What happened to him before he went off this way? What was behind it psychologically?

Shef: He was probably more or less all right until he married this girl, and then being cut off by his father gave him this queer twist. Mother said he was quite a charming boy up to the age of twenty-one, perfectly capable of a normal life.

Bobbie: She said he was perfectly terrified that people were going to marry him for his money. He had that very much on his mind—that people were going to "do him in" for his money. Even when he was a small boy, he had that fear.

Tell me about his father "Rosy" Roosevelt. He's just a name and a shadow to me. I don't know anything about him ... How could he have done that to his son?

Shef: I can't imagine. My mother never understood it. She was completely charmed with Cousin Rosy. He was a great influence on her.

Bobbie: Corinne and I have the theory that she was very much in love with him, but we may be wrong.

Shef: That's a theory that Bobbie has, and I don't believe there's any weight in it at all, but perhaps it's so ... I'll tell you a certain amount about him which to me was always fascinating. He married Helen Astor, then Helen Astor died when their daughter Helen was fourteen, and my mother went over. Mother was over there in London for a certain time and then became engaged to Father in 1895. As a matter of fact, Cousin Rosy rather resented Mother's engagement to Father. He felt that it was somewhat an imposition. They were very happily set up in one establishment, and why should it be broken up? But about that time, or possibly prior to that, Cousin Rosy met Betty [Elizabeth Riley], whose last name I don't know. Betty was the daughter of a country minister in England and was a salesgirl in Harrod's. She was very good looking, and Cousin Rosy and Betty set up some sort of an establishment. In fact, after Cousin Rosy finished with the Embassy in London, he moved Betty to this country ... They were not married, but they were everything else.

But he was furious when his son married!

Shef: Yes, yes. Isn't it queer? Well, as a matter of actual fact, I believe that after he got back to this country my mother told me that he tried to persuade Betty to marry him then. But Betty said, "Oh, no, it wouldn't do ... This is very comfortable, this is fine, but we shouldn't get married." Then Cousin Rosy had to have an operation. He was in Poughkeepsie at the time. Cousin Rosy was always a little apprehensive of operations and felt that he was going to die. It was not a very severe operation—I can't remember the nature of it. He telephoned Mother and asked her if she would come over the day before the operation. Mother got over there and Cousin Rosy said, "I have to have this operation and I know I'm going to die. I'm going to marry Betty first." That is how he happened to marry Betty. Then the next day he had the operation and two days after he was perfectly well again ... And, of course, Betty became a very intimate friend of Sara Delano Roosevelt, Cousin Sally, Franklin's mother. Cousin Sally was living in the large house at Hyde Park. Then Cousin Betty, Mrs. James [Rosy] Roosevelt, was living in the red house at Hyde Park, the one that Helen now owns. They were only a few hundred yards apart and the two women were more or less of an age...

What did he do for a living?

Shef: He fiddled around in the diplomatic service; he loved to fish; he used to have a place up in the Upselquitch River and fished salmon up there. He used to fish in Norway. In fact, he used to take Betty over to Norway fishing with him, which is one of the places they were able to set up a little camp and entertain people, and all that sort of thing—Cousin Rosy's men friends. He loved to shoot. He was a very good shot. He gave me a shotgun at a very early age, which endeared me to him.

Bobbie: He didn't ever really do anything except be a gentleman of leisure and have a very pleasant time.

Sheffield: Cousin Rosy was Franklin's half-brother. And their father was Dr. James Roosevelt, who lived at Hyde Park. I think he was a doctor but didn't practice. I could be mistaken [James was, in fact, a lawyer and a businessman]. But in any case, the family decided that my mother should marry him. He was I think, about twenty-five years older than Mother. Mother was taken up to Hyde Park frequently; it was hoped that she would get engaged to Mr. James Roosevelt [Franklin and Rosy's father]. She couldn't make up her mind to it and often spoke of how different her life would have been had she acceded to the family's efforts to get herself engaged to Mr. James Roosevelt in Hyde Park...

Bobbie: This was when she was quite a young woman, before he married Cousin Sally. Cousin Rosy was about two years older than Mother-in-law.

Shef: Yes. It's awfully complicated, that relationship. It's a very scrambled relationship. That, I believe, to be a correct statement ... Mother stated that unequivocally. She always mentioned it as a fact. They never got engaged, but the effort was made.

Who made the effort?

Shef: I always gathered from Mother that Mr. James Roosevelt, among others, made the effort. And I think my mother's father was sympathetic to the idea. But I think the original suggestion came from Mr. James Roosevelt. Later on, the family intermarried several times, of course, Franklin and Eleanor; Teddy Robinson and Helen Roosevelt, "Rosy's" daughter.

But Rosy Roosevelt is still a shadowy figure to me. What did he look like?

Shef: He looked like King Edward ... Charming, a man of the world, very elegant, great fun, a sense of humor. He had a very well-dressed beard.

Bobbie: A terrible snob! ... If you were a friend he'd be as snobbish for you as he was for himself, you know. And if he were selfish, he'd be selfish for you.

Shef: Mother always said that about him. She said, "Cousin Rosy's a very selfish man, but if he's on your side, he'll be just as selfish for you as he is for himself" ... I don't think that Cousin Rosy had more than a very reasonable amount for those days. I think he must have had something because he never showed the slightest sign of doing any work. Cousin Rosy was always keenly interested in investments. He was one of the Astor trustees, and due to the fact that he was interested in investments he was one of Mother's trustees for a number of years. I can remember that when I was a very small boy he came up and explained something to Mother which I subsequently understood, but which, at the time, didn't mean anything to me at all. He had invested in some railroad bonds for her and they had defaulted. He explained that it was really his fault because he hadn't looked into them enough. He bought them back himself at the price that he had invested in them as a trustee ... A very descent, nice thing for him to have done. I imagine he was quite intelligent about investments. I imagine he followed that closely and perhaps did more work than we credit him with. I think perhaps he worked down at the Astor office to a certain extent, but he must have taken it, as they all did in those days, quite lightly. It never interfered with his various sporting activities.

Was his fury at his son because he felt his son had married so terribly, terribly beneath him?

Shef: It was because he had besmirched the Roosevelt name. He had besmirched Cousin Rosy's name. I think that's what he felt and why he turned against his son.

His relationship with the fair Betty was perfectly all right...

Shef: Oh, that was quite different because that was his own.

Your mother must have given [James "Tadd" Roosevelt] a feeling of family for the first time in many, many years.

Shef: Oh, yes! It was the first time that he'd seen any member of the family for fully eighteen or twenty years. I think I was about two or three when he became of age, and I was twenty-four or twenty-five when [he] came up to

	Farmington. It must have been twenty-three years that elapsed between his seeing any members of the family. And it was quite pathetic because [Tadd] told Mother at the time that he himself had a very strong feeling about the family and every year bicycled up to Hyde Park and laid some flowers on his mother's grave, going past his father's door to do it! And never stopping in. It's a fascinating story.
Bobbie:	It was really like Rip Van Winkle. He was astounded at the things we were doing. He was so conservative that smoking was shocking to him. He was shocked that his sister Helen took a glass of sherry before lunch. He had the Victorian ideas of what women did!
Shef:	It was a matter of some discussion whether we ought to ask him whether he would have a cocktail or something of that sort. Mother said, "No, we always have sherry and we'll ask him to have a glass of sherry with us." But no, absolutely not—he hadn't touched it for twenty years! Anyhow, the most peculiar thing in life is the hermit!

Did this gal that he married have any particular job?

Shef:	I think she was a nightclub girl of some sort, or of the theatre. I know that Helen at one time felt that it might be worth exploring the question of what [Tadd] was going to do with his estate. And he said that he had thought that over at great length and had decided to leave the whole thing to the Salvation Army—and that's the way his will is written. That was when I last heard from him, but that was a little while ago.

** Corinne Robinson Alsop enters **.

Bobbie (to Corinne):	We were trying to recreate Mother-in-law's early life. Certainly, she was the one who ran the house—managed it.
Corinne:	When she was fourteen she took over. I don't think Auntie Bye liked Grandmother [Martha Bulloch] Roosevelt...
Bobbie:	She was slightly jealous of her, maybe, because she adored her father so, or else they were temperamentally unsuited to each other.

Corinne:	They were completely temperamentally unsuited to each other, in every way, from what Mother said. Mother, on the other hand, adored my grandmother in a totally different way from the way she adored my grandfather. Grandfather gave her all the things that he gave your mother—enjoyment, pleasure, fun, excitement, riding, dancing—all of those things. But my grandmother gave Mother instead a great love of beauty. According to Mother, my grandmother had an innate taste of real beauty, whether it was linen, whether it was china, whether it was paintings, whether it was anything that was beautiful. My grandmother who had been brought up an untutored, uneducated—in one sense—a Georgian girl in Savannah at the plantation, she nevertheless, according to Mother, had an innate appreciation and taste. To my mind, from my point of view and all the letters I have, and all my mother told me, she and Aunt Annie Gracie were the people who gave whatever humor we have.
Bobbie:	And the looks.
Corinne:	Well, of course, we never inherited looks, any of us, but whatever looks there were, were there. She was very lovely looking ... My grandmother, according to Mother—of course, I never saw her—was *really* lovely looking. She had a skin as Mother described it always, not like peaches and cream but like coral. It had that coral color of pink. She had black hair that had no grease in it whatsoever, but *real* black hair, and blue eyes and a wonderful mouth, a perfectly charming smile. I think you can see that in the pictures. She really was an enchanting person. She never was on time for anything. Mother described to me one time when she was in Austria with my grandfather [Theodore Roosevelt, Sr.] and had been invited to go to a great dinner of the Emperor. She had a beautiful dress all ready for this, but she never got dressed in time. She never got there. Then she ordered the coachman, Dan, every afternoon at 3. He would pace up and down—you know how cold it was to sit out on the box—and at 5 they would tell him to go away because she never would get dressed in time to get down. Then she had an absolute

	passion for cleanliness. Well, it was a phobia. She really must have been just a little crazy, to be perfectly frank, in the last five years. I think she must have been. But my mother never felt that, except in her actions—not in her conversation. Mother always enjoyed Grandmother's conversation. Mother would, with peals of laughter, tell me the things she would do, and it would sound to me exactly as though she were talking about a crazy person. Not to be able ever to be on time...
Shef:	Grandmother's management probably drove her nuts.
Corinne:	Nuts! Oh, yes, there was no question about that. But my mother was young and enjoyed her. My mother's real love, of course, was Mrs. [Anna Louisa Bulloch] Gracie [her maternal aunt]. She was like her mother as far as the relationship went...
Sheffield:	Uncle Jimmy Gracie [James King Gracie] used to appear and bring us lovely toys for Christmas and birthdays.
Corinne:	He was the great angel of the world—and he had money. I don't know what his business was. He had a place in Oyster Bay and we always went down and spent three weeks with them in the summer right next to Sagamore. But my grandmother, as I say, was the person that my mother enjoyed hugely because of her humor. Her letters show that, much more than anybody else's in the family. When my mother was coming out my grandmother couldn't bear the thought of her in late at night and not being sure that it was she. She locked her door at night and then her instructions were that when Mother came home from a dance she'd stand outside the door and say, "How doth the little busy bee improve each shining hour."
Bobbie:	The code signal!
Corinne:	Of course, my grandmother was very calm. Nothing affected, troubled, or bothered her. She never was on time for anything, she never did any of the things that your mother did for her, she just sat and was clean! She had a white chenille net that she wore on her hair to keep the dust out. She always took two baths—one for the soap, and then she got out and it was run again by the maid and she then got in again so as to wash the soap off... Then when anybody came to see her if she was in a

	bed a large sheet was put down, particularly if the doctor came. And when she said her prayers a sheet was put down so that she wouldn't touch the floor.
Shef:	She was crazy!
Corinne:	Oh, yes, of course, she was; but crazy, according to my mother, in a perfectly delightful, charming and very companionable way. She told stories better than anybody. According to Mother, her ability to describe something was inimitable. And so it was with Auntie Gracie. Both of them had this humor. Now if you look at the letters, the thing that to my mind is interesting is that my grandfather's were fine, good and sound; but my grandmother's letters were terribly funny.

How true was it that your grandmother once hung out the Confederate flag from the 20th Street house after a Southern victory?

Corinne:	I should think it was probably very true, but I don't know. From what I can gather about my grandmother, I think it might have been very true. I always felt, you know, that Uncle Ted [TR] was belligerent because my grandfather didn't go to war. He was ready to volunteer for anything and everything ... I think it was always a real—not exactly a shame—but he felt he had to explain ... about the father he admired so hugely...

Did your mother ever tell you anything about those Civil War years? They must have been very difficult.

Corinne:	Well, of course Mother was no age at all during those years. She was born in 1861 ... Life in the Theodore Roosevelt, Sr. family when the children were young is not so gay at all. Everybody is always very sick. Uncle Ted [TR] is always very sick, everybody is sick, the whole time. Someone is always just getting over something that's perfectly awful...

The relations of your mother [Corinne] to her sister Anna were very close, weren't they?

Corinne:	Oh, she adored Auntie Bye. There was 7 years' difference between them. They were totally different types, to my mind, *completely* different types ... Mother was much more of a dreamy character than your mother (to Shef)...

Bobbie:	Mother-in-law was intensely practical and intensely "on the ball," so to speak, about everything. And rather impatient about people who weren't equally so.
Shef:	She didn't suffer fools gladly…
Corinne:	But she suffered fools gladly very sweetly in front of their faces. In *front* of them she suffered them beautifully.
Shef:	I never knew anybody who could demolish a character for you in about two sentences as quickly as Mother did. She did it completely. She didn't do it to everybody; it wasn't back-biting at all. But if she decided that somebody really needed the knife, she could give it to them in a couple of sentences. She could change my feeling forever about that person by saying two sentences, and quite often did. Am I correct in that, Corinne…
Corinne:	I had quite a time with your mother. The thing with me was that you never would have been able to tell anything except just that she was perfectly devoted to me. I think she *was* devoted to me.
Bobbie:	I know she was.
Corinne:	But on the other hand, when I first came up here, on account of her devotion to Joe [Corinne's deceased husband Joseph Alsop IV] she thought I was young—which I was—and not up to the job, really, in one sense, and she also thought I liked New York—which I did. And I heard these things that she was saying. And my aunt, Mrs. Cowles, was a person who could frighten you, don't you think so, Shef? She was such a tremendous personality that you wanted to be in her favor, you know.
Shef:	Well, she could so tremendously influence people if you weren't in her favor. She could do it indelibly. She couldn't undo it afterwards. She had *done* it. She had done it in a couple of sentences, very quickly.
Bobbie:	And you could never think of that person any other way than in those two sentences. It was a most devastating quality that she had.
Shef:	And it was always done with a lot of humor … It would make you laugh at the time, but you'd never forget it … Among Mother's nephews and nieces of your generation, Corinne, she had some very distinct favorites. Teddy

	Robinson was one ... Kermit Roosevelt was very much one. Alice was very *much* one. F.D.R., curiously enough.
Bobbie:	That was through Eleanor.
Shef:	Not entirely. It was on his own. She always thought he was charming and debonair…
Corinne:	One of the most fascinating evenings I've ever spent in my life was here with Franklin, your mother, and Mr. [William Amory Gardner the co-founder of Groton School for Boys]. Mrs. Cowles was, of course, in her wheelchair, Franklin was in *his* wheelchair, and Mr. [A]mory Gardner was going backwards up these stairs reading Trollope because he had a heart condition. He could go up only very slowly so he took Trollope with him. The three were the gayest, most delicious things you've ever known in your life. Franklin *hurled* himself from his wheelchair into a little tiny wheelchair—I don't know how he did it—and Auntie Bye had this [hearing aid, a] huge box, you know, because she was always so very, very deaf, and they were so gay and so delightful and so enchanting that evening that it will always be a red-letter evening in my life. You felt such *gallantry* in all of them, you know, such humor, such complete elimination of any problem about bodies.

I've heard this extraordinary story of her death. Is it true? That she came down to serve tea?

Bobbie:	Oh, she did. The day before her death.
Corinne:	We were out playing golf, do you remember? Well, we three and Helen Scarth [Mrs. Cowles's personal secretary] had just been taking turns all the time with Auntie Bye because she was dying, and we all knew that she was dying.
Shef:	So, did she.
Corinne:	Oh, she knew she was dying, too. We had all been with her a very great deal and therefore had been housed also. It was a perfectly beautiful afternoon and Shef and Bobbie and I decided to go out for a half an hour and play a few holes of golf. Helen Scarth was going to remain here. We'd gotten to the second hole when suddenly we saw

this car come right near that pond. Helen Scarth got out of the car, came over to us and said that we must return immediately, because Mrs. Cowles had made up her mind that she was coming down and going to be at tea. She always had tea at that time in the front room, so the service was always brightly shining—and it was a rite. So, Bobbie and Shef and I got into the car with Helen and dashed back. We got here to the door—it's as vivid to me as though it were yesterday. We got here to the door and Hopkinson [Mrs. Cowles's butler] was pushing her down the hallway and into the other room. There was this woman who you knew was dying! She was taken in and put in front of the tea-tray. We went in—at least only I went in for one moment, because of course it was absolutely impossible for her to do anything—and in a few minutes she was taken back again. But it was just a definite compulsion to go through the thing that she had gone through every day. And that night, or...

Shef and
Bobbie
(together):   Early the next morning...
Corinne: She died. Is that right? Is that what you would have said?
Bobbie: Absolutely...
Corinne: I'm so glad to have you and Bobbie to corroborate that, because it was so terrific that I have felt all these years as though I might have been making it up.
Shef: No, it happened. It happened. I remember it.
Bobbie: I'll never, never forget that.
Corinne: It was the most dramatic thing that I had ever seen.
Bobbie: You had to go through with your part of it, you see. We had to be there as though we were having tea and as though nothing were going on. We had to play our part with her in it, which was the thing that was so terrific! You knew the pain that she was in, you knew that she was dying and yet you must ignore it, because she was ignoring it. It was perfectly magnificent!

* * *

9 December 1954

I'd like very much to hear about the trip you took with Mrs. Robinson to the Republican National Convention in 1920.

Corinne: I went out with my mother and with my brother and sister-in-law, Theodore and Helen Robinson, and a number of gay other people who were going out. You know, conventions were not completely serious at that period!

We got out to the Blackstone [Hotel] and were assigned our rooms, then came one of the most exciting weeks that I've ever been through, because of course we were all working very hard for Leonard Wood. There was Leonard Wood, who had an enormous headquarters; there was [California Senator Hiram] Johnson, who had an enormous headquarters; and there was [Illinois Governor] Frank Lowden who also had a headquarters—so there were three of them who were attempting to be nominated for the presidency. We went to all kinds of thrilling and exciting things, and there was a great deal of those at headquarters, but I'm afraid I was not too much help to Mother because Mother said at the end of the week that the only thing she could really remember about me was a very small, very wet little pile of underclothes in the middle of the floor when she woke up in the morning because ... it was so unbelievably hot. It was one of those terrible Chicago heat waves.

I think that Mother took the place, really, by storm when she did the seconding of the nomination of Leonard Wood. It was extraordinary! But by that time it was recognized that the probability was that neither Johnson nor Leonard Wood would be satisfactory to the organization ... So, we went through all the agonies and all the excitement; but at the end, of course, Warren Harding was nominated.

One incident that fascinated me was a call that we made. Mrs. Parsons, who was Mother's most intimate friend, was out there and tremendously enthusiastic about Leonard Wood. She, my mother, and I ... decided we would go and see [Warren Harding]. He had no real headquarters, only a tiny room. He had the most pale-faced, tragic looking little character who was the only person in charge. She happened to go up in the elevator with us, otherwise we would never have been able to find his room. We went down a long corridor with the pale-faced creature and found Mr. Harding, who at that time was Senator [of Ohio]. He who was a candidate whom nobody wanted, *nobody* in the whole place wanted, whom nobody really thought of at all. We paid a call on him ... We went into this little room and there he was with his large white shirt-front-bland, patronizing in a certain way, you know. He was a curious, strange character. Then, of course, came the great convention ... and during the convention the decision was made to shift every one of the votes to Warren Harding. We then went back to our rooms perfectly desperate and depressed. My last sight of Chicago was ... as we were getting on the train, this frock-coated character, Warren Harding, walking down the platform, looking like the cat that had swallowed the canary. He came up to my mother and said, "You made a very remarkable speech. I wish that it had been for me."

Mother looked up and said, "But it *couldn't* have been for you!"

He couldn't have been taken aback by anything. You know, he had that kind of bland, white-shirted front, both mentally and physically. That was in July of 1920. Warren *Gamaliel* Harding. I think his name alone was just impossible!

Please tell me something more about your mother. She must have meant a lot to the people who knew her.

Corinne: It was extraordinary, that feeling in all the letters that came after her death—that feeling that she was the important person in their lives due to some instant in which she had been able to give them help or understanding or sympathy. And she was a person you wanted not just merely for sympathy in any sorrow ... Mother you wanted for the fun of life! She was so gay, she had such zest, such a wonderful sense of humor and such a delight in companionship.

I remember when my oldest boy, Joe [Alsop V], who hated anything like a dancing-class or anything of that kind; he was a fat, little, completely uncoordinated little boy who had the most tremendous interest in all kinds of beautiful things with the greatest observation of any child I've ever seen. I made up my mind that I would have him in dancing lessons because I felt it was so important for him to learn to move better and to have greater coordination. It meant my taking him over the mountain and home again once a week ... It was a ball-room where there were red chairs, great chandeliers, red damask curtains ... that part rather fascinated Joe. But to see him dance was one of the funniest things I have ever seen.

Mother was in New York, and I just couldn't bear to see this thing myself. I longed to share it with Mother, so I telegraphed her and asked her whether by any chance she could come up ... So, she did, and Joe never knew that ... we were absolutely in hysterics. I don't think I have ever laughed so in my life, Mother and I together. Joe never realized it. Then she came home and spent the night. We have the most wonderful time! That's just merely an example—not any craving or longing to have her with me because I was sad, but I just wanted to share something with her that was so funny...

She always had people at the house. It was just a Mecca for every kind of person. One of the entries in her engagement book was on, let's say, the 16 December. There were things that she was doing, she was speaking, there were entertainments of all kinds, people at dinner, etc. She always wrote out everything that she was thinking, even in her engagement book. So, she put down on top of December 16 page for the evening, "Want to be alone."

That night, after it she wrote, "Couldn't be alone," and then she described all the people who had come for dinner. The humor of it!

And then she and I had the most heavenly time when I was down there for just one day. I wasn't very apt to go down often. On her pin-cushion there was a piece of paper. On it said, "Remember Mary." She always was writing notes to herself, in every direction. I came down about three days later and below "Remember Mary" was "Who is Mary?"

I lay down on the bed absolutely in hysterics. Josephine [her maid] was helping her to get dressed, the telephone was ringing and everything was happening of every variety. We sat down and I said, "Now, darling, we've just got to sit down and try to remember who Mary is. I don't want to come down another week and find, "Can't remember Mary."

We did a lot of work as to who Mary was, but we never found out. Oh, how I laughed! I would no more think of putting down in writing, "Who is Mary?" than the man in the moon! I don't know anybody who would write out those words.

* * *

28 December 1954

Tell us more of the relationship of Mrs. Cowles and Mrs. Robinson with Mrs. TR. That's fascinating to me. I recognize that in the early years they felt they had to move very gingerly.

Bobbie: Oh, very! Because, they said, that if in any way they jeopardized that relationship they'd lose it with Uncle Theodore.

What did they feel about the marriage in the first place?

Bobbie: I don't know that I've ever heard Mother-in-law discuss that very much. Of course, she loved Alice, the first wife. She said she was an enchanting creature, but I think Mother-in-law, by and large, felt his marriage with Aunt Edith had been a great thing in his life. I don't think I ever heard her critical along that line ... I think they felt not only that they had to go gingerly with Aunt Edith, but they had to go very gingerly with the children. That Aunt Edith didn't want any other influence on the children [and] that they had to be very careful how they acted with them or advised them—no interference...

The children were here a great deal ... Mother-in-law was very, very fond of Kermit. I don't think she was ever fond of Archie. She was always rather critical about Archie, and she didn't like Gracie [Hall, Eleanor's brother] very much. She loved Ethel, was devoted to Ethel ... Archie and Gracie were here very rarely. Kermit and Belle [his wife] were here a good deal. Ethel was always here a good deal. And Ted and [his wife] Eleanor less often, but then Ted in those years was being very active and was everywhere else but this country ... And Eleanor [Mrs. Franklin Roosevelt] would always make every effort to come up here, quite frequently. And I think she discussed things a great deal with Mother-in-law. I think that all the nephews and nieces felt what I feel—her great wisdom. And I think they often, when they had problems, wanted to talk them out with her. Mother-in-law had brought Eleanor up, to a certain extent, after her father [Elliott] died, so she always had a very, very warm place in her heart for Eleanor.

One could get that from Mrs. [Eleanor] Roosevelt's autobiography...

Bobbie: You know Uncle Elliott died in a strange way ... Didn't he fall off a coach, going up Broadway? I think so. And he was taken first to his mistress's apartment on Riverside Drive; and when they went to move him from there, there was a large portrait of his wife on the mistress's bureau, which was rather a fascinating combination of things! But that's the way the accident happened. Mother-in-law was told the story...

I got the picture of his having been ill for quite a long time and moving out to Long Island somewhere...

Bobbie: I gathered from Mother-in-law that the accident was the cause of his death, and prior to his death there was the difficulty of removing him from his mistress's place ... He was in Paris for quite a while. They all were living in Paris. There is a big batch of letters about that. That was a very difficult time, when Anna [Mrs. Cowles] was living in Paris with the children [Eleanor and Gracie] and Elliott was behaving so badly ... There were gals everywhere, always. I know Mother-in-law used to say that it was kind of like a continued story, and she always thought she should call it "La Nounou et le Caporal," which was apparently a continued story which came out when she was at school in Paris as a young girl; and she used to say that the latest instalments would come in these letters from Paris.

I think that when TR was Police Commissioner there was a crisis and he had to go over to do something about it.

Bobbie: I think there was. Mother-in-law was always very reserved about all those times. She kept all the letters. At her death I sent them all on to Eleanor.[5] She felt that Eleanor ought to know the whole story ... Elliott had evidently been very charming, apart from the unfortunate thing with the drink.

Mrs. Alsop found a diary of his, with two entries, one at the time of his father's death; apparently Elliott was the only one of the family who stayed the whole of the 13 hours with his father when he was in his death agony ... And then, at the end of it, he suddenly realized that he had promised Theodore to let him know if there was any danger. In the throes of everything he had not done it, and hoped that Theodore would forgive him ... What is it in the Roosevelts that alcohol so often gets them?

Bobbie: Corinne and I have often, often discussed that with the thought that our children might fall heir to it. The women never seem to crack up. They go on triumphantly. But the men are the ones who, if they can't get the goals that they set themselves, go to pieces. They all have such strong vitality and with it goes a strong ambition, I think. And if that ambition in some sense or other is not fulfilled, they seem to crack up.

I suspect that TR recognized the danger in himself, that's why he practically never touched alcohol.

Bobbie: I think that may be. I think it often is, when you have the example ... [Kermit Roosevelt] was the most tragic of all. Kermit I really loved. He was the one of all the boys that Shef and I were the closest to.

I think that in his case he was frustrated with his career.

Bobbie: I think that had something to do with it, and also the malaria that he had, had a good deal to do with it. You know he never lost those bouts with malaria that I suppose he got in Africa or in India or in South America. He might have gotten it in any of those trips. I have seen him at dinner—he would never go to bed no matter what fever he had—and I have seen him with the perspiration literally spouting like a fountain out of his forehead, and you knew he had a raging fever, but he would not give in to it for a minute. I'm not sure that *that* didn't undermine his system to the extent that the alcohol took hold more easily ... Kermit really should have been in the army. He was the type of fearless person. He was at the height of his life when he could brave everything that was coming his way ... He was absolutely in the wrong groove. And he had so much to offer, too! Again, he had a great capacity for friendship...

In your mind, how does Alice Longworth fit into this whole family picture?

Bobbie: Of course, she's a most engaging and fascinating character to me ... I simply adore her. I think everybody, everyone in the family adores her [and] is a little bit frightened of her. She can be very crisp when she feels like it ... very caustic, indeed. She never will write ... It's one of her "isms." You very much wonder whether she'll open the letter if you write it, so you don't usually write her. If I have occasion to write her, I usually write on the outside: "Maybe you'll be interested in the inside; but, if not, throw it away." And that usually makes her at least go that far and take it out of the envelope ... On the other hand, the moment anything happens, nice or otherwise, she's on the telephone; and you know that she *is* devoted to you and you know that the moment you see her you'll have the most glorious time with her ... Alice is just a law unto herself and letters are just one of the things she won't cope with. But she will go to any amount of pains for you. There's nothing she won't do for you. Oh, Shef and I love her!

I'd love to know some of the constructive things that have been effected through her in Washington.

Bobbie: That would be much harder for me to give you any help on. It would be through her friendships with, of course, [President of the United Mine Workers] John L. Lewis, with [Idaho Senator William] Borah, with [Ohio Senator] Bob Taft—those were all intimate friends of hers.

And yet she speaks awfully snootily of Bob Taft.

Bobbie: She turned against Bob Taft toward the last year or two of his life. Up to that point she adored him ... I don't know what happened there ... Because even when we were still in Washington at the end of the war, he was very intimate. You never dined with Alice that Bob and Martha [Taft] weren't there. I don't know what issue they split on, because she was isolationist, of course, and so was Bob. It might possibly—this is just guesswork—have something to do with the Taft-Hartley [Act that restricted labor union activity].

You mean that John L. Lewis might have influenced her?

Bobbie: On that basis ... Alice has never been a very constructive person. She has always been *de*structive, has always been *agin* something. I've never really heard her *for* something ... The one purpose that came into her life was Paulina. That made all the difference to Alice, I think, having that child. She had always been very scornful about children or talking about children. I think she'd always wanted children very, very much. And then, when she had Paulina it brought purpose to her life. When Paulina married a man that she didn't care for in the beginning—it was a great blow to her—then she forced herself into taking him and making a friendship there, which she did ... Alice is rather more a cat that walks by herself, though, than any other member of the family. Alice can be away from people for months on end and it doesn't bother her ... Do you know, she told us once in Washington that her father had never spoken of her mother to her ... That's the most extraordinary thing, I think...

Can you say anything about Eleanor—Mrs. FDR—and her part in this whole picture?

Bobbie: I think probably Corinne has already told you that that generation all felt terribly badly when she got engaged to Franklin. They all had been a good deal together and they felt that Franklin wasn't up to her ... Corinne had written in her diary, I think, she'll tell you this, that she went for a drive with Franklin. They were all down at Orange [NJ] ... Eleanor, Franklin, Helen [Roosevelt Robinson] and a whole group of young ones, and that she'd gone for a drive with Franklin and in her diary, she wrote, "He was very charming, but the truth is not in him." Which I think is very amusing. That was her reaction to him at that young age, I suppose they were seventeen or eighteen around then. And I know that Corinne was devoted to Eleanor and I know that was her feeling at the time.

In what way would she feel that? I'm just curious.

Bobbie: I don't know. But he was thoroughly un-liked by his own college contemporaries. He told Shef something that interested me: When they came back from the war—the First World War—Shef was detached from the Marine Corps to be Franklin's aide just to get him back to college. Strings were pulled to have that happen, and on the boat coming back, Franklin told him the greatest disappointment of his life was not making the Porcellian [an all-male student club at Harvard University]. Franklin was Assistant Secretary of the Navy at that point; he was a man of thirty-five, and that still rankled...

As I gather from Mrs. Alsop's autobiography ... she felt that Eleanor was quite indifferent to Franklin for a long time.

Bobbie: I think that may have been. I think it did take him quite a while to persuade her. I think I remember her telling us that. But, of course, all that era I only heard from hearsay. I think that with Eleanor, I don't think the relationship could have been quite satisfactory or she wouldn't have gone so hard for causes. And I know that Mr. [Endicott] Peabody [Founder and Headmaster of Groton School for

Boys], [found Eleanor difficult]. My boy [William Sheffield Cowles III] went [to Groton] and I was up one weekend when Eleanor was there with one of her lady friends. When I went in to see Mr. Peabody, I said, "What's the latest success story?"

And Mr. Peabody replied, "Thank heaven you take that attitude because Eleanor always comes and asks me what's been going wrong with her children!"

I know that Mr. Peabody felt very strongly that she took the attitude that all her children were going to turn out badly instead of they are going to turn out well.

Wasn't it because Sara Delano took over?

Bobbie: That was a terribly difficult relationship for poor Eleanor to grapple with. They have a door-through between their two houses and Cousin Sally could come in any moment. That must have been very hard. She gave them their house and she had the house next door and on one floor you could go from one house to the other. And then of course their summer was always spent at Hyde Park where they were in the house with Cousin Sally.

** William Sheffield Cowles enters **

What was the relationship between the Franklin Roosevelts and Mrs. Cowles in later years?

Shef: Oh, I think they were always very close. And, mother, of course, had the highest regard for Franklin. She always considered him a very charming, debonair person and was very fond of him ... She was all for him when he was Governor of New York. And enthusiastic about him, and very fond of Eleanor. And Eleanor was very fond of her.

Bobbie: Mr. Hagedorn asked me: Eleanor never lived formally with your mother?

Shef: She was with her a great deal, but I don't think she ever lived formally with Mother. To tell you the truth, I can't remember. When I was in the Marine Corps in the First World War, after the armistice, I became Franklin's aide in Paris. And after a few months in Paris, we came back on the boat together, and I saw a great deal of Eleanor on the

	boat coming back. And Eleanor always told me that she patterned her reading a great deal after my mother's reading. And mother always had a great influence on her from the point of view of certain types of reading.
Bobbie:	Mother-in-law always kept a pile of books she called her "mental maneure"—ones you couldn't read right through, but were there to sort of fertilize your mind to go on to other reading. I always loved that expression and I always have a pile on my own right table of the same variety. She read as widely as all the rest of the family. Always piles of books on the chair in the front room. She read a great deal.

Did she read as rapidly as her brother?

Shef:	I don't think she had quite the memory her brother had, but she was an omniferous reader.
Bobbie:	She always complained that she hadn't had any education, but was the most cultivated person imaginable. I'm just going to say of all the reading that is done, Alice is the most extraordinary, probably in our generation. I think maybe some of Ted's boys have that same quality—for instance she's very knowledgeable about Gypsy law and language. When we were in Washington, a big group of gypsies appeared at the hospital. One of them was ill and they all camped in the hospital and all around it. And the only person who could keep them calm and quiet was Alice, to go down and tell them everything was all right. She knew how to talk to them and what to do and in Greek. She has the most extraordinary knowledge because she reads till four and five and six every day, every night. She's never up in the mornings, never before eleven and even that's a little early for her. But she'll come up here and you'll see by the number of cigarettes she smoked, what hour she probably has read. And out will come the queerest things out of the bookshelves that Alice decided to read that night. She really has an extraordinary knowledge … You'll find every kind of queer sideline she's gone down. She's done great reading in Hindu philosophy, for instance. The facets of what she's been interested in is just extraordinary. You can hardly find a subject that you won't find Alice hasn't—at some moment—given a real reading to. And she, of course, also has a wonderful memory.

Now look here—you're opening up something entirely new! We've only seen Alice from the outside, so far...

Bobbie: Well, you'll find that if you bring up almost any subject that Alice will have gone rapidly through it at some point in her career. It's great fun to talk to her about. And she also has miles and miles of poetry by heart, the way that all that family have...

Tell me about her friendship with John L. Lewis. Was there anything constructive there in their relationship at all?

Bobbie: I wouldn't really know that well enough. We were only there [in Washington] for two years watching Alice operate in Washington, otherwise I've just seen her when she's come through. But a thing of going to her house: they were the ones you almost always met there. Alice is a great one for having a few people for lunch and at the club and always one or the other would be—she'd always have people without their husbands or wives—they're just much easier that way. You bump into one or the other inevitably.

Can you tell us about Nick Longworth, her husband?

Bobbie: Well, of course, Nick was very interesting. He must have been an extraordinary person. I never knew him. He died before I had known Alice. I think it was a pretty dim [marriage], in one sense. Nick was always very keen about other ladies. He was, according to Shef, a most extraordinary person. He got no sleep. He always drank very heavily, but not to the point he was obnoxious. But he would be up all night and would be up early to the House [of Representatives], dapper as could be. He always looked, even after the latest kind of night, as if he'd just stepped out of a long happy night's sleep. And, of course, he was very musical, which Alice isn't. He played the violin beautifully. And he loved to gamble. At one-point, Alice rather enjoyed that but I think she got tired of that. She still likes Bridge, but they used to play poker till all hours. I remember a story Shef always told of being down there when he was in the First World War when he had come up from Quantico or Parris Island or something in the Marines

Corps and he went on a picnic with them ... Nick was lying, chatting with a lady, I think perhaps they were even holding hands or something. And Alice, walking by and [the lady with Nick] looking up and saying, "Oh, hello Mrs. Longworth," in this kind of formal fashion, as Nick was being very intimate with her on the ground, amused Shef as a young man intensely. I think probably Alice's real relationship was with [U.S. Senator William] Borah. I think the family have always felt that probably Paulina [Longworth] was Borah's daughter rather than Nick's.

She played a decisive part in the debate over the League of Nations.

Shef: She was very against that ... I was extremely surprised, in coming back to this country at the end of the First World War, over Alice's attitude on the League of Nations. As I said before, I had been an aide to Franklin Roosevelt. We had been over there and we came back on the same boat as President Wilson and Mrs. Wilson. We heard nothing but the League of Nations—and the great advantages of the League of Nations. I went straight down to Washington and stayed with Alice [upon returning home] and reported everything I heard about the League of Nations and she immediately broke down my arguments in favor of the League of Nations. In fact, she completely changed me on it in no time at all. My mind was not at all fond of it. But I was extremely surprised from being in one media in which the League of Nations was the ultimate and desirable thing to attain to Alice's house where I found it was the absolute worst thing in their opinion that we could do for this country.

Did she feel it was getting involved in foreign entanglements?

Shef: I think no. I think it was more because she was violently anti-Wilson. I think her politics were somewhat on a personal basis. She was dead against Wilson and Wilson was for the League and she was against the League. And, I think, that lined her up with [Senator Henry] Cabot Lodge who was a natural friend of hers anyway through family friendship. And I think she worked very hard for and with Senator Lodge in trying to defeat the League. I

	think that [her anti-League work] was the strongest, single political point that Alice was keen about…
Bobbie:	I haven't heard her get very excited about any political issue. Of course, she was deadly against Franklin.
Shef:	She was dead against Franklin.
Bobbie:	You know, she's a wonderful mimic and she does Eleanor to the Queen's taste. And it got around Washington that she was doing it, so Eleanor asked her to [do it] for her, which she did … She'd do Bob Taft for you…

It's too bad her political influences have all been on the negative side.

Shef:	And she was quite a friend of various people like [Michigan Senator] Homer Ferguson, who we met at her house, occasionally. John L. Lewis we met at her house. Speaker [Joseph W.] Martin was in her house occasionally. She saw a great deal of the Republican top political group in Washington and had them around to the house a lot.
Bobbie:	My, she had a queer life in those days. She had nobody in the house. [Nick died in 1931, Paulina went to boarding school in 1938, and then college before getting married shortly thereafter]. Everything came in the evening. A butler came in in the evening. A cook came in. All the queerest. If she's lonely it's of her own choice. I mean, I think people are very devoted to her.
Shef:	She always led very queer hours. She believed the time for reading was from 11 o'clock or 11:30 pm on. And she would read until 6 in the morning and got up very late. I can remember one-time she was staying up here and she arrived that afternoon, had dinner with us, and we chatted at dinner until about 11 o'clock and she went up. The next day when she appeared, which I would say was for a very late lunch, she had by that time read one book that was in the room she was in, which is my mother's room … and had gone through the good part of another [book]. In other words, she read until about 6 in the morning. And in Washington she led very curious hours. She wouldn't get up until 3 or 4 in the afternoon. Tea in the afternoon was her first appearance. It's very hard to get her in the mornings. She has curious idiosyncrasies. She

never answers a letter. She hardly ever answers a telegram. A telegram is the only hope if you wish to get an answer out of Alice. She's perfect on the telephone...

I was asking [Bobbie] in the afternoon about your mother's relationship with Mrs. [Edith] Roosevelt—[if] Mrs. Robinson and Anna [Mrs. Cowles] were scared of Mrs. Roosevelt.

Shef: I had a feeling she was always on a slightly cautious basis with Aunt Edith, but on the other hand, I think so much had gone by that time that it mellowed somewhat. Wouldn't you think Mags?

Bobbie: Well, they had a great admiration for each other ... I think with Aunt Corinne, she was devoted to [her sister] but very impatient. I think [Mrs. Cowles] thought that Aunt Corinne was too sentimental. And I think somehow—she always a little implied that if you could be that spilling over that the emotion in back of it wasn't very deep. That was a little bit her implication about Corinne. "Darling Corinne, she's putting it on—she's acting out, but I don't think it really means that much to her, as she makes out it does." I don't think that was true in Aunt Corinne's case. I think Aunt Corinne was far, far more accepting of Mother-in-law in her affection as Mother-in-law was about Corinne.

Shef: I think that's true. Yes, Mother, I think, was distinctly reserved in her feeling about Aunt Corinne. Slightly critical, perhaps that's a better way. I never thought Aunt Corinne was critical about Mother, but I always felt that Mother had a slightly critical feeling about Aunt Corinne...

Bobbie: Mr. Hagedorn was asking me about the reaction of the family when Eleanor married Franklin. Can you remember anything about that?

Shef: I can remember the wedding. Just slightly ... I had a feeling that it was one of those marriages that was more or less arranged by both branches of the family ... I think Corinne was rather anti-FDR at that time. She didn't like him much. They rather felt that he wasn't one of them, somehow or another. That sort of feeling they never entertained about Helen Roosevelt [who was] thoroughly accepted. But FDR not. Mother was always a great friend of Cousin Sally [FDR's mother] and always got on very well with her. Oh, very well. They were very chummy, very close. Mother used to go up for rather long visits to Cousin Sally at Campobello in the summer.

** Corinne Robinson Alsop enters **

Can you give me a picture of the house where Eleanor Roosevelt was brought up by her grandmother and aunts?

Corinne: It was a house on 37th Street with one gas jet in the hall and a staircase that went up straight—you know. They went to Tivoli, New York, in the summers. The Hudson River was beautiful, so that part was very good for them when Eleanor and [her brother Gracie] Hall were growing up.

I'm a little bit concerned about saying these things, on account of Eleanor. Now these are things that I heard, not things that I know.

Bobbie: All of this, Corinne, is confidential, nothing that will be appearing to hurt Eleanor, and much that explains her! That she was called "Granny" by her aunts would condition a child to a role that none should ever be made to play, don't you think?

Corinne: Her mother died when she was 8 and her father a year and a half later. After her mother's death she and her two brothers lived with their grandmother in that 37th Street house.

Bobbie: Eleanor didn't go into the really horrible aspects of her childhood in her book. She knew she'd had a ghastly childhood but she really didn't realize how ghastly it was.

Corinne: I told her perfectly frankly after she gave her book [*This is My Story*] to me, "I have never imagined anything as stark and as grim as the description you give of your childhood." I think it was a perfectly extraordinary book.

She went abroad to school, to the same school I went to [Allenswood Boarding Academy]. That was her salvation.

Bobbie: That gave her the chance to be on her own for the first time.

Corinne: That wasn't the important thing, really. It was the question of Mlle. [Marie] Souvestre, who loved her, understood her, made much of her and gave her tremendous responsibilities. She was really the head pupil, the person Mlle. Souvestre counted on and made the favorite...

What kind of woman was Mlle. Souvestre.

Corinne: She was one of the most curious people ... My aunt, Mrs. Cowles, was at her school near Paris. Then in the 1870s after the 1870 [Franco-Prussian] War she moved over to England. I went to that school in 1901. She had already been established for 25 years over in England.

[Souvestre] was an enchanting person. She was not as tall as she should have been for her remarkable head. It was a beautiful face but it was a *big* face, a face for a person of real stature, a sculpted face, and her body was not tall enough for the beauty of the face. She had never married. She'd had delightful friendships with many intellectually prominent people of that period. The library was one of the most remarkable rooms that I've ever remembered, and there were [Pierre] Puvis de Chavanne pictures and books of all kinds. Her father had been Emile Souvestre who wrote a French book called "Le Philosophe sous les Toits." She was intimate with Charles Wagner and with the Stracheys; I went to lunch with her with [British novelist] Mrs. [Mary Augusta] Ward and I met many of the Stracheys. She had a real—well, not a salon; I don't mean that—but she was recognized at that period as being a very remarkable person.

She was an unusual person, in one sense, for a headmistress, because she always had favorites. Eleanor happened to be a very great favorite, and because I was Eleanor's first cousin, I then became a favorite. Every evening she and I would read aloud. Oh, she was the most stimulating, exciting person that you could ever imagine. It gave Eleanor love and it gave her tremendous interests...

Then you must have been with her quite a lot during your own childhood?

Corinne: She came to and fro. She was a person somewhat apart. She didn't seem to have any sense of humor, you know. Do you have to put that down?

Why didn't anybody ever do anything about her teeth?

Corinne:	Her grandmother was old. I always used to laugh and tease Mother about it.

I suppose there was not too much money at that time in the Hall family.

Bobbie:	Well, I'm fifty-four, Corinne, and I'm passionately interested in my grandchildren's teeth and various portions of their anatomy.
Corinne:	Well, you probably haven't had two drunken sons and four *very* beautiful, fatiguing daughters, and you are not having your grandchildren right there with you every moment.
Shef:	Eleanor and Hall [her brother] always had a certain amount of money.

I was wondering why Mrs. Robinson or Mrs. Cowles didn't do something about it—or Mrs. Theodore Roosevelt?

Corinne:	I always told Mother that I thought she had been completely derelict in her duty, so I don't know. I think it was terrible.
Bobbie:	I don't know what you could do except pull them out.
Corinne:	Oh, no. She could have had them all straightened. Oh, it was terrible, Shef, that she didn't have it done!...
Shef:	Well, she's had them out now and they look much better.
Bobbie:	Mr. Hagedorn was also asking me about the feeling in the family when Eleanor got engaged to Franklin. I said you all had been very depressed about it. Is that right? That was the impression I got from you all—that you didn't like Franklin.
Corinne:	Oh, no, I don't think you can say that.
Bobbie:	You told me of that part in your diary about Franklin...
Corinne:	I know, but I wasn't depressed about it; because I loved Franklin in one way. I was awfully fond of him, but I just thought he was a hypocrite.
Bobbie:	I thought you hadn't approved of it when Eleanor got engaged to him. Was I wrong on that?
Corinne:	Oh, no, I never did *not* approve of that.
Shef:	I thought you felt that Franklin wasn't one of the boys, so to speak.

Corinne:	He certainly wasn't one of the boys. But it wasn't the question of my disapproving of Eleanor marrying Franklin, as far as he not being one of the boys...
Shef:	Why wasn't he accepted at that time?
Corinne:	I never can describe Franklin to anybody. He was just—well, as I told you before, he was called Feather Duster. He was so completely superficial then. He did no athletics at all. I mean if he got on a tennis court, he couldn't do anything. He had such peculiar friends, Shef. He was the type of person who just didn't make attractive friends. He was just not in the group of attractive friends. You can look at [his roommate at Harvard] Lathrop Brown, you can look at any of those men that he saw at that time ... It's awfully difficult to say exactly what I'm trying to say; but he didn't have the fundamental reality about him. He had very, very narrow eyes, you know, very, very sloping shoulders. He was handsome ... this is perfectly awful to put on a recorder!

This can be sealed.

Corinne:	Well, let's for heaven's sake seal it! There used to be satin handkerchief boxes—did you ever know those satin handkerchief boxes? ... And on the top of them there were painted figures with a gentleman dancing a minuet with a handkerchief in his hand, you know, just doing this way [illustrating]. In our family we called a certain type of "handkerchief box-y," which meant a kind of dainty quality...

You mean effeminate?

Corinne:	No, Franklin wasn't effeminate. I don't think you can say that. But he wasn't rugged. There was nothing that was—well, as Shef said, "one of the boys." He really didn't have that quality ... I told you all that I was terribly surprised by my own diary because I hadn't remembered much about Eleanor's engagement as to when and how and what. I also had rather visualized the feeling that Franklin was handsome and Eleanor was plain and that Eleanor had loved and Franklin hadn't particularly. I had remembered that he had always been fascinated by a pretty girl

called Dorothy Quincy [Roosevelt] who was very attractive, from Dark Harbor.

But in my own diary I have items that completely fascinate me! I hadn't come out by then. I was up in Dark Harbor and Eleanor was staying with me. I had had a very, very bad accident with my leg so that I was completely housebound and not able to do very much. Caroline Drayton [Phillips] was there and we all read Browning together. Franklin appeared on his yacht called the *Half Moon* and gave parties. He tried to see Eleanor and [I wrote,] "I feel very badly for Franklin, that she really doesn't love him! He loves her and I really am very sad about it." It always surprised me until I found my ridiculous, very dull little diary with all those notations in it. Then, in that same little diary, they come to stay for a house party in September. And at that time, I take a drive with Franklin. That was the time where I said, "I have always called him a hypocrite; but he's not only a hypocrite, he's a liar!" But all the way through I'm very fond of him. I'm not anti-Franklin in the diary but I don't think he's particularly attractive. However, I'm very fond of him.

On the 30 November Eleanor tells me that she's engaged. I think that Eleanor may have been charmed by older people rather than of that age. But how Franklin did it I really don't know. If his mother had wanted him to do it then I would have seen the reason for it because her influence on him was as great as any mother's influence on a man that I've ever known.

Shef: Well, do you think that was not the cause? Perhaps it was.
Corinne: I don't think it was.

Did [Sara Delano Roosevelt] approve of Eleanor?

Corinne: Well, I think that she didn't want him to marry at that moment.
Shef: She was perfectly horrible to Eleanor for most of the rest of his life.
Corinne: Simply terrible.
Shef: Yes, really nasty to her. I mean, visibly so to us who were staying at Hyde Park ... Saying "Why can't you dress decently"—you know, before us!

Was that just her natural possessive motherhood? Would she have been that way with any other woman who might have married Franklin? Or was it just that she disliked Eleanor?

Corinne:	I would say that she would have been that way anyway ... I've never seen such possession in my life...
Bobbie:	Mr. Hagedorn asked me whether there were other people in the Roosevelt family who had taken too much alcohol, and asked about Uncle Robert [Barnhill Roosevelt, TR's uncle]. I said I thought he drank a certain amount but that it wasn't a problem that way—he was just a completely unconventional character and didn't care what he did or said...
Corinne:	I thought that tendency came from the Bulloch family [TR's mother's family]. The drinking didn't come from the Roosevelt family.
Bobbie:	Were the Bullochs alcoholics?
Corinne:	Not Jimmy [James Dunwoody Bulloch] and Irvine, but I thought that there were Elliotts—your mother-in-law felt that it was my grandmother's blood that wasn't so "hot" in that direction.
Bobbie:	I remember she always referred to the two miniatures that we have—one was a Bulloch or an Irvine and one was a Cowles—and she'd say, "See the difference between the ones who spent most of their time *under* the table from alcohol and the ones who sat very rigidly above it."
Shef:	I must say, the Bulloch looked more attractive!
Bobbie:	Far more attractive.
Corinne:	I don't think that Irvine or Jimmy Bulloch drank, but I had a feeling that it was the Stewarts or Elliotts [Martha Roosevelt's maternal line], I think they come in.[6] I think that there were characters in that part of the family ... and I have the feeling that there were all kinds of stories about one of those...[7]

When did [Mrs. Robinson] have time to write her poetry with all of her social engagements?

Corinne:	Well, the tremendously active period of her poetry was the years after Stewart died. That was the very active period of her writing. That put her in a position of being

	a great deal with contemporary poets ... Really, nothing was ever published before then.
Shef:	Aunt Corinne cried the whole of that summer.
Corinne:	Yes. I was telling Hermann that she was a very mercurial person, you know. She could cry and then she could laugh, like sunshine coming after rain. That used to bother your mother.
Bobbie:	It scared *me* to death. I can remember when I went up there when we were engaged, to see Aunt Corinne, that she cried on my shoulder because Shef reminded her of Stewart. Our family were so self-contained in showing emotion that I didn't know what to do. I was absolutely lost and terrified if somebody was crying. After I patted her on the back, I didn't know how to go about helping her. To me it was bewildering ... You learned it was just her way of showing what she felt and it wasn't bothering her. But in our family if anybody cried it was really a crisis. To cry over somebody who died—it must have been 10 years before—that was upsetting to a person who wasn't used to showing emotion that way.
Shef:	For a year or two after Stewart's death, Aunt Corinne used to burst into tears at meals and things like that, then it would sort of pass over...
Corinne:	Well of course, Stewart's death, Mother never got over—never. Her whole life was affected tremendously by Stewart's death...
Bobbie:	Well, I think she was gay, in a sense, throughout her life, too. The two strains were side by side.
Corinne:	Well, she had that tremendous capacity which I think Auntie Bye had, too—but I think Mother had it perhaps almost more—and that was such a consuming interest about other people that if they were gay, she could be gay, too. If they were sad, she was sad, too. But, as I say, of her own life, Stewart's death had the most tremendous effect upon her—of all her life.
Bobbie:	Do you think she felt in any way responsible, Corinne? That he hadn't been handled properly or anything like that? Was that part of it?

Corinne:	Stewart? Oh, no. Stewart's death was by complete entire accident. She and he had the most wonderful relationship. He was the gayest, most enchanting boy! Of course, he was *my* most companionable person of my whole life. I had never known anybody with such humor…
Shef:	Was he rather like Monroe [Douglas Robinson] or like Ted [Douglas Robinson]?
Corinne:	You mean drinking? Oh, no. He wasn't like Monroe. Not like Ted, not like Monroe. Not like any of them. He was tremendously loveable, gay, humorous, absent-minded, didn't concentrate properly on his lessons, but it was the most delicious companionship. He was just *fun* to be with!

How did the accident happen?

Corinne:	There had been some sort of a game at the party, during which he had hit his head on the newel post and was knocked out—and cut himself. They did take him back to his room.

He was knocked unconscious?

Corinne:	Probably, evidently. The thing could perfectly well happen. In any event, they took him back to his room. The window, when he opened it, was very low. It was one of these low windows. His friends thought that either Stewart, who used to crawl from one window to another on the outside ledge and frighten the boy in the room next to his—he'd often done it—had done it again and lost his balance, or else he had just gotten dizzy opening the window and fallen out. What happened nobody knows. But he fell out of the window. There had been no problem, no difficulties, no anything except that he was very much in love with Elizabeth [Parrish] Starr … they were engaged. There wasn't any question of [suicide]. Oh, he was a very sunny character with blue eyes and kind of thatched yellow hair—and just *great fun*. When Johnny, [Corinne's youngest son John deKoven Alsop] is at his most relaxed, he reminds me of Stewart. You know, at that period in our lives there weren't sudden deaths because there were no automobiles. Sudden death for a very young person was a *shattering* experience for those left behind!

Do tell us more about the Franklin Roosevelts.

Shef: Well, it was at the time that I mentioned to you before. I was a Lieutenant in the Marine Corps and an aide to Franklin after the Armistice at the end of the First World War. We came back from the Peace Conference on the same ship. We were walking up and down deck and Franklin was talking a little bit about his life. He said he'd had one great disappointment, by far the greatest disappointment in his life, and that was that he was not taken into the Porcellian Club at Harvard—which to me was an extremely interesting and significant fact. At the time, he was Assistant Secretary of the Navy, he was an important man, and, from the eyes of my generation, he was a much older man. To hear him say that that was the greatest disappointment in his life struck me as extremely odd. And he wouldn't have said it if it hadn't been true.

Corinne: That had the most terrific effect upon him ... for him it was his most important goal.

Bobbie: Sheffield always felt later that the attack on Wall Street, or on the bankers, was largely because of the Porcellian fellows. He was getting back at his own!

Shef: [J. P. Morgan Partner and CEO] George Whitney, I feel, was one of the reasons why he attacked J. P. Morgan and the banking fraternity. George Whitney was about his time in Porcellian...

My, that's a rather grim aspect of his life.

Shef: I think it's a very true one and a very significant one. I'm convinced of it.

... I never was convinced that he was very profound in his social ideas or his economic ideas, but I've come reluctantly to the conviction that he was right on a lot of the New Deal, that it was something that was long overdue in this country. It has given us a balance...

Shef: And a greater stability...

Bobbie: I agree with you there, but I'm not at all sure that that isn't in a strange way due to Eleanor ... It was a combination. I think he used Eleanor as a yardstick. I think it was an extraordinary lucky political combination because she was so eager to do good, and she was in such touch with the needs—so agonized over the needs—that I think he could pick out highlights.

Corinne: I don't think either of them were the basis. I think Louis Howe was the basis.

Bobbie: All of it?

He was the source of it? Was he really a social philosopher?

Corinne: Well, he was politically—he knew very definitely where he thought Franklin should go, and I think Louis Howe had the most extraordinary effect on both of them. He was just like a little Svengali. I shall never forget it ... Well, perhaps I shouldn't say Svengali. I meant more that he had his hands on what was going on. It wasn't that he did abracadabra on him...

Bobbie: He was the one who said Franklin was going to be president, right from the beginning.

Corinne: I was there just after Franklin had had his paralysis. I had never met Louis Howe before. I came home and said to Mother, "Who is the little man who controls the whole of the Roosevelt family?" It was like complete control. I went into, first, one room where Eleanor was having tea—and Louis Howe was there. Then Louis Howe took me into Franklin's room—Franklin was paralyzed and in the front room. Louis Howe came with me and we had this little man with us; he completely controlled what we talked about and what we said. It was the most fascinating picture of control!

Bobbie: And, of course, after Franklin was President, Louis Howe was always there until he died. And Eleanor always took him for a drive every afternoon, in that early part when he was so ill.

Corinne: And I had a long talk with Eleanor in which she analyzed the difference between Louis Howe and [FDR advisor] Harry Hopkins. It was very interesting.

Bobbie: That would have been very interesting, Corinne. Can you remember the details of that?

Corinne: Yes, very well. She didn't like Harry Hopkins. She didn't tell me that but I just knew that. She said that Franklin had to have someone on whom he relied on completely. The difference between Harry Hopkins and Louis was that Louis could analyze and tell Franklin what not to do and what he'd done that was wrong, or what he would do that might be wrong; and that Harry Hopkins just merely was a yes-man, giving Franklin the praise and adulation that he needed.

Shef: It's extraordinary how some of the conversations that you have with Franklin stick in your mind. I also remember, coming back on that same ship, we fueled two destroyers at sea. Franklin said, "If I'd followed what was best for me, I'd have resigned as Assistant Secretary of the Navy and enlisted in the Navy and been an officer in that destroyer. It would have been much better for my future."

Then again, I was terribly impressed one time when Bobbie and I were staying at the White House in 1935. We'd had tea with Eleanor and we were to see Franklin at 6. We were led to Franklin's study and had about an hour with him. That hour, I may say, was interrupted several times by Eleanor coming in and asking Franklin, "if that bill could go through," and Franklin saying, "No, it cannot go through."

Then she came in again and said, "*Can't* that bill go through?" and he said, "No, it is *not* going through!"

What the bill was we never knew. It was evidently some piece of social legislation that Eleanor was interested in at the time. But Franklin spent most of the hour talking to us about Japan and Japan's Asiatic ambitions and the fact that Japan wished to make the whole western Pacific *their* ocean; how they intended to expand down toward Australia and expected to get control of a strip of the Chinese mainland and Korea, and one thing and another. He was *extremely* conscious of Japan at that time and during one of Eleanor's entrances and interruptions Eleanor

	said, "Oh, you shouldn't talk about this, Franklin," and Franklin said, "It's on my mind and I'm going to talk about it." He went right on and talked for pretty nearly a full hour about the threat of Japan.
Corinne:	...what I thought was so fascinating was that I didn't think he was a success originally, socially, but that I think he *became* a very real success in his power over men, utterly charming! That's what I meant.
Shef:	Oh! He upset the standards for success for a generation.
Bobbie:	You went in feeling allergic to him, as I did, politically, and at the end of an hour you were completely charmed. You felt: here was somebody who *really* was thinking about the problems. When he talked to you about them, they sounded quite sensible for the moment. Then you got away from that honeyed voice, you began to analyze the things he'd said, and they didn't really make sense. But for the time being, you felt it was really the most exciting thing you'd ever heard! At least, I did. I probably was gullible.
Shef:	He could make it awfully interesting ... Something happened there—the combination of his running for the vice-presidency in 1920 and his illness immediately afterward made him a much more important personality.
Corinne:	Yes. I think there are some people who are destroyed by power, as far as their personalities go, because they become arrogant, something unattractive. But Franklin had a great sense of humor, and, I think, achieving confidence was essential to the development of his charm.

CHAPTER 5

First Lady of the World: Anna Eleanor Roosevelt

Fig. 5.1 Eleanor Roosevelt at Val Kill (1947), National Archives and Records Administration

Harry S. Truman called Eleanor Roosevelt the "First Lady of the World" in recognition of her work for human rights. Biographers credit her with much more, and her family more still. Some Roosevelts say that Franklin's achievements as president originated with Eleanor, from New Deal policies to the growing influence of the United States on the world stage. Historians might dispute her role in the administration, but they concur that Eleanor made an undeniable contribution to women's and civil rights. Her outspoken opposition to segregation and social inequalities match her deeds. She invited African Americans and women to the White House, raising the issue of discrimination in public forums, and she petitioned for substantive legislative programs for equal pay or anti-lynching.[1] Yet her activism provoked a certain friction within Eleanor, between her wealthy patrician class and the desire for social justice. The conflict was personal. "The revolution in our social thinking appears in capsule form," she said, "in one family I know well—my own."[2] Transforming the nation, or the world no less, began at home, and for Eleanor it started with the Roosevelts.

As the daughter of Elliott Roosevelt, TR's younger brother, Eleanor spent her childhood among the Oyster Bay set. Her youth was tragic. Her father suffered a likely, but undiagnosed neurological condition that prevented him from attending college and, as family members believe, led him to alcoholism and drug use. He married Anna Hall, a member of New York's upper crust, and they had three children. The joys of fatherhood failed to settle Elliott and his substance abuse intensified. Intoxication combined with resentment of his brother Theodore's success and Elliott had bouts of violence and absence from his children. His marriage deteriorated and family members—including Theodore Roosevelt—encouraged him to seek treatment, which he did. Still, his recovery suffered many setbacks. When an affair resulted in an illegitimate son, Elliott returned to overindulgence, and Eleanor bore the emotional trauma of her father's neglect. Worse, her mother prematurely died in 1892 of diphtheria and the following year, her brother Elliott, Jr. died of scarlet fever. The hammer fell again in 1894 when her father's drinking drove him to suicide. He jumped out of a window, survived the fall, but agonized from debilitating seizures that claimed his life shortly thereafter.[3]

Eleanor and her brother Gracie moved upstate with their maternal grandmother. They spent many days with Oyster Bay relatives, especially Anna Roosevelt Cowles, TR's sister. Mrs. Cowles nurtured Eleanor in the absence of her mother and ensured that the tragedies of her childhood would not keep her from her cousins, most of whom lived in stable households. Biographer Joseph Lash wrote that Eleanor's childhood led her to believe she was an "outsider," but one who's "unhappiness made her even more determined to succeed."[4] She kept close to her aunts and cousins, especially those sympathetic to her. Conversely, she came to eschew those who were unkind. She developed a tumultuous relationship with Alice Roosevelt Longworth founded on personal jealousies from their childhood that manifest into political differences in adulthood.[5] Numerous biographies situate Eleanor Roosevelt's tragic adolescence alongside her relations with the Oyster Bay Roosevelts and these familial bonds had an undeniable impact on her personal development.[6]

The Hagedorns interviewed Eleanor Roosevelt on 18 January 1955 at her apartment in New York City. They did so after speaking with family who believed she could shed further light on their stories. The questions, therefore, follow the channels by which the Hagedorns examined Alice Longworth, Bobbie and Shef Cowles, and Corinne Alsop. Eleanor confirms and expands on much of what they say, but with her own perspective, an interesting angle because of her place in the family. Notwithstanding the considerable tension with her cousins, the idea of "devotion" to the family appears as strong in Eleanor's reminiscences. Indeed, her testimony avoids mention of family differences, unlike her cousins who amuse the Hagedorns with unkind stories about Eleanor's teeth, her occasional poverty relative to her class, and how they ostracized her. Eleanor's testimony bears no sense of resentment.

The most powerful parts of Eleanor's account come with regard to women in politics; she discusses the evolution of feminist attitudes in the twentieth century. While her Auntie Bye disapproved of women voting, Eleanor rubbishes the notion that women like her had "a man's mind" in a man's world. Instead, she maintains that women have always had strong opinions and valuable insights, and that her Auntie Bye played an important role in politics without voting. She celebrates her aunt's achievements and abilities, while ignoring the different opinions they had on equality and feminism. Her approach is constructive; it seeks common ground and points to her family's ability to transcend generational boundaries. That observation closely follows the sentiment of other family members and the image Eleanor casts of the past seems inclusive, of an attentive family with grandparents mixing with great-grandchildren, and of wits sharpened by that interaction.

Despite being a vital figure in American history and foremost personality in the Roosevelt family, the first lady's testimony was not included with those collected by Columbia University as part of the oral history project. The transcript—edited by the Hagedorns and amended by Eleanor Roosevelt—was archived with the Theodore Roosevelt Centennial Commission documents. No recording exists. The version presented here has been minimally edited. Some questions posed by the Hagedorns have been removed, as well as some of the exchanges in which Eleanor Roosevelt indicates that she has no recollection of note. Given her centrality to American politics in the mid-twentieth century, one wishes the Hagedorns had spent more time asking about life in the White House or her work for human rights at the United Nations. Disappointingly, they did not and her testimony is among the briefest in the collection.

* * *

As far as Auntie Bye is concerned, I think there was one outstanding thing that most of us who were younger remember. When I was a young girl back from Europe, 18 years old, she was already beginning to be very deaf. She lived in Washington and still was active, did everything, but she was very deaf, so that when you went there you know that she labored under a disability and yet it never seemed to affect her. She never complained, though she had rheumatism already, but she would go and walk with Aunt Edith or she would make herself available to Uncle Ted at any time. I never heard her complain. She took such an interest in all the younger people that all of us, I think, were ready at any time to go and see her. We would rather have a chance to talk with *her*, even though she always provided us with plenty of young people there. I don't believe there was one of the younger generation who would not have preferred to go and sit down and talk to *her* and have a chance to discuss any problems or any situation in the world, because she was so interested. She was interested in everything and she never gave you the feeling of being bored or that you were bringing her things that didn't interest her. She was *always* interested. That was a very remarkable trait, I think.

Alice made a very interesting comment. She said that if Auntie Bye had been a man, she would have been the one who was president.

Well, I think it might easily have been so. You know, people are so apt to say a woman has a man's mind. People in talking about Auntie Bye and Aunt Corinne always said that Auntie Bye had a man's mind, that she was much more calculating in what she did and was not as feminine as Aunt Corinne. I have never quite been willing to accept that category, because I think many women have that type of mind—and it *is* a feminine mind. Many women are quite able to think into the future. It's not confined to men only. And there are women who, like Auntie Bye, are very good in making an analysis of a situation, which she was very good at. I think that she just had that type of mind, but she didn't seem to me one bit less feminine.

I never remember the time when she didn't have a great many men friends. She always had some man much younger than herself with whom she had a particular relationship—like Bob Ferguson all the years of his younger life, and Joe Alsop [IV], too. There was always that quality in her, which some women have, I think, of enjoyment of every age. It didn't have to be her own generation at all. She could move into another generation and if the person had something of interest, she had the quality that drew it out.

And I suppose identification with that other person's age and experience, too, in a way.

No, but she just wasn't of an age. Of course, she had very close friends of her own age; Mrs. [Olivia Peyton Murray] Cutting, for instance, was one of her very close friends. And I've heard people say, "Well, Bamie always happened to have people whom it was an advantage to have as a friend." I don't think that was the case. I think she genuinely liked a great variety of people. She could appreciate people in a great many different categories. Because if you look over the people she knew, they weren't all rich people, they weren't all society people, they were of many different kinds and from many countries.

She was not tied to age. That's why all we young people felt so free to go and talk to her and enjoyed it so much. She never made you feel that you were less interesting than an older person—and you *weren't* less interesting to her because she had that *quality* of interest. I have an idea her father had it, too ... I have always felt that Auntie Bye's father must have been very close to her because of her back, which he struggled so to have straightened, and his closeness with the doctor who helped—which was the start, of course, of the Orthopedic Hospital. I have always thought that the man who could send so many youngsters from the Newsboys' Lodging House out West—and I think his statement was that only two had failed to repay him—did the kind of thing that Auntie Bye would have been perfectly capable of doing, too, had she had the money. She would have enjoyed it, because she loved young people—*all* people. She was interested.

Of course, Auntie Corinne had that quality, too, of great interest in people, and I would agree that Auntie Corinne had to a far greater extent a certain literary and artistic charm, which Auntie Bye did not have. Auntie Bye had a much more analytical mind and not that great charm of imagination and admiration for beauty. There was something really very lovely about Auntie Corinne that you felt the minute that you came into the room with her.

I loved going to see them both, but they were always very different people to me. You didn't take problems to Auntie Corinne. You went and enjoyed her and had a lovely time with her. But Auntie Bye you took any problem to because you felt that she would give it her best judgement—and it would be a good judgement.

I was wondering whether her experience in England might have helped her brother, because he was pretty much of an "American Firster" in his early days, and yet he was so warm towards England in particular and the other countries, later. I wondered whether Mrs. Cowles had any part in the changing of his thought along that line?

I imagine that Uncle Ted just normally was interested as he went to places. You see, Uncle Ted's change came about as he went. He was interested in *people* always; from the time he was a young man.

As he accepted responsibility he grew and matured enormously, in his relations to other nations, too.

And I think that was a case of his own development. But I think he put a great deal of trust in Auntie Bye who helped him a great deal, I believe, in analyzing situations. I know that he often came to see her to talk out problems in Washington. They were a wonderful family because they enjoyed each other so much, enjoyed the play of wit and had such good times together. They enjoyed so many of the same things. Uncle Ted loved to read aloud, and he loved to read poetry aloud. Auntie Corinne loved that. Auntie Bye, not quite so much—but still she would love it if they did it. They were a *wonderful* family …

Auntie Corinne was more emotional and less wise, I think, and of course had tremendous charm. Occasionally, she made mistakes, actually because she had more easy wit and sometimes couldn't quite resist making a witty remark at the expense of someone else. Auntie Bye never did that.

She wasn't tempted by her own wit. She didn't have it quite so easily as Aunt Corinne. It came so easily to *her*.

Both Shef and Bobbie [Cowles] have pointed out that Mrs. Cowles could be pretty caustic.

Oh, yes, but that was because she felt it, do you see. But never, never just as a casual thing because it was amusing. When she was caustic it was because she really meant it, you see, and she really wanted you to get it.

But with Auntie Corinne, the minute she'd done something she'd be sorry because she'd realize that it had been done for the sake of a witty remark and that it had hurt. Then she'd try very often to make up for it. Sometimes, she didn't realize she'd done it, even. But, I think, on the whole, Auntie Corinne had the greater artistic ability of expression and the greater charm. Auntie Bye had, on the other hand, the quality of making you want to discuss problems.

Do you remember any instance during the White House period, for instance, showing relationships between Mrs. Cowles and the president or Mrs. Cowles and Mrs. [Edith] Roosevelt?

Well, I remember staying with her and having her go to walk with Aunt Edith, who practically every day took a walk. It was one of the things that Auntie Bye was still able to do and she would go down and walk with Aunt Edith as a regular thing.

Auntie Bye did something which I've always thought was very lovely to do. She always tried to be at home at tea-time. Auntie Corinne did that, too. She always made a good deal of a ritual of having tea and quite a good deal to eat, and so forth. People dropped in. Uncle Ted would often drop in at tea-time and got started on interesting conversation. He would often stay when he should have gone home, and then he would suddenly say, "I should be—oh, Edie will be wondering what has happened to me!" Then he would rush off.

Did you get any hint of certain relationships between Mrs. Cowles and Mrs. Roosevelt which were quite harmonious?

Oh, I would say there had always been difficulties. Mrs. Roosevelt was, in a way, a very jealous person—and a very wonderful person; one who, I think, was quite extraordinary in the way she kept her personality in spite of being with a man who had such a strong personality that it was difficult to remain as much of a person herself. But she *did* manage to.

There were times, I think, when she would be annoyed with Auntie Bye—I think even with Auntie Corinne, though for not quite the same reasons. I think that was a case of a very natural feeling. A president has so little time and she would feel, I think, sometimes, that he enjoyed being with his sisters so much that it would take time, which she wanted for herself and her children. For instance, I remember very well Mrs. [Martha "Patty"] Selmes, who was a great friend of Mrs. Robinson's and great friend of Uncle Ted's. Uncle Ted liked her very much; Aunt Edith didn't like her at all! No, not at all, because Mrs. Selmes had the quality of exciting his mind, and Aunt Edith wanted to excite his mind. She didn't want to share that!

And Mrs. Selmes was rather beautiful, too, I take it, wasn't she?

Mrs. Selmes was not so beautiful; she was interesting looking. She was never like Isabella [Ferguson], but she was an extraordinarily interesting person, quite exciting as a person to talk to, and Uncle Ted found her exciting. Aunt Edith never like that very much ...

In the letters of Mrs. Roosevelt to Mrs. Cowles there's a degree of affection that is perfectly remarkable in view of the fact that I know there was friction there. There was basic devotion, I think.

There was basic devotion, but there must have been friction. How could there be anything else, when two women really cared as much about a man and they had such different qualities ...

I don't know that I have much to tell you because—Auntie Bye was very thoughtful. She always had us come to see her. She always asked us to come. And, of course, when I was a little girl, before my father and mother died, I used to go and play in her house on Madison Avenue, because we had a house just near her one winter. You always had a sense of the closeness of family feeling. She had a great deal. And so did Auntie Corinne ...

I'd love to find out sometime the situations, the issues, the questions in which Mrs. Cowles had a part when Mr. Roosevelt was in the White House.

I don't really know that.
 One remarkable thing was that when my husband went into politics, Aunt Corinne nearly always wrote him a letter wishing him well and wanting him to succeed, regretting that they weren't on the same side. But she

never gave you the feeling that she was opposed to him in any way. I was awfully interested by that, that she could take such a detached point of view about someone in the opposite party.

I felt it was very fine that she would not take part in the 1932 election.

She would not take part. There was something quite remarkable about it. But way back, farther than that, she would always write Franklin, every campaign he ever was in, and would write me saying how interested she was—and would do it on a personal basis even though she was on the other side.

Shef and Bobbie told us how much it meant to Mrs. Cowles to have Mr. Roosevelt, your husband, come to see her when he was governor, and talk to her—how much she enjoyed it!

I think she always enjoyed it. And when he was, of course, assistant secretary of the Navy and we were abroad, he brought Shef home because he felt Auntie Bye was ill and didn't want her to worry any longer. She never forgot anyone who cared about her, you know. She was very loyal ... The war was over and it was possible for him to bring Shef home, and he brought him home because Auntie Bye was really miserable then.

CHAPTER 6

The Scions of Sagamore Hill: Ethel Roosevelt Derby and Eleanor Butler Roosevelt

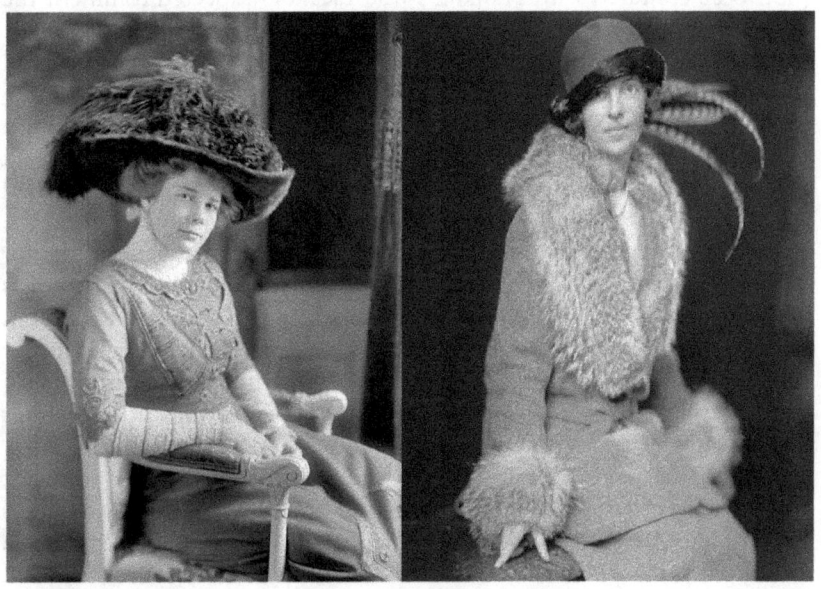

Fig. 6.1 Photo portraits of Ethel Roosevelt Derby (1908) and Eleanor Butler Roosevelt (1905), National Park Service and Library of Congress

The evening before he died, Theodore Roosevelt asked his wife Edith if she, "will ever know how I love Sagamore Hill."[1] The Long Island estate, where TR built his house in 1884, had been the epicenter of the Oyster Bay family. During his presidency, it became the summer White House, a beloved retreat from Washington. Besides traipsing the wooded grounds, identifying bird species, and rowing in the bay, Roosevelt raised his children there. When away, he longed to return.

TR's death left the property spiritually vacant. Edith remained in residence and visitors still came, if less frequently. The vibrancy of the place had dissipated. TR's namesake Ted, and his wife Eleanor Butler Roosevelt (not to be confused with Franklin's wife Eleanor) expected to inherit the property and planned to revive the site, but Edith resisted. In 1938, Ted and Eleanor instead built a substantial house called Old Orchard behind the main house. Their residency was brief. Ted reenlisted in the Army when war broke out in 1941 and died in Normandy in 1945. Edith Roosevelt died three years later, in 1948, and before her death, she sold the house to the Theodore Roosevelt Memorial Association, which had long desired to make it a shrine. The memorial association restored the house to its appearance during TR's presidency and charged visitors for the experience. In 1953, it opened to the public. When the first tourists came to Sagamore, they could catch sight of Eleanor Butler Roosevelt, who stayed on in Old Orchard. The last resident of the estate, Eleanor died in 1960, and sold Old Orchard to the memorial association. Two years later, in 1962, the memorial association donated the entire grounds to the National Park Service.

One of Eleanor's regular visitors to Old Orchard was TR's youngest daughter Ethel Roosevelt Derby, who lived nearby. Described by family as the best liked of TR's children, Mrs. Derby had a distinguished career as a nurse, philanthropist, and social activist. She worked closely with the Red Cross for more than 60 years and sat on several charity boards, many of which had long associations with the Roosevelt family. She also took a leading role in her father's memorialization. She steered the Roosevelt Memorial Association in the absence of Hermann Hagedorn who died in 1964, and cultivated Sagamore Hill as an attraction. Ethel made her presence felt by helping to inform curation and preservation efforts until her death in 1977.

From the available transcripts, it is unclear who interviewed Mrs. Derby and Mrs. Roosevelt. We might assume it was the Hagedorns, or one of them, but unlike the other collected testimonies, theirs includes no mention of dates, location, or circumstances. Given the questioning, it seems likely that Alice Longworth prompted the Hagedorns to interview them. If we accept that, we can also assume that the interviews occurred in 1954 or 1955. No recording exists. Equally frustrating for researchers, the transcript is clearly truncated and heavily edited. The surviving transcription strays unnaturally from one topic to another with gaps where the interviewer's questions would be expected. While it is impossible to account for the deviation in practice, the transcription still provides a glimpse into the lives of the Roosevelts. As Alice Longworth predicted, her sister Ethel has a sharp memory and lucid recall. Her reminiscence begins with food and social life at Sagamore, including the interactions the family had with servants, but also offers a description of their privileged upbringing and the idiosyncrasies of the Roosevelt family, from TR's dislike of telephony to the role of women in the household. Eleanor Butler Roosevelt explains what it was like to come to the family as an outsider—a daunting proposition. Although brief, their commentary will be of particular interest to those who wish to learn more about life at Sagamore Hill.

* * *

Mrs. Derby: For the servants it was at least a 12-hour day, with a couple of hours off in the afternoon. The man outside lit the stove in the early morning and the servants breakfasted at 7. Breakfast for the family was generally at 8, unless someone had to get an early train for New York.

The servants were Mame (who had been the first to hold my mother in her arms at birth)—she was our nurse; Molly, the seamstress; Mary [McKenna], Mother's maid, and her sister Rose who was the parlor maid and waitress; and Annie O'Rourke the cook. Then there was Seaman and his helper, named appropriately Gardner, and the coachman Frank Hall. Frank Hall lived in town with his family and was very rarely if ever called upon to drive in the evenings.

The laundry was always sent out.

In 1912, we had a "second man," George, who was a thief. He stole jewelry from Father, a watch-fob Father had given me with silver dollars in it, and a wallet with the inscription "Thou shall not steal!" These he took; other things he stashed away in the pantry, probably intending to pick them up later. After two days and very clever detective work, he was caught at Coney Island.

Mary Sweeny left after the "rumpus" brought about by George. She took up a job in a candy store with great enthusiasm about all the free time it would give her after hours. However, when the Roosevelts returned from a trip and got in touch with Mary, she couldn't wait to come back! She said the work in the store was nothing but trouble, and she couldn't have her tea in mid-morning and afternoon!

In 1910, after Annie O'Rourke retired, Meta Batt was the cook. Mathilde, a French woman, followed her and stayed until 1914. During the war, servants were very hard to get. It was a reign of terror as far as servants were concerned. Another Annie followed Mathilde. Finally, Mary Sweeney got Bridget Tubridy who became the proverbial treasure.

One of the favorite preserves was quince preserve.

Yes, for breakfast, a raw egg was served with the hominy but was always stirred into it!

Breakfast was served at the Emlen Roosevelts, down the hill, at 7 a.m. The boys used to run down and have breakfast with them, then return for their own at home!

Mrs. [Eleanor Butler] Roosevelt: In 1912, when my husband [Theodore Roosevelt, Jr.] and I used to visit at Sagamore, Mathilde was the cook and I remember that the food was awfully good. Prior to my marriage in 1910, when Annie was still at Sagamore, I was too scared to eat so cannot really compare the two cooks.

Mrs. Derby: I remember that there was always delicious Yorkshire pudding!

Mrs. Roosevelt: Ethel, your mother told me that when she was first married and came out to Sagamore, Douglas Robinson said to her, "Now remember, you're going to have just half as much money to run this house as there was to run it before." There were any number of times, she said, that she would decide not to go to New York because of the expense involved.

	(Neither Mrs. Derby nor Mrs. Roosevelt remember Mrs. [Edith] Roosevelt making cocktails during Prohibition! Cocktails were made and served only by the Roosevelt men.) The eggnogs Alice Longworth refers to may have been sherry flips.
Mrs. Derby:	I don't remember Father in connection with them! We were brought up with consideration of servants. Because of that consideration of others, we were allowed to be 10 minutes late to breakfast, but no longer. If we were later than 10 minutes, we had to wait an hour before eating.
Mrs. Roosevelt:	In 1912, I had the most terrible time getting used to a large family who never seemed to go to bed at night and then got up so early! I went back to sleep after they woke up, then the little nurse I had for Gracie [Roosevelt McMillan], my daughter, brought up my breakfast.
Mrs. Derby:	When Alice speaks of home responsibilities, mine was of a different pattern. I helped arrange the flowers in the house and taught Quentin to read before he went to school. I also taught a colored Sunday School class in Washington, and taught Sunday School in Oyster Bay for years! As far as servants' transportation to church was concerned, the livery stable sent for them Sunday mornings. They were brought back to serve our breakfast at 9. On weekdays, breakfast was usually at 8.

How early was breakfast when Mr. Roosevelt went to the Outlook office every morning?

Mrs. Derby:	He always drove to New York. Our parents gave us a lot of trust and confidence. I brought Archie and Quentin from Washington to Oyster Bay when I was 12. Mlle. Drolet, the French governess, went along, but I was the member of the family in charge.
Mrs. Roosevelt:	At Sagamore, in 1912, the house was not geared for a small baby. When we were there, Gracie could never go to sleep in the afternoon. Your mother said that her children never went to sleep in the afternoon! So, I used to take Gracie riding in the car with the chauffeur. During the drive, Gracie, who was then a year old, would go to sleep.

Mrs. Derby:	We had a "high phaeton" [horse-drawn carriage] with which we drove to church. It was the special Sunday conveyance.
Mrs. Roosevelt:	When the family came back from Washington in 1909, they were discovered planning to take out the telephone. Mr. Roosevelt said that boys from town could carry all messages that were important to Sagamore Hill! You were all staying with me in San Francisco in 1911. Mr. Roosevelt was called to the phone; the president of the University of California wished to speak to him. I gave him the message and left the receiver off the hook. After 10 minutes I found the receiver still off. When I inquired if Mr. Roosevelt had answered (his bedroom door had been shut), he replied that he hated to talk on the telephone and hoped that if he didn't go to the phone, the university president (Dr. Benjamin Ide Wheeler) would get discouraged and would come to see him!
Mrs. Derby:	At Sagamore, during the "summer White House" days, when one of Archie's friends called him up, Father answered and said that Archie wasn't there, but that this was Archie's father. When the boy said, "You'll do!" Father said afterwards, "It's so nice to think that the president of the United States 'would do!'"
Mrs. Roosevelt:	When Gracie was just through school and the question came up as to whether she should go to college or not, Mrs. [Edith] Roosevelt remembered that the daughter of a diplomat had gone to college and had said later, "Before I went to college, I was a little pearl pin in a box. Now I am a glass pin on a pincushion." Mrs. Roosevelt said, "I want Gracie to be a little pearl pin in a box."

Were there ever any battles between the children and the servants?

Mrs. Derby:	There were no battles. They were very good to us. We loved them and they loved us. When we were small, we would all have tea in the kitchen with them. We had a passport to the lives of the servants. But after you were called "Miss," the change came, and there wasn't the same camaraderie. Then formality came in.

	Annie O'Rourke was a wonderful Irish presence in the kitchen, with her big white apron. She had brownish hair and blue eyes—wonderful person! Mary and Rose McKenna were very shy Irish girls. Mary married in Washington a man named Norris and Rose came to live with her. Mame had false teeth and left them in a glass of water at night. There was great excitement when a mouse was discovered, drowned, in the glass with the false teeth! Whenever Mame was reprimanded by Mother—and anything less than hearty approbation could be interpreted as a reprimand—she would retire to her bedroom, read her prayer-book in tears and say that she wondered how her "little girl" could ever speak to her like that!
Mrs. Roosevelt:	Alice had a maid, Anna, who started in Albany. With her, Alice couldn't call her soul her own! When Alice went to the White House, Anna went along; she went with Alice when she left the White House after her marriage. Anna would never light the fire in the bedroom, but would always get the housemaid to do it, because Anna was above that sort of thing! ... Mrs. Longworth's walking ability was always phenomenal. She walked to Oyster Bay and back ten years ago, and could at a pace which no one could keep up with. She walked to Center Island and back, a distance of about ten miles each way!

Mrs. Longworth spoke of home remedies which Mrs. Roosevelt kept in the medicine cabinet. She mentioned spirits of nitre.

Mrs. Derby:	Yes. We used to have three drops in a tumblerful of water and were given a teaspoon every hour. That was for colds, etc. We were also given syrup of figs at times, too. After Sagamore Hill became the Summer White House, Duncan was added to the staff, as a butler. James Amos also used to come. He was Father's valet besides being a butler. Delaney, the barber, lived in the village and used to come up to shave Father.

Mrs. Roosevelt: On rare occasions, Mr. Roosevelt used to go through a pantomime at the dining table of a man looking for a pocket knife in one of his pockets, then in others—with appropriate gestures, grunts and exclamations—until finally, at long last, he found it. He would always have the children in hysterics. He apparently had great acting ability! And for a special treat, perhaps a birthday, he would do opera in the living-room, taking all the parts in turn—the prima donna, the hero, the villain, everyone. The fact that he had no ability to carry a tune didn't seem to matter. He would do this at Mrs. Derby's birthday party, at her special request.

PART II

Neighbors

CHAPTER 7

A Grande Dame: Georgiana Farr Sibley

Fig. 7.1 Photo portrait of Georgiana Farr Sibley (**1908**), Library of Congress

Georgiana Farr grew up in Orange, New Jersey. In her youth, that semirural township's most famous resident was Theodore Roosevelt's sister Corinne Roosevelt Robinson. "Georgie's" parents, the Farrs, had settled in the affluent suburb of New York a generation before the Robinsons arrived with their four children. Both families had wealth and social status, and with children of similar age they struck up a close friendship. As Georgie recounts, her family visited the Robinson house for tea almost daily, and there she met Theodore Roosevelt whose children became lifelong friends to her and her brother Barclay. Ethel Roosevelt would stand as bridesmaid at Georgie's wedding, and Kermit Roosevelt as groomsman in Barclay's.

Georgie married into the Sibley family from Rochester, New York. In her testimony she recalls how Fletcher Harper Sibley, the grandson of Hiram Sibley who cofounded the Western Union telegraph company, asked for her hand multiple times before she finally agreed. Her decision to hold out should not occlude the fact that their relationship had developed into a strong partnership. Observers referred to their marriage as a lifelong love affair. Indeed, Georgie insisted on being referred to as Mrs. Harper Sibley throughout her life. The Sibleys had six children, but Mrs. Sibley did not stay confined to the house. She collaborated with her husband on academic pursuits, and specifically on the improvement of agricultural science. During the 1930s, when Harper worked as president of the U.S. Chamber of Commerce, she spoke at business conventions, and during World War II, when Harper was president of the United Service Organizations, she spoke at military bases around the country. After the war, she supported civil rights, women's rights, the ecumenical movement, and advocated for refugees. Her activism, similar to that of First Lady Eleanor Roosevelt, set Mrs. Sibley out as a woman ahead of her time. She also operated like the women of her generation, leading social crusades behind their politically connected husbands. Mrs. Sibley attempts to explain this in her reminiscences.

Harper Sibley died in 1959, less than a year after the couple's golden anniversary. Naturally, Mrs. Sibley mourned her husband's absence, but grief did not impede her work or prompt a retreat into seclusion. In Rochester, where she had long been considered a powerful figure, she brokered race and labor disputes for the town's biggest corporations, Xerox and Kodak. By the 1960s, her reputation had gone far beyond the confines of Rochester and she was invited to the Vatican II Council as an observer. Mrs. Sibley even featured alongside Alice Roosevelt Longworth in a 1968 *LIFE* magazine feature on America's "grande dames.[1]

Mrs. Sibley's account, taken by Mary Hagedorn, tells of the close personal relationships she shared with the Roosevelts, including stories about their upbringing and life among other wealthy and connected elites. Of particular interest are her recollections on gender roles and specifically how the Roosevelt women contributed to politics without the same agency as men. Sibley's testimony was recorded at Theodore Roosevelt's Birthplace in Manhattan, and although no date for the interview exists, it was likely conducted around the time of the Roosevelt Centennial in 1957, before the death of her husband. Portions of the recording are inaudible, but the Hagedorns also produced transcripts of the interview. The following chapter includes as much of the original recording as possible. At times, Sibley corrects her testimony, and in such instances the published transcript conveys her intended expression.

* * *

Mrs. Sibley, could you give us some of your earliest memories of Mrs. [Corinne Roosevelt] Robinson?

Oh, I'd love to Mary. Of course, I don't remember the times when I didn't know them. When I was a little girl, she was part of our life here in Linden Valley, a far more simple life, in Orange, New Jersey. And perhaps the most outstanding early memory is one that I blush when I think of it. My mother and father were away. There had been quite a bad coasting accident on a hill where we all enjoyed it, and that particular day, I had been told not to coast, but I couldn't resist and went out and coasted. And when we came in Mrs. Robinson said to me, "Did your mother say you could coast?"

And I said, "Yes, she did."

And then she came in and asked my nurse, Alice, who was one of those characters, "Did you say that Georgie could coast?"

And Alice said, "No, I said it was bad to coast."

And Mrs. Robinson, who I admired more than I can possibly say, caught me in a lie. And perhaps that did more for my experience from telling lies [and telling the truth] than any other experience you can imagine: to be caught by somebody you admire so much. And yet she was the kind of person that never mentioned it again, never brought it up. And yet it made such a deep impression on one's little tiny self.

Perhaps she intuitively knew that a very positive effect had been made on your life.

She was an amazingly conscious person. She was more a radiant person than she was a reformer. She didn't have any of the reformer's zeal. But she just somehow seemed to radiate this great personality.

Mrs. Sibley, did Mrs. Robinson say anything to you when she realized that ...

She just said, "Oh, Georgie," and that was such a reproach that I went up to my room and just cried and cried that she should have discovered me telling the lie.

Please tell me some more stories of her.

Well, of course, she was always so much fun. She was always planning the most delightful picnics. The one I perhaps remember best was at a place called Lush Meadows. And when I look back, knowing the reputation for mosquitos the Orange Mountains had, I wonder how we survived, but I don't remember a single mosquito. But she knew all the names and all the most fascinating plants. She knew where to find the Lady Slippers and the things that would come in the Spring. She knew the birds. She knew the bird notes and she would hear them when nobody else did. I remember trying to find the bird that she was hearing. And then such wonderful stories and just the *gaiety*! I feel an aura of gaiety about her, whenever I think of her, although I saw in her, times of deep, deep sorrow. Nevertheless, as I remember her, particularly through those early years, it was laughter and gaiety in everything she did.

I understand that she never got over her great grief at Stewart's death.

I think no one could. I think it was the shock of it and he was so young. Perhaps as the youngest child he was her Benjamin [youngest son of Jacob and Rachel in the Old Testament]. I don't think there is any question of which she loved most, but perhaps because he was younger and his two older brothers were picking on him that she would be standing up for Stewart a good deal. And so, when this *tragic* news came of his death at Harvard University where he had such promise, I think something in her died with him. And we felt ever after, even in her laughter, there were tears. And we did feel a difference from that time, I think, I would agree with you at that point.

Can you describe the way she looked as she was when you first knew her?

It's curious that I'm more conscious about personality than I am about looks: her way of talking, her way of laughing, her way of throwing her head. Of course, I've seen pictures of her in recent years, but it was really a spirit that she had with us, a spirit of joyousness, of youth, of exuberance and vitality. Perhaps those are the words.

I understand she was a very beautiful person.

You know, I've never thought that side of it. I suppose she was, but I don't think we thought of her much in those terms as we did in her interests. She was one of these people that at any kind of a party, picnic, dinner, anything—I think everyone in the room—young or old, man or woman, child, grandmother—would want to sit and talk to her more than anybody else there. She had the extraordinary quality also of being able to concentrate on the person to whom she was talking. That made her relationships so very vital.

That I understand, too, was the quality Mrs. Cowles had.

Oh, in a wonderful way. Of course, my memory of Mrs. Cowles is much more after she was so lame and, in a wheelchair, but it wasn't the mobility or the activity and yet the same humor, the same laughter and the wonderful ability to tell a story.

Wonderful women they were.

One other thing that was in my mind: I remember when I was more grown up—in fact, I was quite grown up because I had come out and I had on some of my good clothes—and she was working evidently very hard with her secretary, which in those days meant nothing to me. I didn't know what she did, but she immediately left her there—left the secretary—and I remember took me into the little "white room" as it was called. It was a parlor, set apart a little bit. And she wanted to know everything about what I was doing and she thought my dress was so pretty. She was interested that the fur had come off a dress that had belonged to my grandmother. All of those different things, and today when sometimes I'm in a heaped-up mess with *my* secretary, and some young person comes in and just wants to talk, I try to remember what it meant to me that day. She didn't even give me the feeling that I was interrupting her—that she was just so glad to see me. And I try to pass that on to some other young people even when inside I'm a little restless.

Mrs. Sibley, in connection with Monroe [Douglas] Robinson [Corinne's middle son] and his problems, which amounted to an illness. His mother never let that affect her use of alcohol when she entertained in his presence, when he was there. Can you give me some light on that?

That's a tremendously difficult thing, of course. I was young in those days. We didn't realize the *disease* of alcoholism and many of its aspects. And, of course, when you say "the use of alcohol," I don't think she even used it. She served it a great deal. I don't mean she took nothing, but never interested in it particularly. But, I think, perhaps, she belonged to that group of people who put hospitality so *very* high in the category that she wants her guests to have everything they want, without, perhaps, the discipline that is sometimes needed, if you have a particular situation. And, yet, I'm not sure it made any difference because, of course, if he didn't get it at the table in one of the bad moments, he could have gotten it somewhere else. I think we'd have to know a lot more about it, but I do think that she put hospitality very high, and was one of the reasons she was such a *wonderful* hostess and made everyone want to come and made them feel so at home.

I'd love to tell you an amusing story that Mrs. [Anne Elder] Munn, who was the sister-in-law of Charlie [Charles Allen] Munn, who was such a great friend and was incidentally my father's best man when they were married. Mrs. [Anne Elder] Munn, I remember hearing her screaming to my mother one day about Mrs. Robinson and how everyone would rather go there for a party than anywhere else and she said, "I do believe that cracked lampshade"—it was the day when we had china lampshades around—Mrs. Munn said, "I do believe that cracked lampshade has been around for 5 years and I don't think Corinne even noticed it." And I thought that was the most marvelous quality. And so today I have, perhaps not a cracked lampshade, but a very torn silk lampshade, and then I tried to remember that doesn't have too much to do with hospitality. She had a great deal of influence on the many ways, perhaps at the time that I hardly realized.

Oh, give me some more of the ways, can you?

Well, her great diversity of interest. Of course, the fact that her brother—in the days I was growing up—was vice president of the United States and so whenever he came, we all were there helping with the tea or helping pass the ice cream or something. And I remember the group of interesting people that were there and just listening to the conversation about every part of the world. But, perhaps, she had the same quality that Theodore Roosevelt had that I remember so well when one woman came up and spoke to him and said, "My son was one of your Rough Riders, Colonel Roosevelt."

And he immediately was at an enthusiastic grand stand and said, "Jimmy! I'll never forget Jimmy! The day we went up San Juan Hill." And then he enlarged in this great description.

She had that same ability both to remember and apply the incident or situation to please the other person. Perhaps it was a word, that in those days I never heard, but which has come now to be one of my most important words: the word "empathy." She was able, as he was, to put herself into the other person's place. Young or old, man or woman, poor—because many, many poor people were at her door. The maids also worked in our house loved her and I'll never forget the suffering that she used to share with my mother because we lived next door. My mother, she'd come over and pour out her heart with various problems about children and our households. There was one maid who she didn't feel was quite right. And finally, I remember hearing her say to my mother, "[The maid] sewed it on a high button shoe." She had sewn a shiny cut-jet button. She knew the maid must go to a mental hospital! She didn't seem concerned and wouldn't allow any of the other idiosyncrasies that anybody told her—wouldn't have anything to do with them. When finally, this strange button appeared, she decided [the maid] needed help. She was the most human person.

Oh, that's wonderful. I understand that Mrs. Robinson didn't take an active part in the League of Women Voters, although she was very active in American politics as a woman, and that originally, she wasn't for women's suffrage. Was she similar to other women in other ways generally orthodox ones—rather than the League of Women Voters friends?

Well, you're so nice and young that you don't realize that in the days I'm talking about, women didn't have the vote. There was no League of Women Voters in the early days and her pattern was completely set, you see, before any of these things came into existence. She was an older woman—very much older. Well, she wasn't in her first youth at that time, because she must have been born in [18]65. Do a little mental arithmetic. Do you see? And so, her pattern was already established before. She belonged, and my mother belonged, to the Victorian Era when one expressed one's self much more through one's husband, one's brother, one's sons and so forth.

And you'll be horrified to know that I was an anti-suffragist, too. [We were] under that influence because our premise was this; the premise of my mother, and Mrs. Robinson, and that whole group: that the family was a unit. You realize the family in those days was so strong? The family had a vote, and therefore the women were expressed, because in English fashion the husband would talk over the political situation, particularly with a woman as brilliant as Mrs. Robinson, or as very thoughtful as my mother, having great, tremendous influence. But, at that time, women were not independent in industry, with their own incomes, and so forth. And, of course, today I can't imagine how I ever felt that way. But as I go back, I can't imagine that I will ever feel as I do today. That's what time does. Does that interpret it a little bit?

Yes, it's interpreted very definitely. Because she as a woman and as very definitely a part of a family and in her contacts with other people—as the wife in the household—had more influence than, I think, many, many people who tear off on tangents, do outside their main role.

Well, then, of course, a great many men were tremendously wanting to talk to her. Cabot Lodge, Senator Cabot Lodge—all those people used to be people who would come and visit, you see. General Wood, I remember all of these and sometimes sitting listening to the conversations because we would go over for tea almost every afternoon. There used to be the most wonderful, what she would call "damp" sponge cake—moist sponge cake, mother's sponge cake. And once in a while it wasn't quite the way it was expected. And there were all these little things that stand out so clearly. And the children would go and play in the sandbox or the swing and they all had their cake or their tea or whatever it was. It was a great center in all those days, and perhaps you'd like to hear about the Christmas house parties because they turned out so interestingly. You see, a number of her young relatives really didn't have a mother: there was Eleanor Roosevelt who afterwards became the president's wife, whose mother was dead. She always came for Christmas. And one of the things I'll never forget: Mrs. Robinson being so disturbed one Christmas because Eleanor had grown a great deal since the Christmas before and had the same blue dress. And this Christmas it was wider to her knees. We wore patent leather pumps and long black stockings. And Mrs. Robinson looked at Eleanor and wondered what she could do, and it was the night of the party. And so, they put some kind of a ruffle on it or something. And I remember how she suffered over the problems. It was Helen Roosevelt who later married

[Corinne's] son, Teddy Robinson, as we called him. And, of course, Corinne Alsop and a wonderful man called Courty Nichols and then Alice Roosevelt Longworth always was there. And Erskine Willard and some of the others in this great big house party and we all had a country club dance that was considered the one dance of the holidays that was considered just a *complete* festivity. And they did all these gay things—sleigh rides, skating—[Mrs. Robinson] skated beautifully, danced beautifully, rode the hounds. She was one of the most versatile people and then came home and wrote poetry with very real understanding. And one of the quickest wits. Her repartee was brilliant! I know some shy people who went, including my husband, who was afraid to say anything. The wit would be too sharp for him. And he never felt as comfortable [as I did] because he hadn't grown up in it. It was very all-enveloping, the kind of family and group of friends that a shy person—they always called my husband "Young Lochinvar" because to them Rochester, New York was the West, and he came out of the West! And we live now in Rochester and are practically on the Eastern seaboard.

Do tell us the story about your telling President Roosevelt about your engagement. I think that's delightful.

I think that's a wonderful story. It shows his extraordinary memory, in the first place, and his ability to personalize things. It happened that we used to be at Oyster Bay, both my husband and I. My brother Barclay [Harding Farr] was, of course, one of Kermit's best friends, and Kermit was one of his ushers as Ethel was one of mine. And we became engaged down there at Sagamore Hill on 4 July after one of their wonderful celebrations which they used to put on for President Roosevelt was when he was president. And we said nothing about it, and the following October we went back to Oyster Bay and before the president moved to Washington and I went in to tell him I was engaged to Harper Sibley and the president looked at me with that wonderful smile and said, "I'm not exactly surprised, Georgie," and then he said, "Is anybody surprised?"

And I said, "No, Mr. President, nobody but Harper." Because as a matter of fact, Harper Sibley had asked me several times and I had refused and so he was a little surprised that finally I said, "yes."

Well, the point of this is that the following May, I went down to stay with Ethel Roosevelt, now Ethel Derby, at the White House. And it was simple days when there was no office building and the president just walked around the White House and would meet one conference in one room and one in another. And as I walked in the front door—Ethel having met me at the train with the carriage and she had a wonderful coachman—and I walked in: there was President Roosevelt walking from one room to another and he said to me, instantly, "Georgie, I'm so glad to see you; and how is the surprised Harper?" The ability to associate and remember when the things of state were on his mind!

Another thing I want to add about him and I shall never forget: we used to have breakfast in a little breakfast room there just to the right of the entrance door [at Sagamore Hill] and Quentin was just a little boy. And the president would be very engaged. He was one of those people who concentrated so completely and he'd be reading his paper or reading something he had to know before he went to a meeting. And, you know, I remember one morning when Quentin's governess came in late and instantly, the president of the United States rose, and pushed in her chair. Absolutely the *instant*—courteousness—that was so deep in him and was so bred in the whole family. You could never forget those things because today important people are so important that sometimes they forget these courtesies. And to me it's part of greatness and it was part of his greatness.

And his *lovely* relationship with Mrs. [Edith] Roosevelt! I remember that particular evening we were just there alone at dinner and he had carved; and he carved in his usual vigorous way. It was a roast of beef. He splattered some of the gravy—the juice I should say—on his shirt front, so it was quite red. And there were some Senators coming to see him, some rather unfavorable senators. And Mrs. Roosevelt, in that lovely way, said, "Theodore darling, don't you think you'd better go up and change your shirt? Senator so-and-so is coming and you know those tales about your drinking—this looks very suspicious."

He said, "Senator so-and-so! I will wear this shirt and he can think what he likes!"

I think that's a lovely story.

Mrs. Sibley, do tell me some more about Mrs. Robinson's impact on your life and its future expression.

Well, I think her reading poetry was one of the things that made me love poetry. She read so beautifully, even before she began writing very much. She loved and lived poetry and, of course, when she read aloud it was done with such vitality that she lived in the poem. And I think her ability to help and encourage young poets and to build up their morale and make them feel they could do better work. She never was sentimental about poor work. She was a very real critic, and didn't hesitate to say, but she never left them with a feeling of despair that they couldn't do better, simply pointed out to them why it wasn't better poetry. And I think that's very important because I think the person who's sentimental does the other person really no good and leaves them just as badly off, thinking the world is against them. And instead of feeling that they themselves are not doing the best of which they might be capable of, you see.

She also, I think, perhaps in her capacity for concentration, she always talked to the person at dinner as if there was no one else at the table. And I think of that in contrast to my husband's idea of sitting next to some hostesses where they—he says—they were always talking to the waitress and telling her to give more butter, or something else. She would never let it, just like the cracked lampshade, from the time in the beginning. She wouldn't know any of those things. She was concentrating, and in fact, there was a story they used to tell about her. That she concentrated so completely she practically had her elbow in her soup plate! And so, it was one of the slogans that so-and-so had their elbow in the soup plate. And with the concentration so great then it would be equally so to the man on her other side.

But at salads the conversation always became general and when I say "salad," I don't mean California salad, which is at the beginning of the meal. In those days, if it was a proper meal, the salad followed the fish, the meat, and then the salad. And so, the conversation was always individual until it came time for the salad or taking salad plates from the table, and then the conversation became general and she had a way of throwing in a most interesting question: "Also, now I think everybody will want to hear what Senator Lodge has been telling me," and he would then speak to the whole group. After that would come the most brilliant, and fascinating general conversation, *always* remembering to have our hostess tell some funny story that he had just heard, to bring Douglas in, or tell something she thought was the funniest thing she ever heard. And Douglas with stentorian tones and tremendous laughter would tell his story. And then very often if someone else didn't seem to be entering in, she had that kind of a quick eye. Not in the first place when she was concentrating, but in the second place when she became almost the presiding officer of the dinner table with the quickness with which she included everybody and they made their contribution. She was one of the great hostesses, and she probably came nearer to having a salon than anyone I know. Her Tuesday afternoons—wasn't it 422 Madison Avenue, am I remembering that right?

It was my childhood practically when she was always at home Tuesday afternoons with the really most fascinating conversations which isn't always easy when you're at home to anybody. It was an extraordinary quality and always bringing out the person—their most interesting side. I don't remember her ever being small, or petty. And I never heard the sharp tongue—sharp wit, yes. But I count that as something a little different; even though I don't think we should ever get a laugh at the expense of someone else. It was such a brilliant rapier wit.

She had a great caring for people, didn't she?

Tremendously! ... She also had a tremendous capacity for friends, both men and women, both old and young. I remember Douglas Robinson telling my father with white indignation that he had to put in another telephone because Corinne was talking to her three most intimate friends and he couldn't even get his office on the wire. Because her three most intimate friends telephoned her every morning and talked so long! He had, of course, a twinkle in his eye with great indignation.

In connection with their other children, I understand that she gave them a tremendous lot in connection with nature, the fields, the heavens.

And their friends—don't forget her house was *always* open, for any number of Monroe's friends, Hall's friends, and Corinne's friends and all the different [kids]. I wonder now as I look at the house because it's still next door to ours in the Orange Mountains, although it's no longer alive as it was when she lived there. I just wonder where you put all the people that used to come there and stay. And, remember those were the days when one had one bathroom, and not one on each floor! And yet, the great joy and warmth of her friendship and of her hospitality.

And what amazes me is all those of the early Roosevelt family—they had as children, constant illnesses and yet, as they grew up, they had terrific vitality and energy. I've never been quite able to understand that.

I think it's a vitality of the spirit. I really do. I think the way that Theodore Roosevelt conquered his asthma and conquered his illnesses. And in a way [Corinne] rose above hers and then when she had the trouble with her eyes, the way she *still* was able to keep her interest. It's a great interest in other people. And even though they were tremendously dynamic persons, they never were so egotistical that they were not interested in what the other person was doing or what the other person was thinking. That, I believe, is part of their self-forgetfulness and their great vitality.

CHAPTER 8

The Worst Friend of the Worst Boy: Barclay H. Farr

Fig. 8.1 Kermit Roosevelt with dog Jack (1902), Library of Congress

Of all the stories about Theodore Roosevelt's character, the most endearing and humanizing are those that describe his family life. An active outdoorsman, Roosevelt took his children on point-to-point hikes, swimming in Oyster Bay, horseback rides, and nature hunts. The children kept unlikely pets, sat for lunch among distinguished guests and, sometimes, orchestrated epic pranks at the White House or Sagamore Hill. The children avoided scolding, not because TR had set his sights on matters of state over household discipline, but because he delighted in their antics. Historian Sidney Milkis referred to Roosevelt's family life as "his own private circus" and while the impression of TR as "one of the boys" might sound cliché, it is also true.[1]

In Barclay Farr's testimony we get a flavor of that circus atmosphere. Barclay, the younger brother of Georgiana Farr, shared an affluent upbringing in New Jersey. Barclay was the same age as TR's son Kermit; the two boys attended Groton from 1905 to 1909, graduating in the same class. These years proved formative. Kermit would remain a dear friend throughout Farr's life, and it is no wonder when you consider their childhood hijinks. Farr's reminiscences tell of their dangerous dalliances with firecrackers on the Fourth of July and vandalizing the White House pantry. Their capers loomed so large that when TR met Farr's mother, he introduced her as "the mother of the worst friend of the worst boy in the world," a good-natured jest that nonetheless gave a sense of how epic the boys mischief-making had become. Farr, for his part, developed an abiding admiration toward Kermit's father. He talks of TR as a role model, and of striving to become a man in his likeness.

Farr attended Princeton University when Woodrow Wilson still taught politics and government. Wilson lived on campus until moving to the White House after the 1912 election; the first Democratic president since Grover Cleveland loomed large over life at Princeton. Despite this, Farr regarded Roosevelt as the greater of the two and, before his graduation in 1912, invited Roosevelt to campus as the presidential campaign reached full swing. Farr hoped the visit would inspire fellow college students to vote Progressive. For many students, the invitation seemed audacious given Princeton's association with Wilson and, according to Farr, the speech made little dent in Wilson's popularity on campus.

The characterization of Wilson and Roosevelt in Farr's story—Wilson as a stoic and introverted intellectual contrasted with an ebullient and extroverted Roosevelt as the man of action—has since become a prevailing impression.[2] We also get a sense from Farr's recollections that young men of college age gravitated to Roosevelt as much for his personality as his policies. Farr had the opportunity to experience Roosevelt's private sides from childhood, an impression best exemplified in his remembrance of the pair playing tennis. Roosevelt was a clumsy partner on the court. As historian Ryan Swanson puts it: "To Roosevelt the game was meant for exhaustion and competition. He cared little about decorum."[3] Farr describes the president's lack of finesse in endearing terms and remembers his boundless enthusiasm much more than the missed volleys and blown serves. On the stump or on the court, TR's stature grew each time Farr interacted with it.

Farr's interview catalyzed the oral history project. Hermann Hagedorn interviewed Farr at Sagamore Hill on 5 May 1953, along with Columbia PhD candidate Harlan "Bud" Phillips, a seasoned interrogator who had conducted several oral history interviews working for Professor Allan Nevins and the Columbia Oral History Project. After taking Farr's testimony, Hagedorn determined to cast a wider net for reminiscences. It is easy to see why. Farr presents a playful portrait of TR, and no doubt Hagedorn knew that this kind of portrayal would endear Roosevelt to a generation that had no chance to meet the man.

No distinction is made between Hagedorn's questions and Phillips in this chapter, as doing so would only distract the reader's attention. The omission has no impact or bearing on the testimony. This version of Farr's account also omits some peripheral conversation between the interviewers for clarity.

* * *

I remember the very first time that I came to Sagamore Hill when I was a boy—I think I was about 14. [Future Long Island Congressman William] Kingsland Macy and I drove over from Islip on the other side of Long Island for lunch with the president and his family. That must have been 1904 or 1905. We arrived late because of the fact that the boiler of our old white steamer kept leaking. We had to stop every few miles to replenish the supply of water. I remember that it was a rather large lunch party. I don't know just who were there, but I do remember Ethel, who was then a young girl several years younger than I was, a very attractive young lady, I thought. Of course, Kermit was there as we had come over to be his special guests. He was our classmate at Groton School. I don't remember too much about what happened that day except that when the chauffeur came to take us home, he told us that, going down the steep hill, a wheel had come off the car. He had lost the ball bearings and had had to go back to retrieve them one by one, and put the wheel back on, before he could proceed into Oyster Bay for his lunch. The next time I was here was on the Fourth of July of the following year. That must have been 1905 or 1906, I should think. It was either 1904 or 1905. I shall have to check this against the record of the guest book.

If it was 1904, I was wondering whether you heard anything of the political campaign which was raging just then.

I don't think that came up at that luncheon any way. I remember that there were almost always members of Congress or politicians there. They were coming and going constantly. As boys, we rather kept out of their way. I don't really remember anything to do with it. The first time I remember anything about a political campaign was in 1912, when I was the president of the Roosevelt Club at Princeton University.

I don't remember anything except the excitement of being in the home of the president of the United States, and meeting Mrs. [Edith] Roosevelt for the first time. She was a lovely, lovely person. I met the other members of Kermit's family. I already knew Theodore, Jr., who was at Groton School with me. He was a few years older. But it was mostly just the excitement of being at Sagamore Hill and getting to know the family of my Groton classmate.

Did you get any definite impression of Theodore at that time?

Oh, I got a tremendous sense of his friendliness and his warmth. As I said, we were late to lunch, and he got up from his place at the head of the table and came out to welcome us boys and bring us in to lunch. It was that sort of complete informality which one always felt here. I had to pinch myself to realize that I was in the presence of the most important person in the United States. Chiefly, I remember him as being very informal, as a friend. On other visits, I was invited to ride horseback with him. I remember on one occasion I was allowed even to ride Mrs. Roosevelt's horse, which was, I felt, one of the greatest privileges any youngster could have. I remember playing tennis with him, and I was his partner. I was panicky—when I was serving and he was playing at the net—at the thought of hitting the president of the United States in the back of the head with a tennis ball!

Would you tell that story in full?

He was couched at the net. I remember serving the first ball and lobbing it over his head and its going way beyond the server's line. The second and third serve followed very much the same trajectory. Finally, the president turned around to see what in the world I was doing. I was serving so far out of court. Then, when I saw him looking at me, smiling at me with all his teeth showing, I remember having a sense of horror that I might hit him in the glasses and break them and perhaps put his eye out. So, the next ball went over the backstop and disappeared into the woods beyond the tennis court. He was much amused.

Tell us something about TR's tennis game. I've heard it described as the worst tennis anybody in the world ever played.

I don't think any of us could claim to be very good tennis players. I think we were all about on a par. He may have been a little worse than I was, but if so, only because I happened to be playing on my mettle with him. He played at many sports with tremendous enthusiasm, but I don't remember his playing any of them with great skill. Of course, he was a very good horseback rider. The thing that impressed us very much was that which has been spoken of so often, his "strenuous life." He would go for a horseback ride in the early morning, come in, open his mail, and dictate his letters. Then he might play tennis with us boys. Then he would come in, take a shower and have lunch. He would probably then return to his desk to work on one of the books he was writing, or to transact the business of the government. We never knew just what he did in his study. Then he would take Mrs. Roosevelt out rowing on the bay, and come back for tea or lemonade. In the evening he would return to his desk, after having perhaps read a book while the rest of us were sitting in the trophy room, talking and laughing. I can picture him now over in a corner in his rocking chair, rocking back and forth. He seemed to turn the pages almost as fast as he could get his finger between them, and apparently read a whole book in the half-hour or so that he gave to being in there with us before going back to work again. That was his program almost every day, as I remember it.

I remember an amusing incident. I wasn't actually present when it happened, but I did see the bathing suit all darned and patched. Miss Grace Potter [a family friend] was visiting the family. She and the president decided to go down for a swim in the bay. It so happened that a short time before, Ted and his cousin had been given new rifles. They had gone down to the beach and had put a target up against one of the bath houses to shoot at. They got into quite an argument as to which gun had the higher muzzle velocity. They decided to shoot through the bath houses to see which one would carry through the most partitions. It so happened that the president's bathing suit was just on the other side of one of the partitions in the line of fire. It was literally riddled with shot. The president put it on, and not noticing anything wrong, swam out to the diving raft with Miss Potter. He was pulling himself up on to it when he happened to spy the holes, and quickly slid back into the water. He stayed there until Miss Potter returned to her bath house.

Who was Miss Grace Potter?

She was a great friend of the family's, and used to come down here frequently. That was one amusing incident that I can only vouch for by my memory of seeing the darns in the bathing suit. I actually wasn't present at the time they swam together.

Then another time, I remember an overnight camping trip on the beach. Dr. Alexander Lambert, [TR's personal physician and Cornell University professor] was also visiting there. He and the president rowed out in a rowboat to the spot we had selected. I don't know just where it was. I remember sailing across the bay with Kermit and Archie. It was on the other shore; I think beyond the point. What is the point across the bay ... Cold Spring Harbor? It might have been around that point. It turned out a very rainy and foggy night. We managed to pitch a tent we had taken along, and also, we dragged up on the shore a sailboat in which the boys and I had sailed over. The sail protected us a little bit from the rain. We lighted a fire and cooked our supper, then sat around while Dr. Lambert and the president regaled us with hair-raising stories of their adventures. We were fascinated and sat up late into the night listening. None of us slept much that night on account of the rain and discomfort and the sound of the foghorns blowing at frequent intervals, quite close to us. That was one of my memories: of his just being one of us boys.

Was he approachable?

Oh, completely so. Completely. You could go up to him at any point and talk to him. There was no formality. In my memory, he was just like the father of any of my friends. There were times when obviously he would be preoccupied with the business of state. There were other times when he would come out and join us on the porch. We would discuss anything that was current. He was very much interested in all the doings at Groton. He would ask Kermit about the teams. I remember some of the boys getting on the lawn one day and turning handsprings, and walking on their hands, much to his entertainment. Theodore Roosevelt was definitely approachable. There was no sense of standing in awe of him, except, of course, we did respect the fact that he was the president of the United States. He obviously was a very important figure. But when we were at ease with him, he was very friendly and asked us all sorts of questions of interest to ourselves.

Was he a boy with his boys?

I would say so. I would say he was very much a boy with his sons. He entered into their games and all of their interests. You can see that, I think, from his letters. I have been reading his letters to Kermit. He knew what his children were doing. He knew who their friends were and what they were up to. He had very much that same attitude when he was with us here, finding out what we were doing. We didn't always tell him, but when he found out he could laugh about it.

What was your impression of Mrs. [Edith] Roosevelt?

She was always very reserved. She was a lovely person and a wonderful companion to the president. She was always available to do things for him. As I say, they often went rowing or riding together. But she usually kept herself very much in the background. She was a charming hostess.

I was wondering if TR had any rules of thumb. If he played as a boy with his sons, for example, how did he draw the line between having the responsibility as a father? We see a president, I tend to feel, in a most one-dimensional setting. I would assume that being a father is somewhat different than being president. Where would he draw the line in their deviltry? Did he take delight in their deviltry?

Well, Theodore Roosevelt certainly winked at our deviltry. He must have known what we were doing, yet to my knowledge he never scolded. There was certainly nothing ever said in public. There many have been some reproofs or reprimands behind closed doors. But never to my knowledge did he lecture us, or tell us we would have to be more thoughtful of the neighbors. He simply expected the best of us, I think, and assumed that we would act like well-trained gentlemen. But when we did some rather wild things, he never rebuked us—not to my knowledge, anyway. I never remember getting any rebuke. There was always great friendliness and openness, and willingness to share in our adventures, where, of course, he could, as an adult.

I wonder, if in this connection, you would put down the firecracker story and the neighbors as an item of the kind of pranks in which you were involved.

One of Kermit's, his cousin Philip, and my chief activities down here on the Fourth of July was, after midnight on the third, to put on old clothes and load ourselves down with packs of firecrackers of all sizes, shapes, and loudness, and then proceed to wake up the neighbors in the wee small hours. I remember one adventure we had. It was a very damp night, with a drizzling rain, and foggy. I didn't know the countryside at all. I remember clinging to Kermit as he led us across country and through the woods to the home of one of the neighbors for whom he apparently wanted particularly to make life miserable. It being so wet, we went closer than usual to the house and began placing our firecrackers right under the porte-cochere in front of the house. We had a string of about 500, starting with small ones and ending with giant dynamite things. Just as we were about to light them—we had some difficulty getting the first one lighted, because of the dampness—a window was thrown open just above the porte-cochere. A head came out and said, "You get out of here! I've got a gun and I'll shoot!"

We all ran. There were three or four of us on that particular escapade. We scattered in different directions. I remember running straight out from the house and suddenly finding myself falling through space. After falling some distance, I landed and picked myself up and began running again. I repeated the same things three more times, and found that I had been running off a series of terraces each of which dropped down six to eight feet. Why I didn't break my neck I don't know. We had confederates who rowed along the shore, and we eventually gathered at their boat. They were carrying our supplies as we wanted a particularly large supply of firecrackers on this occasion. We discussed what we would do next. We had abandoned our best and biggest bunch of firecrackers under this fellow's porte-cochere in the excitement. Finally, we drew lots and the lot fell on Kermit to go back and set the firecrackers off. The rest of us stayed at a safe distance to watch and warn him. He managed to keep his punk lighted by shielding it under his coat so that it wouldn't get wet. He lighted the pack and came racing over and rejoined us. We weren't quite sure whether we heard firecrackers or shots from a gun. We quickly made our escape.

Then we went to the Landons [another wealthy New York City family that summered on Long Island]. I remember their son's name was Henry [Hutton Landon, Jr.]. There was Cornelia and Agnes [Landon]. As it was still raining, we decided to put the firecrackers right on the porch. We placed them on the door-mat, and lighted them and ran.

The next morning, we heard that somebody had gone down to investigate, found the door-mat on fire, and discovered that the firecrackers had jumped up against the white door and had burned black marks on it so that the whole doorway had to be repainted. We boys felt that because we were operating out of the president's home there was some sort of aura of security around us. We were untouchable and could do these things without anybody daring even to report us to the president. But I think he found out in some way because of little remarks that came out of him now and then. They usually were accompanied with a chuckle, however. They never came out with a reprimand.

Well, of course, TR had a very warm feeling for the kids about the Fourth of July. The Fourth of July was not a safe and sane sort of one. He used to supervise all day long and just see that there were no casualties. But of what went on he probably was well aware.

Yes, I think he must have known about our midnight escapades because it was a regular tradition. The boys had been doing it for several years before I arrived on the scene. I always felt that I was just a follower. I wasn't really a leader, and I never felt that I deserved the title which he gave me years later—"the worst friend of the worst boy in the world."

I suppose Quentin was too young to be in on any of this?

Yes. It was Quentin and Archie who were the "White House Gang," because they were living in Washington whereas Kermit and Ted were at boarding school and college while their father was president.

Wasn't it Quentin more than Archie? Archie was never in the White House Gang himself.

They were both living in the White House when the president was there. You see, Kermit went off to boarding school in 1902. We were at Groton together until 1908, when we graduated. That was practically the whole time that Theodore Roosevelt was in the White House. Then, of course, in the summers they all came to Sagamore Hill. So, Kermit was really only in the White House for the Christmas and Easter vacations, whereas Quentin and Archie were there practically all the time. I think Archie came to Groton about 1907 so he would have been in Washington during most of the time that Roosevelt was in the White House.

Did you see anything of Alice at all?

I saw very little of her. Alice, of course, was married, so she was Mrs. Longworth when I first met her.

Did you ever see her up here at Sagamore Hill at all?

I never remember her at Sagamore Hill.

Do you remember any special incidents showing the relations between the president and Mrs. [Edith] Roosevelt? Did she have a way of keeping him in line?

Yes. She was a very calming influence, but she also had very definite ideas. I can remember her sometimes coming out with some very firm remark, giving the president some very sage advice. I don't think I can tell you specifically what it was, but she was not at all the kind of person that could be relegated to the background. She kept herself in the background, but at any moment she would express her feelings, very definitely. I felt she was a very stabilizing person, and a lovely person. I remember her for her charm and tact. She was always a perfect hostess under difficult conditions. I remember on one occasion when we were just about to sit down for lunch and the telephone rang. Six or eight congressmen had just arrived in Oyster Bay. They asked when they could see the president, and she said, "Oh, come right on up for lunch." The table had to be all taken apart. She asked James [Amos], the butler, if there was enough food to go around. James shook his head and said, "Well, I guess there is, but it's a little late to let me know." He had to add two or three more leaves to the table. We all sat shoulder to shoulder, our elbows practically in the other person's plate. That was a fairly typical occurrence there. I can remember that happening on more than one occasion at Oyster Bay.

In Washington, it was more formal. They had more warning about such things, and also a larger table and more supplies, except the time we raided the pantry and ate up the food that James had prepared for the president's meals the next day. That is one of my most vivid memories of my visits in Washington. We had come back from a dance, about fifteen or twenty of us, boys and girls, in the wee small hours. Somebody suggested that we go up on the roof of the White House. We all went up through the attic and out on to the roof, and clambered up the mansard to the flat-topped roof, where we sang and made merry for some time. Finally, we started down. When we got into the trunk room of the attic of the White House, who should be standing there but the president himself, in his pajamas, without his glasses. He was rather amused, at the same time realizing that we had perhaps overstepped the proprieties a bit. He made the remark, "Mrs. Roosevelt is very angry. You must go *right* to bed you naughty children." His daughter, Ethel, and Kermit rushed forward, each seizing an arm, and led him back to his room. The girls slunk off to bed. We boys started to go to our rooms but decided we would have to have something to eat in the pantry before we retired. We tried in every way to get in, but James

Amos had locked it up, having warned us the evening before that, the next day being a holiday, he would have no way of replenishing the supplies in case we ate them up.

We finally made our way to the basement where the kitchen is located. Kermit caught sight of the electric dumbwaiter, which was down in the basement, but the door had been left open up in the pantry, so it couldn't operate. This did not deter him long. He finally located a meat saw in the drawer of the kitchen table, and sawed a board out of the top of the dumbwaiter. Then he climbed up the greasy cable, having removed his dress coat, but still in his dress shirt and white tie, and shut the door in the pantry so that one by one we could get into the dumbwaiter and go up. The last chap who went up was the son of the publisher Henry Holt. He was about six feet, three [inches] tall, and his chin was resting on his ankles in this dumbwaiter. When he got between floors, some unkind soul opened the door, and the dumbwaiter came to a stop. Henry's bellows came up the elevator shaft, "Let me up! Wait 'till I get my hands on you!" I being the considerate member of the party finally shut the door and pressed the button. Up came the dumbwaiter, out shot Henry like a jack-in-the-box. He seized anything he could lay hands on, food and everything else, and hurled it around the pantry.

It really was a terrible thing we had done. We had not only eaten up the food which James had provided for the president's meals the next day, but we also had made a shambles of his pantry. Without bothering to clean up we eventually went to our rooms, which had been turned into dormitories. There were a number of cots in one of the large East Wing bedrooms. We continued this rough-house until we fell, exhausted in our beds about four o'clock in the morning. Henry Holt had been hit on the nose, which unfortunately bled all over the mattress. Somebody else managed to tear the sheet on the bed in two. A third member put a cigarette on the white mantel and burned a black mark on it, so that that had to be fixed up after we had left. But we never heard anything from the president about it. Kermit may have.

Did you hear from Amos?

Well, he told Kermit a few things. But the Roosevelts were very considerate of their guests. They never really told us what they felt about me. There's an amusing aside on that escapade. I don't know whether it should be recorded for history, but Amory Gardner, one of the founders of Groton School, and a great scholar of Greek and Latin, and other subjects, had the room next to us. I suddenly thought, "Wonder what in the world he's doing, with all this rough-house going on in the adjoining bedroom," and so I peeked in. We found him sitting up in bed, reading Dante's *Inferno* in the original! He waved two fingers at me, but didn't discontinue his reading of Dante.

The next morning, he got even with us by coming in at what we thought was the crack of dawn—it was probably about nine o'clock—singing a song. "The lark is high in the heaven, Wha-ha-ha-ha-ha, Wha-ha-ha-ha-ha, it must be after seven, Wha-ha-ha-ha-ha, Wha-ha-ha-ha-ha!" We had been students under him for six years. But now we had graduated and at this point were freshmen in college, most of us at Harvard, I at Princeton. So, we were out from under his jurisdiction, and we could afford to take liberties with him. Shortly after that we found it impossible to sleep because the Marine Band started up in preparation for the New Year's Day reception. We all felt very privileged characters. We could go through ropes, under ropes, and when the guards challenged us, we would just say, "One of the boys," and they would let us by. We really had the complete run of the White House.

Was this New Year's Day reception the occasion for the remark that you were "the worst friend of the worst boy in the world?"

It was another one. It wasn't a reception at which I was present. It was a previous one, and I think it was apropos probably of the things we did down at Sagamore Hill.

I think you ought to jot that in with some background, because that's a good story.

Yes. My mother was invited by a friend of ours—it was the congressman from our district, Representative Wayne Parker—to go to a New Year's reception a year or two previous. As her name was announced, "Mrs. T. H. Powers Farr," Mr. Roosevelt said, "Mrs. Farr—the mother of the worst friend of the worst boy in the world! I'm delighted to see you! Come behind the ropes. I want to see more of you after the reception is over." My mother kidded me about that for the rest of her life.

Did the boys ever, as far as you know, verbalize on their feelings toward their father, or were those some of the things about which they kept pretty silent?

They were all devoted to him. I never heard them say anything critical. They were devoted to both their parents. They sometimes talked about the problems he was up against in his office, but it was always in terms of tremendous admiration and affection. I never heard any of them make a disparaging remark about either their father or their mother. They were always protecting them. They had a feeling that somehow a president was a fair target for people to make criticisms of and make cracks at. They were always very defensive. If anybody made any remark at any time which was at all critical, Kermit especially, I remember, would jump to their defense, and tell people some of the difficulties of being the president. I think that was their general attitude towards their father.

As I was saying before, each one had some special, inherited characteristic. Kermit, the one I knew best, inherited particularly the literary side of his father. In their letters they would write back and forth, talking about books that they had read and characters in the literature that they had both enjoyed. Of course, Kermit was also interested in the explorations and the frontier life of his father. That was something that he enjoyed. Later on, when Theodore Roosevelt had left the White House, they went on a trip together to the River of Doubt in Brazil.

I wonder if, unless there is something more you want to add, we couldn't move on to some background at Princeton and the 1912 campaign that you came into.

There was also that interesting time when I went out on the president's yacht, the *Mayflower*, to welcome the [Great White] fleet back home in 1909. There is one particularly interesting incident that I recall about that. After the battleships had all passed the president's yacht, each giving the salute of twenty-one guns, we followed them into Norfolk. The president went aboard the flagship to congratulate the admiral. As he was congratulating him on the successful termination of the trip, and on what it meant to the country, in the middle of his speech, he stopped short and beckoned to a sailor who was seated up on one of the gun turrets, some distance away from him. I don't know how he recognized him, because I remember that there were 600 or 700 men, all looking like peas in a pod. But he *did* recognize this man, and beckoned to him. The man at first wasn't sure that he was the one the president was speaking to, but finally his crew mates pushed him forward, and he climbed down and came toward the president, rolling his cap in his hands. Mr. Roosevelt said, "Aren't you the sailor who presented Mrs. Roosevelt and me with a loving cup when we went down to Panama several years ago?"

"Yes, Mr. President. Yes, Mr. President."

"Haven't you shaved off your moustache since that time?"

"Yes, Mr. President. Yes, Mr. President."

"I'm delighted to see you. Congratulations on the trip."

This incident shows his tremendous human touch and his memory for faces, which was, to me, fantastic. I saw him do the same thing on another occasion. I was at the officer's training camp in San Francisco. I had come to hear him speak at the World's Fair, the Panama-Pacific Exposition, at which time he was urging the country to get into the war, assuming that eventually we would have to, and thinking that we should do so immediately. Afterwards, I pushed my way up to shake his hand. Out of the hundreds of people who were all crowded up there, he spotted me, called me by name, and invited me to come to breakfast with Mrs. Roosevelt and himself at his hotel the next day. He had an amazing touch with people, and an ability to remember names, which I have always envied. It seemed to me uncanny, the way he could do it.

The story you have asked me to recall is when he was a presidential candidate in the Spring of 1912. John Gilbert Winant, later the Ambassador to the Court of St. James, who was in the class behind me at Princeton, and also Joseph Duff, who was the brother of Senator [James A.] Duff from Pennsylvania, and I were the prime movers in organizing the Roosevelt Club at Princeton. Most of the undergraduate body felt a loyalty to Woodrow Wilson, who was living in Princeton at the time, and who had been the president of Princeton University while we were undergraduates, and who had taught many of us, including myself. But I felt so much loyalty and admiration for Mr. Roosevelt that when Winant suggested that we organize this club, I gladly and enthusiastically joined in with him. The first thing we did was to ask President John Grier Hibben, the newly elected president of Princeton, if we might have Alexander Hall for Mr. Roosevelt to speak in. It so happened that President Taft had come from Washington a week or two before, to the inauguration of President Hibben, and President Hibben was afraid that, in extending the use of the University hall, he might be criticized, particularly if anything derogatory was said about Mr. Taft. He took our request under advisement, and in a day or two called us in again. He said that the trustees and he had discussed the matter, and they felt it would be all right, provided Mr. Roosevelt would promise not to make any derogatory remarks about the president, William Howard Taft.

We didn't know quite what to do, but finally I wrote a letter to Mr. Roosevelt, who was campaigning around New Jersey and New York at the time, inviting him to come, but with this limitation in his speech. I got a typical wire back from his campaign manager: MR. ROOSEVELT

CANNOT CONSIDER ANY LIMITATION ON HIS SPEECH. HIRE OPEN-AIR BALCONY. So, we made arrangements for the day and hour that Mr. Roosevelt was planning to come. We hired a brass band and placarded the countryside with notices. We got all the undergraduates out to listen to him. It so happened that his train broke down, and he was delayed several hours. I had to dismiss the crowd, telling them that he would give them notice when he finally would arrive. We recalled them, and he came driving through the crowd in the dusk of a June evening. We practically carried him from his car, up the stairs, and out on to the balcony. I had prepared a very flowery introduction, this being the big moment of my life, introducing an ex-president, and I hoped, the next president of the United States. However, he, realizing that he was being waited for in other places, particularly Jersey City, where a crowd was already assembled, cut me short in the middle of my speech by saying, "Bully for Barclay. Barclay's all right!" and slapping me on the back, much to the amusement of all my friends among the undergraduates, who have since greeted me on all occasions, particularly at reunions, when they've had a few extra drinks, with a hearty slap on the back and a "Bully for Barclay." But I was very proud, actually, to have this accolade.

Then Roosevelt made a speech which was along the lines of the opportunities and responsibilities that college graduates have. No remarks were made about the president of the United States. He could perfectly well have made the speech in Alexander Hall. He finally was whisked away by his campaign manager, and dashed off to Jersey City. There was an amusing aftermath, however. When we paid off the band, the Wilson Club of Princeton immediately hired the same band, captured our crowd, and marched around to Woodrow Wilson's house around the corner. In the cool of the evening, and knowing his audience, he made a very fine speech, and, I think, captured more votes than we had done by having the former president speak from the balcony.

In terms of the two personalities, Wilson and Roosevelt, is there anything there that is worthy of recording here? As an undergraduate at Princeton, you had as much contact as one can have, I suppose, with a teacher like Wilson.

Well, we undergraduates always thought of Wilson as a remote sort of an intellectual and an executive figure. He was never the type of person that one would drop in on for a friendly chat. The only time that I remember his unbending slightly was when he came to address the football team on the eve of its big final game of the season with Yale. As he was leaving, he said, "May the better team win!" All of us knowing that Yale was the better team, we didn't feel he had sounded exactly the right note.

That's really enough. I think you've summarized the difficulties of a man with a non-human touch who didn't see that what was required was more than some Olympian-sounding phrase like "May the better team win!"

I felt he was rather a self-conscious person. I remember the first lecture he gave us in a course on political economy. He spent several minutes saying how sorry he felt for us as undergraduates listening to him, because we would have to look at his face all year, and he knew it was not much of a face to look at, or words to that effect. As it happened, he was elected governor of New Jersey in November [1910] and resigned from the presidency [of Princeton], so we didn't have to look at his face very long. There was a certain self-consciousness and remoteness to Wilson which I never felt about Theodore Roosevelt. I never remember any sign of self-consciousness with him. It seemed to me he always reacted instantly. He was a very warm and terrifically human person. As a boy I idolized him. To me he was the perfect man.

I remember several years later, when I read Rudyard Kipling's "If," I thought of Theodore Roosevelt as being the embodiment of this poem. With each line I said to myself, "Well, that just fits him." He could talk with crowds and keep his virtue, or walk with kings—nor lose the common touch. I thought, "That *is* Theodore Roosevelt. There is the man." I wanted to model myself and my life on such a person. I tried to imitate him, but without too much success.

PART III

Political Disciples

CHAPTER 9

The Political Backroom: William M. Chadbourne

Fig. 9.1 Photo portrait of William M. Chadbourne (1918), *Leaders of the Twentieth Century*

The political clubs and associations of New York have long greased the wheels of state and local government. Whether doling out spoils or staging campaigns, the state's political business exists as much in the private clubs as it does in the public sphere.[1] William Chadbourne frequented these political backrooms, becoming a prolific operator in the smoke-filled quarters, if all but unknown to most New Yorkers. A corporate lawyer committed to good government and social welfare, Chadbourne rubbed shoulders with party bosses, the duly elected, campaign financiers, activists, and interest groups. He led Fiorello LaGuardia's campaign for mayor of New York City in 1933, causing a stir by accusing Tammany Hall and the Democratic Party of stuffing ballot boxes and coercing voters. He even got arrested for causing a disturbance at a polling station to protest the fraud. He managed LaGuardia's successive campaigns for mayor in 1937 and 1941. After World War II, he retired from law and continued his activism in New York charities and good government crusades. Modest and quiet, Chadbourne worked gracefully in New York politics from 1905 to 1945. He died in 1964 at the age of 85.

When Chadbourne began his law career, Theodore Roosevelt occupied the White House and the young attorney took an immediate liking to the president's brand of Republican politics. The push for good government, anti-corruption, moderate state welfare assistance, and civic duty particularly appealed. Chadbourne cultivated a network of friends and fastidiously built alliances among New York City's power brokers, and thus Roosevelt came to rely on Chadbourne to keep him abreast of political developments in his home state, while he led the nation from Washington. Some of the most interesting testimony Chadbourne provides is his insight on the relationship between Charles Evans Hughes and Theodore Roosevelt. Hughes ran, and won his race for New York Governor in 1906, but the governor's relationship with the president soured when the press published rumors that Hughes and Roosevelt disagreed on state legislation that would allow for presidential nominees to be directly nominated in a primary election. A seeming political storm in a teacup, Chadbourne reveals that Roosevelt had been considering Hughes as his successor, but chose William Howard Taft as a result of this episode. In fact, much of Chadbourne's testimony to Mary Hagedorn illustrates how backroom intrigues generate significant and long-term political positions.

In 1912, when Roosevelt decided to run for president as a Progressive Party candidate, Chadbourne led the New York State Bull Moose campaign. His ringside view to the 1912 election skews back to 1910 when a local bribery scandal split New York Republicans. As tangential as this episode seems, Chadbourne credits Roosevelt's defeat in 1912 to this forgotten moment, demonstrating the dictum that "all politics is local." Other testimony from Chadbourne speculates on the fate of the world had Roosevelt won the 1912 election. In that scenario, Chadbourne believes Roosevelt would have forestalled the Great War, and thereby a century of European conflict.

Chadbourne served in World War I as a chemical weapons specialist and stayed in Paris after demobilization as an advisor. He brushed shoulders with many leading military figures such as General Douglas MacArthur and Army Chief of Staff General Hugh Drum. Another counterfactual Chadbourne entertains is what the Versailles peace settlement would look like had Roosevelt lived, or if his contemporaries like Taft or the erstwhile Secretary of State Elihu Root negotiated the deal alongside President Wilson. Although such speculation may fascinate, Chadbourne's recollections on New York politics provide the most insightful reminiscences. Here, in the political backrooms, Roosevelt's acolytes and enemies plotted their next moves. One fascinating example begins with journalist and critic Oswald Garrison Villard who converted from a Roosevelt-supporter to unrelenting detractor, but did not let his dislike for Roosevelt preclude cooperation. Chadbourne explains how the progressive "boy" Mayor of New York City John Purroy Mitchel owed his election to the joint efforts of Villard and Roosevelt. The nexus of New York politics, its complexities across state and city institutions and the convoluted networks of myriad motives come to the light in Chadbourne's account. Journalist Nicolas Lemann lamented that "Among the cruelties of popular political history is that almost everyone below the level of president winds up being forgotten."[2] That is not true here. Chadbourne tells the story of Roosevelt's era through forty others, all below the level of president. It demonstrates that political reform requires an army of operatives.

Perhaps because of Chadbourne's lengthy and variable career, his memories jump around from local, state, national, and even international affairs. Listening to Chadbourne discuss one matter at length before quickly moving on to another gives the sense that he has an erratic mind. The recollections are not haphazard, however. At points he asks for a break to gather his thoughts. He returns with sharp and vivid anecdotes that reinforce his earlier testimony. In total, Chadbourne spent nearly two hours on 8 May 1955 answering questions, some of which related to events more than 50 years prior. Half of his testimony survives as an audio recording; the other half was lost or recorded over. The oral history project transcribed the entire interview, and by comparing the audio with the dictation confirms the Hagedorns efforts to maintain a true and accurate record of the original interviews. The Hagedorns did edit for clarity, but sparingly. Chadbourne signed off on their transcript as a faithful reproduction of his statements, and this chapter reproduces Chadbourne's verbal testimony where possible. The variations between the recording and transcriptions are slight, and changes made by the Hagedorns were designed to illuminate, not conceal.

* * *

I was born in San Francisco, California, though both my mother and father were born in Boston. And since one of my forebears was the first president of Harvard, I went to Harvard and spent seven years there, four in the college, three in the law school. I graduated from college in the class of 1900 and law school class of 1903.

Being undecided where I wanted to live after a seven years' absence, save for the summers in California, I took some money that my grandfather left me and spent 15 months going around the world: two months in Russia, a month in Persia, the Philippines, Java, India and China, where I was during the Russo-Japanese War. During that period, I subscribed to the *Outlook*, which was duly mailed to me. And it was running in it at the time, "The Story of Theodore Roosevelt," by Jacob Riis. That had a profound effect on me. And I naturally gleaned what news I could from the papers I was reading in the various countries I visited about Theodore Roosevelt. I recall that when I was in Java, travelling alone, I was naturally gregarious, and made acquaintances. I mentioned Theodore Roosevelt to some of my Dutch friends, who told me that they understood that Theodore Roosevelt always spoke Dutch with his children!

It happened that the last country in which I stayed, before returning to this country, was Japan, where our ambassador was Lloyd C. Griscom, who had been a great admirer and friend of Theodore Roosevelt. Also, I had seen [career diplomat] William Phillips, who was likewise a friend and admirer of TR. Lloyd Griscom urged very strongly that I go to New York, where I did, arriving in September of 1904. A friend and classmate of mine was interested in the Bowery District—James Bryce Gordon Rinehart. And I remember watching in the 1904 election, though probably I had no authority to do so, but conditions as to watching certificates were very loose in those days.

I became interested in what was known as the Roosevelt Home Club, which was organized in a small bedroom in the top of what is now Theodore Roosevelt House by a chap who was a tailor. And his name was Leo Glaser, if I recall it right. I recall being asked by reason of my enthusiasm for TR to speak for a gathering of about twenty in this room. And I created some excitement because the news was given to the papers of my urging that TR should, when he finished his term as president, become the mayor of New York and straighten it out.

The first time I met TR came about in this way. Through some friends in New York, I met Mrs. [Florence Lockwood] La Farge, who was a close friend of TR. And she gave me a letter to him. I was then, with [New York YMCA Secretary] Robert Bayard Cutting, quite active in the Intercollegiate Civic League, which would have a convention in New York once a year [with] people coming from all over the country, sent from local civic clubs in the colleges which were organized through the nation; we would have people from as far away as South Dakota and California. The president of the League was Robert Bayard Cutting, the son of Robert Fulton Cutting, [the sugar tycoon-turned-philanthropist]. The delegates to the Intercollegiate Civic League conventions were undergraduates, who were sent from local clubs in the colleges, civic clubs, who were organized throughout the country and had people from as far away as South Dakota and California. And they would hold a convention at Columbia in New York City during the day, have a banquet in the evening, to which we would invite those who supported the Intercollegiate Civic League, and then they would take the night train to Washington. There they would call upon the president, on the French Ambassador [Jules] Jusserand, on the British Ambassador [James] Bryce and others. I recall presenting Mrs. La Farge's letter on this occasion to TR, and he asked me to tarry behind for a few moments when the others had gone. And I told him about my hopes. And he implied that things like that have got to wait.

I became quickly interested in the Republican organization in the old 25th Assembly District [in Manhattan], which includes the Theodore Roosevelt House and its confines. There was a struggle on at that time between the [Governor Benjamin] Odell forces and a group headed by [Congressman] Herbert Parsons and [anti-vice advocate] Norton Goddard, a group whom TR later supported. We went through a primary fight in 1905, when [Lemuel E.] Quigg who was the lieutenant to Senator

[Thomas Collier] Platt, who was bitterly opposed to Odell helped Herbert Parsons throw out William Halpin, who was the Odell leader in New York County. And in 1906, Quigg joined with Odell in trying to throw out Parsons. The Parsons forces, however prevailed, and the delegates went to Saratoga, where over great opposition, they nominated Charles Evan Hughes for governor. Hughes was elected over William Randolph Hearst. And I recall at the convention that he had the support of TR, without which he could not have been nominated. In the period between 1904 and 1906, Hughes, who had not had great experience in politics, got on not well with the organization, including those who had supported him.

And when the convention of 1906 came—the governor was then elected for two years—there was great opposition to Hughes's re-nomination, which was, as I recall, in fact, was reinforced by TR who was president and had great influence, especially with the Parsons group in New York City.

Was that—that was for Hughes. He was for Hughes, the re-nomination.

Oh, yes. He was for Hughes.

An incident which has been mentioned in the biography of Charles Evan Hughes explains TR's feeling toward Hughes, which later was cold. In amongst the correspondents in Albany was Frank H. Simonds, who happened to be a classmate of mine, and he represented the [*New York Evening*] *Post*, which under Oswald Garrison Villard was bitterly opposed to TR. There was a struggle in the legislature in Albany over the programme of Governor Hughes to put through a law implementing the constitutional provision about racetrack gambling. This bill met with a degree of opposition, in large measure from the group in the western part of the state, a group with which the Wadsworths were associated: [Civil War soldier and state politician] James W. Senior and [state politician] James W. Junior. During this fight, there was taking an active part in it a man called Archie Sanders, who was the collector of the port, or collector of Internal Revenue in Western New York. So then, the word was passed around that because Sanders was a federal officeholder that the administration was against the governor in his fight. During the fight, the Commissioner of Public Works—I forget his name, but he's in the records [F. W. Stevens]—I remember he had an odd beard—went to Washington and told the story to William Loeb [TR's personal secretary]. And Loeb brought him in to see TR. He pointed out that this activity of Sanders was hurting Governor Hughes' campaign, whereupon TR said, "well, now this shouldn't go on." And he had Sanders removed for "pernicious political activity." The news of the removal reached Albany in the morning. In the afternoon dispatch of the *Evening Post*, through Simonds, who disliked Hughes intensely because of some supposed slight that Hughes had paid him on a campaign train, sent a dispatch to the *Post*, reading somewhat as follows: "Those about the Governor Hughes are very much disturbed by what President Roosevelt is doing. They feel the governor does not believe in using political methods to achieve his objectives and the governor believes taking his fight direct to the people."

From the best information I can get, no such statement was made by friends about Hughes, but it was Frank Simonds's way of getting back at Hughes.

When the *Evening Post* reached the White House, TR was naturally furious. He said, "Why, they asked me to do this?"

Hughes, unfortunately, didn't, as he should have, call up the president on the telephone, and say, "Of course, I didn't say any of those things, but I'd rather not take a position in criticizing it, because I'm getting the support of the *New York Evening Post*."

From that date and time, the coolness began between Hughes and TR. And there are many who think that but for that, TR would have supported him for president in 1908, instead of Taft. I have talked about this with both William Loeb, and with TR, who did not know that the story was a plant. And Governor Hughes, who years after I came to know very well, once indicated to me that he had issued no statement of that sort. It is an unfortunate case where Hughes did not communicate at once with TR and explain the real facts.

In spite of that incident, which happened during the first term of Hughes, TR supported him strongly in the convention of 1906, [New York Congressman] Will Cocks being his representative there. And without that support, Hughes would never have been re-nominated. As it was, there was a bitter fight against him in the convention.

In Hughes' second term, there developed a struggle between him and a certain group of rather undesirable Republican leaders in upstate New York, headed by a man called [Jotham P.] Allds. And the fight continued into the beginning of 1910. There was a struggle over the Primary Bill that Hughes wished to introduce. And it was introduced by [New York State] Senator [Harvey D.] Hinman. Many of us who were TR men, but also were fond of Hughes, and wished to avoid a split, supported a compromise bill, which was named after [New York State] Senator [George H.] Cobb who came from Watertown. Hughes was very anxious that this measure—the Cobb measure—go through, which he accepted. In 1910, I was having my tenth-class reunion and I met Hughes on my way to Albany, on my way to Cambridge, and Hughes told me that unless TR came out for the bill, there was no chance of it going through. He said he was going to be in Cambridge at the 1910 commencement because he was going to receive a degree. TR was there as the president of the Harvard Alumni Association. I didn't reach the commencement exercises until the group was emerging from Sander's Theatre, where they were being held and the section of those having a degree, that had received degrees, marched through the yard to President Lowell's house, where they were to have a luncheon. With [syndicated columnist] Mark Sullivan, we were watching the procession. Governor Hughes came by and waved to me to come along with him. This, I did, and being photographed with Mark Sullivan. And we went to Lowell's house. [Hughes] told me that the president was anxious to speak with me because I was deemed to voice, in a measure, the view of the Republican organization in New York County. Reaching the house, Hughes buttonholed TR with me and we had a conversation about the bill, which Hughes urged the president very strongly to support. And TR said, "Will you excuse us for a moment." And he took me into a room and asked me what the situation was. I stated that those whom he had gotten into politics were very anxious that the Republican Party be not upset by the triumph of the Allds group [implicated in a bribery scandal], none too savory over Hughes.

And he said, "What should I do?"

Well, I said, "You'd better send a telegram to Lloyd Griscom."

He wrote out the telegram, which I modestly substituted for my name, that of "your representative" and took it and sent it to Lloyd Griscom.

I felt as I talked with Theodore Roosevelt that there were running through his mind the following thoughts: if I go back to Oyster Bay and become the Sphinx of Sagamore Hill, the entire Republican Party will come to me in 1912 and urge me to run, for Taft had not been a success as president. Yet, as always, the appeal of his followers, for aid, was decisive and TR took the steps he did. Thereafter, came the [New York State Republican] convention of 1910, over which TR presided [in the chair] as his supporters had more delegates than the other group, which was supporting Vice President Sherman. It was a very exciting convention and I recall Abe Gruber, who was one of the anti-TR groups from New York

County quoting the phrase about turning the White House into a shooting gallery and saying that this should not be done to the State House in Albany, by electing [then-District Attorney Henry L.] Stimson. Well, Stimson was nominated and defeated in a close race. We have always felt that if the election had lasted three weeks longer that we would have won because the man who was elected over Stimson—John A. Dix—was probably one of the weakest men ever elected governor of the state, if not the weakest man.

As the campaign of 1912 approached, many men, including Henry L. Stimson, went to Theodore Roosevelt and said that if he would be a candidate, they would devote all their efforts to him, and Stimson agreed to resign [as Secretary of War in Taft's cabinet]. And Theodore Roosevelt said he was not a candidate and told them that they should not do so. What finally decided TR to be a candidate was when the governors, Republican governors, came to him and said that their position in their own states was being undercut by the National Committee of the Republican Party and urged him not to desert them. That was a plea that TR never could resist. He said, "his hat was in the ring." If he had made up his mind in January of 1912 to be a candidate, he would undoubtedly have been nominated by the Republicans and elected, because there was a split in the Democratic Party.

What were his reasons for not running at first?

I could not tell, but I think he felt that probably he had been president for nearly eight years, that he did not want to take the drastic step of being a candidate again, unless it were absolutely necessary. Well, I think the plea of the governors was irresistible, as such pleas always were. Even at the Republican Convention of 1912, I've been told by people who were on the other side, that if it had not been for errors in the handling of the matter by Governor [Herbert S.] Hadley in Missouri, the floor leader [for TR's campaign] and if they insisted on a vote in each delegation, instead of having one vote covering them all, that enough TR delegates would have been elected to nominate TR.

When TR finally threw his hat in the ring, I went to Sagamore Hill with Mark Sullivan and told him I would join the Progressive movement, for I felt that the Republican Convention had not been a fair one. And again, I thought back to 1910 of the talks we'd had at Cambridge. and Hughes' hearkening to the plea of his supporters, which had created the situation, which defeated him. I'm convinced that if he had not taken the stand he did in 1910, that the Republican leaders who defeated him in 1912 in the convention, notably [Republican boss William] Barnes, would have been for him, because they all felt that Taft was not effective.

I might at this stage say that a political leader who was of great importance during the days of TR as president once said that he thought that he was an ideal president both from the point of view of the good government end, and from the point of view of the political leader. Because the political leader, he said, often ... must recommend first a man whom he does not expect to be chosen, but who would be very much offended if he were not recommended. Sometimes TR would, my political friends said, reject six or seven men who were proposed by the leader, all of whom felt that the leader had done all he could for them and then appoint the last one, who he felt was of the caliber to deserve the appointment.

You have asked me whether, when TR campaigned for Hughes in 1916, he knew about the incident of Archie Sanders and Hughes' attitude towards him. He did, because in 1914, when he was campaigning for [1914 Progressive Party gubernatorial candidate] Frederick N. Davenport, I saw a good deal of him and I told him the story. He was amazed that it had happened, and said, why the Commissioner of Public Works [Frederick C.] Stevens, urged me to do it. And I could never understand why Hughes gave out such a statement. I told him that Hughes had not given out the statement, and that it had been, as it were, planned with great skill by Simonds, who felt that Hughes would not want to run contrary to the *New York Evening Post*, which had been supporting [him] so vigorously. Or he may have not thought of it.

Who was Simonds, again?

Frank H. Simonds was a very distinguished war correspondent and political correspondent, S-I-M-O-N-D-S. One of the greatest we have produced and he was very bitter against those who he felt had slighted him. He was a classmate of mine, as was Mark Sullivan.

In the talks I had with TR, during the campaign in 1914 where I saw so much of him, he said to me once that "I am a better critic than I am a creator, that my role is to be a sounding board for those who have good ideas." And by that time, he had coined the phrase about the "lunatic fringe." And when I observed that—during the period, when as president—he was surrounded by men like Root and the others who made up his cabinet, his decisions were better than when he was surrounded afterwards by a good many of the lunatic fringe. This he completely agreed to and, at the time, I had in mind the proposal for the recall of judicial decisions, which I think later he very much regretted that he had ever advocated.

During the 1912 Progressive campaign, I was, as chairman of the Law Committee and the County Committee, and the State Committee of the Progressive Party, I didn't go about very much with TR because I had so much work to do at home. I did, however, get into the Madison Square Garden meeting where he spoke [one month] after he had been shot [in Milwaukee]. And at that time, when I was living directly south of Madison—then Madison Square Garden—37 Madison Avenue, so slipped through the police lines.

Although he probably very wisely never carried out the idea of being a candidate for mayor of New York, he took a very definite stand in favor of good government. Thus, he supported John Purroy Mitchel whose campaign I was very much interested, both times in which he ran.

I've always cherished the notion that if I hadn't been at the Mexican border with the National Guard from June 1916 to March 1917 that Hughes might have carried California. In 1916, I knew [Governor] Hiram Johnson, actually, very intimately and I would undoubtedly have gone to California with Hughes, who I also knew well and should have brought it to pass that the event should not occur in which the [William Henry] Crocker group—who were more interested in defeating Hiram Johnson than they were in electing a Republican president—kept Hughes from meeting Johnson, especially when they were in the same hotel at Long Beach, California. Hughes told me afterwards that he had no knowledge about it until he left the hotel. And then every effort on his part to reach Johnson failed.

I suppose Johnson felt slighted. Did he?

It was the people who felt slighted, the supporters of Johnson. Johnson was elected by a huge majority. Of course, the fundamental mistake was made of ever letting Hughes go into the state while there was a primary contest on. He should wait till the primary contest was over and then the episode wouldn't have happened. His campaign manager, William R. Wilcox, the most estimable gentleman, knew nothing about politics.

Especially California politics.

And especially California politics.

I was very much interested in the proposal of TR to form a [military] division [during World War I]. He asked me to join it, because I had a good deal of experience in handling mules and water trucks, where I had been during the nine months I was on the Mexican border, since I was fly officer of the 12th New York Infantry. When it was announced from Washington that there would be no TR Division, there was talk of TR being sent as special envoy or ambassador to Russia. The idea being that he would have more influence than Senator Root had had. I had a chance to go abroad with the Adjutant General's Department in December of 1918, when I was mustered out, I was told my eyes were no good and I could not have a line job. Having spent a couple of months in Russia, I thought I might be helpful to TR, so I went out and dined with him and Mrs. Roosevelt. I should never forget his comment about Woodrow Wilson. He said, biting his words as he talked, "Mr. Wilson will not send me to Russia. He is not afraid I will be a failure of it, he is afraid I would make a success of it."

This, of course, was a little harsh on Wilson, but it did highlight a Wilsonian quality, namely he had the attitudes of an embittered man towards others.

Wilson did?

Wilson, yes. This was the last time I ever saw TR, because when I was back, he died the end of December, didn't he?

He died January 6th of 1919.

Yes. I was mustered out on Christmas Day, 1918 and did not have a chance to go to Sagamore Hill until the news came and he was no longer with us. But on the transport to France in December, 1917, there were four major generals, including Leonard Wood. I saw a good deal of General Wood, who was eager for an opportunity to go to France, but very doubtful as to whether he would ever be committed to command the division there.

In France, I was assigned to the 42nd Division. I reported to [General] Frank [Ross] McCoy who was the Secretary of the General Staff at Chaumont and he gave me a letter to Douglas MacArthur, which read as follows: "The bearer of this letter is, if it were possible, even keener about TR than are you."

I had several talks about TR with General MacArthur, then Chief of Staff of the division, who asked me to come up and see him any evening I was free, at 9 o'clock, because he said he wanted to have an hour's talk about other things than tactics and strategy before he tried to go to sleep. The headquarters of the 42nd Division was then at Rolampont in the Haute Marne.

Two episodes which will show that no matter how hard a fighter TR was, his shafts had no barbs and left no sting.

Not even with Wilson.

I'm taking Wilson out of it.

At the [New York State] convention of 1910, Elihu Root was a delegate and supported TR. And there had been very sharp passages between them. Yet, I recall being present when Elihu Root put his hand on TR's shoulder, and said, "Theodore, you are still the great same overgrown boy as ever."

Lloyd Griscom—whom you should take the recordings of when he comes in towards the end of this month—brought about a meeting between Taft and Theodore Roosevelt, of which a good deal has been written. I feel sure, however, that he bore no rancor towards Taft in the later days.

I have previously referred to the pre-Republican convention campaign in 1912. If TR had announced, made it clear earlier that he would be a candidate, a great many people would have come to his aid. Men became committed, so that a number of those who came out for TR were men who had been rejected by the party and were seeking a chance to get back. A number of those were carried over into the progressive organization and they caused us a great deal of difficulty since none of them are in the land of the living today, perhaps the phrase, *de mortuis nihil nisi bonum* [speak no ill of the dead] should prevail.

A good many men who were devoted to Theodore's principles, amongst the Republicans, didn't support him. This was, in part, on account of what they conceived to be the Third Term issue. I remember Herbert Parsons, whom I know very intimately and to whom I was deeply devoted, telling me that this was the reason why he could not support him...

May I continue on what I said before about Theodore Roosevelt and the party system? After all, we have a two-party government and we have a party system. I don't believe there has ever been a president who understood it better. He was able to get what was good for the country out of the Congress and out of the various political parties, but was also able to keep his own party, the Republican Party, contented and had, at the same time, a very high standard of his appointments. The fact that he did so well in this respect was one of the reasons why, I think, people such as Oswald Garrison Villard and others, who were men of the highest type but had no conception of political methods, instinctively didn't like him; likewise, the group who had demanded of him that he refuse to take any party nomination and therefore were against him in 1898 when he was the Republican Party's candidate for Governor.

I have always felt that if Theodore had been elected president in 1912, there would have been no World War in 1914, because he understood how to reach the important people in the governments concerned, and he certainly would have been able to talk to the Kaiser and other people of importance.

You mention, Mr. Chadbourne, that there were some further things about the Hughes-Roosevelt break that you could tell me.

Yes. I had felt from my talks with TR that if it had not been for what I might describe as the *Evening Post*-Simonds episode—the Frederick Stevens, Superintendent of Public Works episode—that TR might very well have supported Hughes instead of Taft as the Republican candidate for president in 1908. Hughes was an agreeable man, although when he was governor he was not experienced in politics.

Later I recall an occasion when Governor Hughes, at the time between his secretary of stateship in the Harding administration and his going on to the Supreme Court as Chief Justice later, was at my home at a dinner I was giving for the Dean of the Harvard Law School. He made the statement about Woodrow Wilson and the campaign of 1916 that it was probably a good thing that Wilson was elected, that Congress was definitely sure to be Democratic, that we were drifting into war and that a Democratic president could hold the Congress in line and get on with it better than could a Republican president. This, it seems to me, showed that Governor Hughes had a willingness to get on with others who didn't altogether share his views.

Going back to the Republican State Convention of 1908, the emissary or representative of TR was William M. Cocks who was the representative in Congress from Theodore Roosevelt's own district in Oyster Bay. Cocks was a Quaker, for there were a great many Quakers in that part of Long Island. As I recall it, he had a Quaker hat at the convention that made him a distinctive figure.

Hughes could not have been nominated in 1908 except for TR's support. Of course, from the point of view of the presidential campaign of Secretary Taft for president, it would have been most unfortunate if Hughes had been turned down for Governor by the Republican convention, because it might have cost the Republican Party the State of New York.

I feel that the only person who could have averted war in 1914—or at least postponed it—was TR, because TR knew the Kaiser personally. He also knew [UK Foreign Minister] Sir Edward Grey personally. I have always felt that World War I was caused by the *Junker* group [German aristocracy] feeling that the socialists were making so much progress against them that to restore their position it was necessary for them to have a short, quick, successful war. I have also felt that the Kaiser was not a person who really wanted war, but the *Junker* war group were too much for him. It is a fact, I believe, that the group chose the time for the demands on Serbia when the Kaiser was in Norway.

Another factor of importance is that when Sir Edward Grey met with Prince Lichnowsky, the German Ambassador, and Lichnowsky told him that "necessity knows no laws," that the war was about to begin and that Germany must go through Belgium. If, when Lichnowsky had said that to Grey, Grey had told him that if that happened, Britain would intervene, war would not have broken out at that time. With the intimate friendship that existed between Grey and TR, it is entirely possible that Grey might have communicated the dangers to TR and TR might have strengthened Grey. He might also have communicated, as he could have, with the Kaiser. Might I add that once upon a time I heard [Paul-Henri] Spaak, the prime minister of Belgium, state more or less the same thing; that is, that if Grey had told Lichnowsky that in all probability the British would have intervened, war would not have happened at that time.

It might be added that today the government of the United States is telling the Chinese communists what will happen if they make an attack on Formosa—which may, as many people think, avert or postpone a shooting war. And when war is postponed, there always is a chance of averting it.

Which [Secretary of State Dean] Acheson did not do when he said that Korea was out of our sphere of interest...

Precisely. There is a good deal of ground for Senator [Robert] Taft's statement after the attack: that while the Republicans pledged support of the president, the policy of the [Truman] administration had, in effect, practically invited the Red forces to come in [to Korea].

The break between TR and William Howard Taft, as to the details of which I knew very little, seemed to me to have come more from Taft's lack of political sense than from any antagonism between the men. There were, of course, around Taft at all times the men who had, in the Republican organization, battled TR, and they were always pushing Taft in the hope that there would be a definite estrangement between him and TR. I think that if Taft had made efforts to get TR's views as to a number of problems, especially personnel problems—because an outgoing president always would like to see that those who had been close to him are given consideration by the incoming administration—I think that this estrangement would not have happened. Taft was a very kindly, agreeable man, but he was unable to control the important political groups in the various states who set out to make war on those who had supported TR before.

Were there many big business interests that were involved in trying to work on Taft to repudiate Theodore Roosevelt?

I have always thought that, fundamentally, TR's relations with business were better than Taft's. It will be remembered that TR approved the merger of the Tennessee Coal and Iron Company with the U.S. Steel Corporation, thereby drawing a distinction between good and bad mergers.

There is a very interesting parallel in the break between Taft and TR and the break that took place between Franklin D. Roosevelt and Al Smith. Al Smith had been governor [of New York] prior to Franklin's election in 1928 and, in fact, Franklin could not have been nominated for governor without Al Smith's approval. Yet, although Al Smith offered to help Franklin in every way as governor, Franklin accepted very little of that help, and substituted for the group that had been built up around Al Smith when he was governor with a new group of his own; hence the friends of Al Smith resented this and, in a way, tended to create the breach between the two, although Al Smith during World War II showed no rancor and definitely came to the assistance of FDR when FDR needed him very badly.

With respect to TR's position in seeking active military service in World War I, I have the feeling that most military men at the time felt that this was not the field in which TR could make his greatest contribution. In the Mexican Border Service in summer, fall, and winter of 1916 and 1917, it was completely demonstrated that the volunteer system was unjust and inadequate. There were many men in these units who were married and to whom it was a great hardship. They were the National Guard and all volunteers.

When I returned from the Mexican border, I, together with a number of others, spoke at a convention that was being held in the beginning of March of 1917 and argued for the adoption of the draft system of securing the necessary number of men for the Army. I even spoke to [Woodrow Wilson's closest advisor] Colonel [Edward M.] House about it and urged most strongly that he communicate the view to Wilson. I have a feeling he did. Colonel House remarked to me once, "When you see the Scotch Presbyterian jaw of Wilson, you can feel pretty sure that he is going to go through with and force the adoption of the system that will furnish the Army with the proper number of men."

It is a matter of note that less than a month after the United States entered the war, the conscription law was enacted, whereas in Britain it was a number of months after the outbreak of the war before a conscription was enacted, and in Canada none was *ever* enacted. There is, I think, a grave question whether a volunteer division would, under the circumstances, have been a good thing. The men who would have composed it would nearly all have been of officer material and they could do very much better as officers in the National Guard and National Army regiments and divisions that were being raised.

[Army Chief of Staff] General [Hugh] Drum once told me that the German commentators upon the war were amazed at the rapidity with which the company officers were developed in the American Army. The Germans expected that they could hold out until 1919. Later, when they learned about the service, on the Mexican border, of National Guard regiments which were, of course, all volunteers, and of the training that many of these men got who were college graduates and otherwise officer material, they realized that it was from this group of men that the company officers of the [American Expeditionary Force] very largely came. The War Department very properly set up training camps like Plattsburg where these men, and others similarly situated, were able to go. In support of these camps, Colonel Roosevelt had a very great influence.

My feeling was that TR as mobilizer of public opinion, or possibly as a Special Envoy to Russia, or perhaps as Special Envoy to other countries, had a greater role than he would have had in military service.

Then, to a certain extent, Wilson was right in not letting Col. Roosevelt have a commission.

Or command a division. I would feel that Wilson did the right thing, but I'm afraid he didn't do it in the right way.

Yes. If he had been positive about where he felt Mr. Roosevelt could perform a better service, it wouldn't have been such a slap in the face.

I think what you say is so true!

At the time of the Versailles Conference, I was in Paris where I had been since my demobilization in December, 1917. I was there as counsel for the United States Liquidation Commission. I always felt that if

Woodrow Wilson had appointed [William Howard] Taft and [Elihu] Root as Republican members of the commission to negotiate the peace, we might have been brought into the League of Nations. I'm not sure that this would have been a good thing at the time, although I'm heartily in favor of the UN—and especially if one realizes its limited objectives. I talked about this possible appointment with Colonel House, who told me that he had urged Taft and Root upon Wilson, but that Wilson did not like it. House thought that that had a good deal of influence upon the ultimate estrangement that came to pass between him and Wilson.

Commenting further upon the suggestion that there be a division of which TR could have been the major general in command, I would say this: I saw a good deal of General Staff work both at division, corps, and Army levels, and at G[eneral] H[ead]Q[uarters] because I was stationed at GHQ as the representative of the gas service for the eight or ten months of the war. The work of this sort was all highly professional and by men who had been thoroughly trained in the art of war and in the work of the different sections of the General Staff. It was completely different from what went on in the Spanish-American War. The General Staff, of course, was set up when Root was secretary of War and Theodore Roosevelt was president. It was one of the great achievements in the military policy of this country.

I think the same questions arose in connection with General Leonard Wood taking a division to France. General Wood was, I felt from my talks with him, resentful—and perhaps, to a certain extent, justly so—at treatment that had been meted out to him because of the fact that he had been so close to TR and a bit, perhaps, subordinate in supporting the Plattsburg plan and other projects in which TR was deeply interested. I have been told that the matter was put up to General [of U.S. Armies John J.] Pershing and General Pershing said he'd prefer not to have General Wood in command of a division in France. He would rather have some other divisional commander.

Was that because of the prejudice or because of sound military wisdom?

Far be it from me to comment on General Pershing, who was a very great soldier! But a person who is embittered by experience is not always the best subordinate to have, I think.

Then General Pershing was probably wise in his understanding of human nature in that respect?

Yes, and I think that he was a very great general, for he insisted upon an American army. He was supported in this by Newton Baker who was secretary of War—and a great secretary of War—and by the president who backed up Newton Baker. The French and the British tried to have

Pershing removed; the French sent over [Commissioner for Franco-American War Cooperation André] Tardieu, and the British, I think, sent over [Ambassador to the U.S.] Lord Reading, to that end. But the Americans ate different food and there would have had to be different lines of supply; that was one reason. The second reason is that, as I remember being told, in a division there are always artillery liaison officers with the front groups of infantrymen. The theory stated is that that was to establish liaison, but I'm told that one of the real reasons was that inasmuch as some of the shells always drop short, the infantrymen felt that the artillery would be more careful if there were artillery officers with the infantry. I am sure that under British and French divisional and corps commanders there would be a constant outcry that the Americans were given the meanest jobs, and all this would have been most unfortunate.

An episode which occurred prior to TR's nomination and election as Governor of the State of New York in 1898 deserves a little comment, although I know nothing of it from my own knowledge. There was a group of people who were very much opposed in New York State to Platt's control of the Republican Party. This group was composed, I think, of Oswald Villard, John Jay Chapman, Robert Fulton Cutting, and a number of others who might be called "independents." There was a good deal of talk about TR being nominated for governor on an independent ticket. Platt saw the importance of nominating a man with TR's vote-getting qualities on the Republican ticket, and it became obvious that the Republicans would, at their convention, nominate TR for governor. The independent group to which I referred sought to get him to refuse to accept the Republican nomination; when he would not follow their counsel, they broke with him.

This, I think, had an effect on Villard's attitude and the attitude of a good many other people who were always very critical of anything TR did. I think their attitude showed that they had very little conception of the party system and that any man who would refuse to accept support of that sort would not have been wise politically. TR was a Republican; and so long as he did not give any more attention to what Platt said than any public official should give to the suggestions of a political leader, he could not be criticized. This, however, is, I think, the origin of a lot of great bitterness toward TR on the part of certain groups of very estimable gentlemen who were mostly independent in their political views or were Democrats. I think it gave TR many opportunities to express himself with his unequalled gift for phrase!

CHAPTER 10

That Tammany Boy: Henry Root Stern, Sr.

Fig. 10.1 Photo portrait of Captain Henry Root Stern (1918), Library of Congress

New York City government has a long history with political machines. The most disreputable was Tammany Hall, founded in the days of the early republic, and instrumental in establishing the "us v. them" nature of American politics. In the eighteenth century, Tammany waged a political war with Alexander Hamilton and the Federalists, seizing upon the tension between those who wanted greater centralized government and those who did not. In the nineteenth century, Tammany co-opted immigrants landing in New York to boost their electoral base and joined forces with President Andrew Jackson's Democratic Party to take advantage of the federal spoils system. In the Gilded Age and Progressive Era, Tammany reached the apogee of its power, helping elect Democratic mayors for 41 of 50 years between 1875 and 1925. By this time, Tammany had become a catch phrase for corruption, vice, nepotism, election tampering, and intimidation. Crooked as it was, Tammany also did important work for its constituents, advocating for the poor and immigrant class in the city.[1] And Tammany did not operate alone. The Republican Party ran its own version of a spoils system replete with bossism and corrupt hierarchies. The similarity between the parties seemed obvious to Henry Root Stern when, as a young man, he determined to join a party.

Educated at the elite preparatory school Andover and then Yale University, Stern returned to New York City in 1903 to study law at Columbia University. He graduated in 1906 and, following in his father's footsteps, established a corporate law firm in the city. At this point in his life, he sought to enter politics and joined a local Tammany branch, but Stern quickly regretted his decision. Tammany left him disillusioned with city politics, yet his short-lived membership had marked him out as a machine-man and a Democrat. When introduced to Theodore Roosevelt sometime later, Stern was referred to as "a Tammany man." Roosevelt had long opposed the Democratic machine, but he received Stern warmly. Reflecting on his experience with Tammany's old-boy-network, and comparing it with Roosevelt's open-mindedness led Stern to join the Republican Party, although he remained resolutely independent. Stern's story offers an insight into the political culture of a city that forged the careers of so many national figures from Samuel Tilden to Al Smith.

During World War I, Stern joined the Army as an officer and earned promotion to captain before being discharged in 1918 when he returned to his law firm. In later years he moved to Long Island, and became a significant local politician in Nassau County. Hermann Hagedorn interviewed Stern in January 1954 with the recent PhD graduate Louis M. Starr, a leading academic in the oral history movement. Like many of the other recordings, Hagedorn and Starr transcribed Stern's account and had him approve the archived manuscript. This chapter has removed a short and extemporaneous exchange between Stern and Hagedorn at the end of the interview, but otherwise reproduces the interview in its entirety.

* * *

Under what circumstances did you first see TR?

I was in my third year at Columbia Law School, where I was studying for an LLB degree and also an MA degree in the school of Political Science under Professor John Burgess and John Bassett Moore, who was giving us a course in diplomacy and diplomatic history.

About that time, there had been formed in various of the Ivy League colleges, so-called "good government" clubs, and one of these chapters, so to speak, was organized at Columbia, and I was a member. In some fashion, President Theodore Roosevelt learned of the existence of these "good government" clubs, and it was characteristic of his interest in college men and in their entry into the world of government and political affairs that he conveyed to these clubs—in just what manner I do not recall—his desire to meet with their representatives in Washington. I happened to be appointed to represent the Columbia organization.

I should say that a good dozen of us met in Washington. Pursuant to the invitation which we received from his secretariat, we met with the president one evening at about nine o'clock in the then Cabinet Room at the White House. After some delay, the president entered the room. I recall that he was wearing dinner clothes with a black tie, and that on his starched shirt front were some drops of what I surmised had been formally part of the blood system of some wild game, presumably ducks, which had been on his dinner menu that evening.

After introductions and hearty handshakes on the part of the president, exchanged with all present, he started the ball rolling by saying, "You're all college men and presumably gentlemen. It must be understood that what I say to you will not be published or repeated, as I am speaking to you in confidence."

He then entered into a detailed description of some of the more serious burdens and responsibilities which any president of the United States was obliged to shoulder, and of the principle troublesome problems which he was encountering at that time. He said we would be surprised at how many of these problems arose out of serious differences of points of view and attitude toward public questions which the president encounters even within his own party. He illustrated these by describing the stubborn resistance to one of his pet measures, the Railway Rate Act, for which Senator [Joseph] Foraker [of Ohio] and [Senator] Boies Penrose of Pennsylvania were the principal offenders.

He then, in eloquent terms, outlined the advantages of the two-party system, and he urged us, whatever our political proclivities had been up to that point, to join one party or the other—that it didn't matter whether it was the Republican Party or the Democratic Party—but once having joined the party, he urged us to fight out our differences of opinion within the party itself. He attacked in the strongest possible terms the evils of the multiple party system of government, and illustrated this by what had transpired in recent months in France. He spoke of the intemperate action of the Kaiser in having sent a cruiser to Morocco, which act had seriously inflamed public opinion in France; of the weakness in the French *Chambre des Députés*—I believe that's its official title—with respect to what action France should take in response to the Kaiser's aggressive attitude. He said that because there were so many parties, each one standing for some pet, selfish objective of its own, it was impossible to obtain a clear-cut parliamentary decision, as a result of which the so-called Delcassé government had fallen.

He urged us to be idealistic as far as the realities of the situation permitted, but always to be prepared, if necessary, to make a reasonable compromise. If I remember his exact words correctly, he said, "Hitch your wagon to a star, but be prepared to compromise at the drop of a hat."

I think he meant by that that compromise was essential to reach any agreement.

What he meant by that is that you could not get anywhere politically by being a bitter-ender, and if there was to be any progress from a practical standpoint, you must prepare if necessary, to make some compromise, provided it wasn't of the very essence of the principle for which you were fighting.

You have to have the give and take. He learned that when he was in the [New York State] Assembly. At first, he went bullying ahead, absolutely going his own way and be damned with everybody, and was completely isolated. You have to play to those people and listen to their ideas and take them into account.

If I may disagree for a moment to go into some personal political history of that period—I had, some time before joining this good government club, told my father that I wanted to find out what politics was all about.

My father was a member of no political organization, either Republican or Democratic—he was a complete independent. I had no party affiliations or convictions one way or the other, so I asked my father to advise me about what I should do to find out something about the machinery of politics so I would know where I was going if I went further in that field in the future.

He said to me, "Look you've been away at Yale and Andover for a good many years. You're now back in the city where you were born and where you expect to live and practice your profession. New York City is chronically—some people say hopelessly—a Democratic city in the sense that it is in the complete grip and under the domination of Tammany Hall, and certainly as long as I live, and possibly as long as you live, will continue to be so. To join a Republican organization would advance your insight into how government is administered in the community in which you live not one single fraction of an inch. You would be permanently on the outside and in the wilderness. My advice to you, if you are serious about this, is to join a local Democratic organization, and the way that is done, in this day and age, is to join a local Tammany club in your neighborhood." That happened to be the Osceola Club, which was then located on 78th Street near Lexington Avenue.

He said, "The head of that organization, the local leader in that whole section, is Tom Rush, the collector of the Port of New York. I know Tom Rush quite well. If you want to go ahead with this, I'll see that you are properly introduced to him."

I said, "Okay. I have to make a beginning somewhere, and that seems as good a way to start as any."

So, I was introduced to Tom Rush, a genial, gray-haired and very tight-lipped but smiling gentleman. His office in the Osceola Club was on the second floor. It was a small room to which only the chosen were admitted. When I first met him, it was the only time I ever was invited into or ever did enter that room. There was a large room fronting on the street on the entrance floor of this high-stoop brownstone club house where various and sundry characters sat around with derby hats, generally cocked over one eye, and with cigar stumps protruding from their mouths. Their conversation was largely a series of sporadic monosyllables and grunts.

I visited this temple of government quite frequently over a period of six months, hoping at least to make some start toward acquiring insight into politics and government. The result of my efforts was that I was informed that I had been appointed a member of the entertainment committee of the club, the function of which was first to contribute personally and then to raise money from others toward the expense of the annual picnic which the club gave to the faithful. I think it was on what was then known as Blackwell's Island. It finally penetrated, even through my naïve skull, that no college graduate enthusiast for good government was worthy of being entrusted with any of the secret processes. I was clearly suspect, and, as far as I could see ahead, would continue to be suspect. So, I finally gave up in disgust and resigned as a member of the club and joined no other political organization of either party for many years, although nationally I voted the Republican ticket and locally tried to pick and choose according to the personality and the character of the candidate as so many other so-called independents were then doing and still continue to do.

The point of my going into all this, in reference to our interview with the president, is as follows: when I was introduced to TR, or rather, I should say, when I went up, as we all did, one by one, at the close of our interview, and someone, acting as spokesman, presented me by name to the president, he said, "Mr. President, do you realize we have here a Tammany man in our midst?"

Well, the president flashed that characteristic, wide grin of his, grabbed me with both of his hands, and said, "That's bully. That's fine," and again repeated what he had said to us before, "That's the thing to do. Join a party. I don't care what party. If you have ideals for good government, as you must have, or you wouldn't be here tonight, you fight for those ideals within that party. That's the only way you'll get anywhere in your situation." The only trouble with that philosophy was that the president had never been a member of the Osceola Club.

I might add that the president's confidence was one hundred percent respected by every man present. There was absolutely no publicity of any kind regarding what he had said or what had transpired at this interview. Naturally, I told my own family about it, and some of my close friends, as I assume others did, but that's as far as it went. This is the first time that I have repeated, after all these years, what I've said about it to anyone outside of that restricted circle.

Mrs. [Ethel Roosevelt] Derby, [TR's youngest daughter] told me that you told her the story.

Yes. Well, naturally, she's the daughter of the president.

Do you remember any other things that he said on that occasion?

No, but I remember that several years later, I met up with some man who either had been present at that interview—whether as one of our group or one of the president's entourage—and in some way he knew that I had been one of those present. I told him about this exchange in reference to being a Tammany man, and he said, "Do you know that a couple of years after that, the president asked me, 'I wonder what ever became of that Tammany boy?'"

Did you ever know Richard Welling [the activist and founder of the National Self Government Committee]?

No.

Those good government clubs were started way back in the [18-] 90s, and [Richard] Welling was one of those who started them. He was a classmate of TR. These clubs were known as the "Goo-Goo's," and they occasionally got on TR's nerves, because the men were inclined to be a little too idealistic and get off the ground.

Now you see, I may have known of this at the time, but after all these years it's faded out of my memory. I may have known Mr. Welling. I doubt if it was Mr. Welling who said that to me. I have searched my memory and I cannot remember who it was. It was somebody very close to the president, with whom the president had talked about this interview, and in some way learned that I was the so-called Tammany man. After I established residence in Nassau County almost 30 years ago, I became very much interested in local government there, because, that being then such a small political unit compared to New York City, the individual had much greater opportunity, if he so desired, to play some part in political and governmental life. There again, I joined the dominant political party, because again, the reasoning which my father had employed in advising me years before was to a great extent applicable to that situation but in reverse so far as the party was concerned. And also, by that time I had come to consider myself, certainly nationally, as entirely in sympathy with the Republican Party and what it was seeking to do. My experiences in New York City, following 1906, had eventually convinced me that I wanted to be a Republican and not a Democrat.

Do you remember anything that TR said about the Kaiser?

Yes. I can't remember, and I won't attempt to quote his exact words, but I can put it this way: that he pitched into the Kaiser with all the indignation and fury that he could command for what the Kaiser had done and was continuing to do. In short, he characterized his conduct as inexcusable and outrageous.

It very definitely threatened the peace of Europe.

Certainly. TR pitched into him with both fists.

The Kaiser was one of TR's principal headaches during his presidency. Yet they were on a friendly personal relationship.

He visited with him.

The Kaiser was always writing him letters, but the Kaiser was always having these bad thoughts every other minute, you see, and he would come across with some perfectly fantastic idea in international relations. Then TR and [secretaries of state John] Hay or [Elihu] Root would have to find some way of saving the Kaiser's face by telling him not to get involved.

TR was furious, but he was almost equally as indignant about the inexcusable weakness of the French. He thought, to use a modern colloquial term, they were complete milquetoasts. He thought they were impotent primarily because of their political system. Any splinter party could maneuver to the position where it would represent a balance of power on any important question and could demand a price for doing the right thing. He thought that was disgraceful. He had, right at his tongue's end, the names of all these parties. I can't even remember but a few of them now.

Did he stay at his desk during all this?

No. He did not sit at his desk. He stood up. If I may use the expression, he was full of beans. He had just had a good dinner; I should say it was a good duck dinner. That makes me think it was probably during the winter months of 1906 that we were down there. It might have been January or February—the shooting seasons were longer then. At any rate, I think he had been eating wild duck—I would almost swear to it.

It was in the winter and spring of 1906 that the railway rate legislation was foremost.

That controversy raged for quite a while. I don't know, I can't place the exact date. I wrote a letter to my mother sometime later and I referred to this interview. Mother kept most of my letters. If I could find that letter, it would be very interesting. Then it was all fresh in my mind. I'll try to turn it up. I'm surprised I remember so much detail even now in all this period of time—47 years. It surely made a deep impression on me. I was just as embarrassed when I was introduced with, "Here we have a Tammany man," as if I had smallpox or something.

CHAPTER 11

Secondhand Memories: Murray T. Quigg

Fig. 11.1 Photo of Lemuel E. Quigg testifying before the Thompson Committee (1916), Library of Congress

Nineteenth-century journalists had immense power. The newspapers of that era functioned as party instruments. They vetted candidates, promoted them for high office, and issued campaign propaganda. For New York Republicans, the most important newspaper was the *Tribune*, and the most important beat was the Albany desk that reported on state government. It just so happened that when Theodore Roosevelt worked as an assemblyman in Albany, Lemuel E. Quigg worked as the *Tribune's* reporter for the Assembly. Quigg would also follow Roosevelt to the Dakotas, where Roosevelt farmed cattle and Quigg reported on the American West. During his years reporting for the *Tribune*, Quigg established a reputation as a leading party man. In 1894, he filled a vacant congressional seat, and within the year won election to the district. Quigg chaired the 1896 state Republican convention, an honor that demonstrated his substantial command within the party. As Quigg rose through the ranks of the Republican Party, Roosevelt did the same.

It was in 1886, when Republicans sought a candidate for mayor of New York City that Quigg's influence had come to bear upon Roosevelt. Confronted with mounting personal problems from his brother's alcoholism and his failed cattle venture in the Dakotas, Quigg proposed redemption in politics and heaped pressure on Roosevelt to run for mayor, despite knowing the odds of victory were impossibly narrow. Roosevelt finished a laggardly third, one of the worst results for Republicans, but Quigg appreciated Roosevelt's commitment to the party and arranged for him to take up a position on the city's police commission in 1895. Quigg again boosted for Roosevelt when the Rough Rider returned from Cuba as a war hero. By 1899, Quigg had amassed considerable political capital within the Republican machine, and the party's search for a gubernatorial candidate began and ended with his suggestion of Roosevelt. Later, when Roosevelt was being considered as a candidate for vice president on President McKinley's 1900 ticket, Quigg advanced Roosevelt's name and tested the party's responsiveness. On all three occasions—the mayoral, gubernatorial, and vice-presidential nominations—Quigg led the negotiations between a fiercely independent Roosevelt and a party machine that expected deference.

Quigg died in 1919, less than six months after Roosevelt. Historian Edmund Morris called him "an attractive, prematurely grizzled, political schemer."[1] His son, Murray T. Quigg, tells a different story. From his perspective, Lemuel tamed the worst excesses of Republican bossism and helped to achieve reform within party structures. Morris's assertion that Quigg amounted to a "silk stocking reformer" might ring true, but from Murray Quigg's perspective, his father was a reformer, nonetheless.[2] And Murray Quigg should know; he was the editor of the *Law and Labor Journal*, a lawyer that helped the League for Industrial Rights and lobbied on behalf of workers. His secondhand memories provide an account of how Roosevelt wielded power, listened to the party-faithful, and how disagreements manifest in policy. Of course, the nature of secondhand recollections means that we should approach Quigg's memories with some reservation. A son's admiration for his father naturally arouses subjectivity, and the stories here begin with a father retelling one to an adoring son, followed by a son retelling the story for posterity.[3]

Murray Quigg interviewed in February 1950 with Owan Bombard, a staffer at the Columbia Oral History Center. His testimony was taken before the Hagedorns had begun their project. Bombard's questions were omitted from the transcript and this chapter reproduces only a selection of the testimony as it relates to Roosevelt. The remainder of Quigg's interview dwells on his father's many other pursuits. Interestingly, and perhaps to make the point that his testimony had a real basis in facts, the Columbia Oral History Project included letters of correspondence between Roosevelt and Lemuel Quigg.

* * *

In 1881, my father reported sessions of the New York State Assembly for the *Tribune*. There he met Theodore Roosevelt, just out of college and in his first experience in public office. Roosevelt was studying law and desired to lose no study time toward that requirement for permission to take the Bar examination by the fact of his attendance in the Legislature. He prepared a bill providing that time spent in attendance at the Legislature should be considered as part of the time expended in the study of the law preparatory to presenting oneself for the examination. The bill passed.

My father and Roosevelt met again in Montana when my father was there as editor and Roosevelt as a rancher ... On one occasion, my mother had been driving out into the country to seek for wild flowers, and had found a horseshoe. She picked it up and put it into the buggy. On returning to town, the first man she met, whom she recognized, was Roosevelt.

She stopped and they chatted for a moment. Then she handed Mr. Roosevelt the horseshoe, saying: "I hope it will bring you good luck."

He thanked her and took it.

My father and Roosevelt both returned to New York. In 1894, Roosevelt hunted up my father and asked his intercession with Mayor [William L.] Strong on behalf of Roosevelt's appointment as Police Commissioner. During the period of Roosevelt's Commissionership, he and my father saw more or less of each other and so far as I know were sympathetic with what each of them was trying to do.

Roosevelt left the local scene to go with the Civil Service Commission, to become later Assistant Secretary of the Navy, to expound his views on the war in Cuba, to organize the Rough Riders, and invade Cuba. When the gubernatorial campaign of 1898 came around here in New York, the Republican Party faced the campaign with a very unpopular Republican in the Governor's chair. My father and [NY Governor] Benjamin Odell both impressed upon [NY Republican Party boss Thomas Collier] Platt, and other leaders, the importance of securing a more popular man for the Republican nomination and preferably a war hero. They both advocated Theodore Roosevelt.

Platt's objection to Roosevelt was that his behavior was unpredictable. He was quite as likely, in Platt's opinion, to help destroy the organization which helped to put him in office as he would be to protect it. As a result of this situation, my father called on Roosevelt at Montauk, Long Island. Roosevelt was there mustering out the Rough Riders. My father explained to Roosevelt that he could have the Republican nomination for Governor if he would give the Republican leaders through Mr. Platt the assurance that in making appointments, he would consult the organization. He was not asked to commit himself always to follow the advice given him by the organization, but merely to give honest consideration to the advice given him by the organization, and when he thought he could, with decency and good conscience, follow it, to do so.

After these conversations, my father reduced their purport to writing in a letter to Roosevelt. It became the basis upon which he received the nomination for Governor, and his election. During his term in office, he followed the course which he had promised and, on the whole, he supported and strengthened the Republican organization.

In 1898, nine years after my mother had given him the horseshoe, she was a member of a line of persons presented to him at a reception at the Oriental Hotel on Manhattan Beach. The moment he saw her, which was for the first time since she had given him the horseshoe, he called out to her, "Well, Mrs. Quigg, how *do* you do? Remember that horseshoe you gave me? Got it up in my barn now, in Oyster Bay. Brought me luck—excellent luck!"

In 1900, there was a question of strengthening McKinley's ticket and at the same time moving Mr. Roosevelt out of active politics in New York. Some men were motivated entirely by the one purpose and others by the other. I fancy that my father was about equally affected by both purposes. In any event, he used his persuasive powers upon Mr. Roosevelt to accept the vice-presidency which Roosevelt did only after a great deal of hesitation and with much reluctance—lest, in effect, it place him in a *cul-de-sac*.

In 1903, it came to my father's attention that Roosevelt intended to remove George Bidwell, the Collector of the Port of New York and to place someone else in his stead. There was no evidence of the misconduct of his office by Mr. Bidwell. He had, as a matter of fact, proved himself a devoted and hard-working public servant. It happened that he was unmarried. One day, on leaving his office and passing through a room filled with clerks, one young woman fainted as he passed. He stopped to inquire what was the matter.

She said, "Nothing is the matter. I'll be well in a moment." Thereupon she coughed.

He asked: "Do you have tuberculosis?"

She admitted that she did.

"Why is it that you don't quit work and take care of yourself?"

She said: "I'm the sole support for my mother and myself. I can't quit."

After further inquiry concerning her physical condition and the truth of her statements, Bidwell arranged for her to go on leave of absence and to take her mother to some place in the Catskills where the two of them could stay at little expense. He himself arranged to meet that expense out of his own personal money.

Men in New York who were interested in securing Bidwell's position for someone else took stories to the president that Bidwell was maintaining a mistress in the Catskills. This libel came to my father's attention. He went to Washington on Bidwell's behalf, certain that, from his long personal acquaintance with Bidwell, that he knew the truth about Bidwell, and from his long personal acquaintance with Roosevelt, that Roosevelt would set upon it.

On his way to the White House, to keep an appointment previously made, he met Mrs. Hazen and Mrs. George Dewey—ladies who had been very gracious to him and to my mother when my father was in Congress and we were living in Washington. These ladies asked him to lunch and he accepted their invitation, then continued to the White House. He told Roosevelt the actual story concerning Bidwell and that he was being libeled and dealt with most unfairly by people who had nothing against him but merely wanted to get him out in order to put someone else in his place. Roosevelt finally said: "All you say may be true. But I want the place and Bidwell will have to go." Then changing his tone, he asked my father to stay for lunch. He said that Mrs. Roosevelt would be delighted to see him.

My father explained about having met Mrs. Hazen and Mrs. Dewey and having accepted their invitation.

Roosevelt said: "Of course you must go to lunch with them. I excuse you entirely."

My father left the White House. Upon his return to New York, on the evening of that day, he was met by an account in the evening papers of how he had insisted upon having his own way in his interview with the president and when the president had opposed him, had created such a scene that it has been necessary to remove him from the White House. He wrote to [William] Loeb, Roosevelt's secretary, asking that Loeb issue a denial of the story relating to his interview with the president. He used the word: "interview."

Loeb replied that Mr. Quigg should know that the President was never "interviewed," making no reference whatsoever to the false newspaper story. Nothing was done about it.

When next my father met Riggs, the *Sun's* reporter in Washington—it was not an evening paper then—Riggs told him that the president had given him the story himself—that he, Riggs, did not believe it, but what could he do except publish it when the President had given it to him? Thereafter, Roosevelt threw all of his support to Herbert Parsons who opposed my father for leadership of the Republican Party in New York County. Apparently, Roosevelt set about to build his own personal organization and to get rid of any personality in the party to whom he felt that he could not dictate.

The years passed until 1912. When Roosevelt organized the Bull Moose Party, my father was captivated by his dynamic personality and spent many hours considering whether he should not support Roosevelt in that campaign. I spent almost as many hours with him opposing his support of Roosevelt. It has always seemed to me that men of very great pretense and men who show a thirst for power for its own sake are not fitting leaders in a democratic republican state.

In 1913, Mr. Roosevelt set about writing his memoirs. He wrote to my father concerning the correspondence they had had when he, Roosevelt, was at Montauk—saying that he had mislaid it and wondering whether my father had copies of it to put at his disposition. My father did have copies and put them at Roosevelt's disposition. Roosevelt asked him down to Oyster Bay and my father went. They took up their acquaintance again as if nothing had happened to interrupt it for a period of ten years. My father advocated Roosevelt's nomination for the presidency in 1916.

In December, 1918, when Roosevelt was in Roosevelt Hospital, my father called upon him. The evening of that same day, or the day after, my father told me that Roosevelt had told him that day that he had advocated the popular recall of judicial decisions because of the treatment given to Roosevelt's statute, passed in 1881, directed against sweat shops in New York City by the Court of Appeals of New York which held the statute unconstitutional in the case of *In Re Jacobs* (98 N.Y. 98). Thus Mr. Roosevelt judged a great constitutional principle relating to the security of law, upon the condition of his own sentiments as a result of what he regarded as a great personal defeat.

CHAPTER 12

The Account of a College Man: Karl H. Behr

Fig. 12.1 Photo of Karl Behr at tennis court (1915), Library of Congress

Karl Behr's obituary describes an extraordinary life. A tennis star who played well beyond his prime, Behr was named to the U.S. Davis Cup team twice, reached the final of the Wimbledon men's doubles tournament, and beat the world number one Maurice McLoughlin in 1915 on the eve of his professional retirement. Behr graduated from Yale University, passed the bar exam and, despite his success in law, changed careers to become an investment banker of some reputation. He courted Helen Monypeny Newsom, a love affair that led him across the Atlantic. Newsom's disapproving mother took her daughter on a European tour to escape Behr's advances, but Behr persisted and followed the Newsom aboard the *HMS Titanic*. The entire party survived the historic disaster, and the experience copper-fastened the couple's affection. They married in 1913.

Interestingly, Behr's obituaries make no mention of Theodore Roosevelt, but when Behr came to write his memoirs, Roosevelt loomed large. He met TR in 1905 at the White House when the president invited students from the Ivy League colleges to the capital for a conference on public service. Representing Yale at the conference, Behr left the meeting with an abiding admiration that never diminished. He again came into contact with Roosevelt during World War I. Then, the former president and Behr collaborated on the preparedness campaign designed to recruit young men to volunteer for military service. The campaign flew in the face of President Wilson's neutrality policy and marked out Roosevelt as the president's most prominent detractor. Behr's part in the campaign made him a trusted ally of TR and in his account that connection led to at least one remarkable episode. In 1917, after the first Russian revolution installed Alexander Kerensky as head of the provisional government, a Russian envoy told Behr that sending Theodore Roosevelt to St. Petersburg might keep fatigued Russian soldiers in the field, and thus maintain pressure on Germany's eastern front. Behr appealed to Wilson through his closest advisor Colonel Edward M. House, but Wilson rejected the call for fear that Roosevelt could not be controlled. Behr relates a counterfactual scenario in which Roosevelt single-handedly saves thousands of soldiers' lives by bolstering the morale of Russian troops. However unlikely this might seem, Behr's secret mission to send Roosevelt to Russia mirrors the belief of other world leaders at the time, and it has implications for how we consider Wilson's foreign policies. French Prime Minister Georges Clemenceau wrote to Wilson that the "name of Roosevelt has this legendary force in our country," and solicited the president to "send them Roosevelt. I tell you because I know it will gladden their hearts."[1] Roosevelt was seen as a talisman for global democracy, and Behr shared that perception.

The testimony in this chapter belongs to Behr's unpublished memoirs and was not a part of the oral histories collected by the Hagedorns, yet the excerpts are included in Columbia's oral history collection because the reminiscences offer as relevant account. Behr dictated his memoirs to his daughter Sally in 1945.[2] He died in 1949 at the age of 64.

* * *

Ever since college I felt that the country was unprepared for any possible war and ignorant of the future dangers. There was then a tendency to belittle everything military and consider anyone foolish enough to join the National Guard, as I had done in 1907, as a "tin" soldier.

On my wedding trip we met [Mayor Charles Beach] Booth in his home in Pasadena, California.[3] It so happened that on his long redwood living room table, [adventurer] Homer Lea had mapped and planned with [Chinese exile] Sun Yat-Sen the Chinese Revolution campaign, which shortly before Homer Lea had successfully completed [in 1911]. Booth not only told me much of this remarkable soldier of fortune, but gave me his then recently published book *The Valor of Ignorance*. It was what I had been looking for, with its bold criticism of the military inertia and ignorance of danger prevalent throughout this country. Its main contentions were soon to be confirmed by the First World War.

In 1915, I became active in the National Security League. After some months I was elected to its executive committee and, as its youngest member, had the privilege of lunching each Wednesday in a private room at the Bankers Club with this committee. Among those who regularly attended these luncheons were Robert Bacon, former secretary of State, Henry L. Stimson [former secretary of State], [New York congressman] Frederick Coudert, [Jr.], [editor and publisher] Lawrence Abbott, [National Security League co-founder] Franklin Q. Brown, [William Randolph Hearst's financial manager] E. H. Clark, [National Security League co-founder] S. Stanwood Menken, [inventor] Henry [A.] Wise Wood, and others I do not readily recall. Among those who came from time to time were Colonel Roosevelt, [Pennsylvania Senator] George Wharton Pepper, [1904 Democratic presidential nominee] Alton B. Parker, representatives of the

British and French armies, and members of the Military Affairs committees of the House and Senate.

I became chairman of the campaign committee towards the end of 1915. The League not only advocated preparedness, but also universal training. We felt certain we would be drawn into the then active World War. There was a substantial paid office force, and branches and committees were located all over the country.

The League attempted to arouse public opinion and the [Wilson] administration at Washington to its cause, through innumerable mass meetings in New York and other cities and through publicity in the press. These local meetings held at Carnegie Hall, the Astor Hotel, and similar places were, however, generally attended only by the more educated strata and members of the League.

We had long felt that the man on the street should be more effectively reached. To this end I requested permission from the League's executive committee to rent on one night at least four to five halls and theatres which I promised to fill, all on the same night. I told them I would have speakers of a type to draw anyone in the city, each to talk to at least two of these meetings. The League had previously been unable to completely fill Carnegie Hall. After much argument I was finally permitted to rent only Carnegie Hall and the Century Opera House (then on Central Park West) for one evening of meetings.

I at once proceeded to get my speakers, obtaining Col. Roosevelt, General Leonard Wood, Senator [William] Borah, and two or three others I do not now recall. It was obviously that with wide enough preliminary publicity the attraction of these men would crowd the meetings, which actually is what occurred—hundreds being left out on the street unable to get inside the doors.

After forming a small group to run each meeting, I decided to place [banker and public relations expert] Guy Emerson in charge of Carnegie Hall and handle the Century Opera House myself. Both meetings went without a hitch, and enthusiasm was maintained throughout the evening. Col. Roosevelt was the last speaker at the Century and General Wood at Carnegie Hall. The ovation these two men received as they walked rapidly down the main aisle to the stage was almost hysterical. The subsequent publicity warranted all the trouble taken to make these meetings the success they undoubtedly were.

You boys [Behr's sons] always have been interested in the few stories I have told of Theodore Roosevelt. In spite of a natural timidity to dignify my experience with him in a separate chapter when so many others knew him so much more intimately, I have decided to relate a few incidents because his personality and ideas had such an early influence on me. I hope these few pages may stimulate in you boys a desire to read more of his life. He was not only a great personality, the most outstanding of his time, but throughout his strenuous life of patriotic service, always remained a devoted father of an affectionate family. Here was a man who, in a period of international and domestic tranquility, by force of character and achievement alone, became the most famous figure in the world. He had no great war to lead, as had Washington, Lincoln and Wilson, but should fate have caused him to be president in a time of great crisis, he would, I believe, have had no equal in all our history as a national leader.

My first meeting with this great man occurred in December 1905. Congressman Herbert Parsons (a Yale graduate) was much interested in our Yale Government Club, referred to in my chapter on Yale. He somehow persuaded President Roosevelt to invite a group of men from Yale, Harvard, Princeton, Columbia and nine other colleges to the White House with a view to stimulating interest in public affairs and politics among the colleges. I was fortunate in being among those to go from Yale. We went to the White House (dressed in dinner coats) in small groups about 8 o'clock in the evening. After everyone had arrived (there were thirty-three in all), we were conducted to a large room on the second floor. The president, also dressed in a dinner coat, stood at its door and each man was introduced to him as we filed into the room where small chairs lined the walls. Following us, the president finding there were not enough chairs, moved to the end of the room and sat on a large table, suggesting that some of us join him. I quickly took advantage of his suggestion and planted myself next to him on the table. I was just 20, a highly impressionable age, yet even to this day I can recall the magnetism which seemed to radiate from his vigorous body.

He commenced his talk by endeavoring to put us as much as possible at our ease, saying that he wished us to forget for the time being that he was president of the United States; that he preferred us to consider him simply as Theodore Roosevelt, Harvard [class of] 1880. He then said he was anxious to talk to us as a college man, without too much reservation, laughingly referring to recent criticism in the press of his too wide interest in matters not pertaining to the running of government [a reference to his interest in football reform]. In a more serious vein, he asked everyone present for a pledge that nothing he discussed be repeated so as to get into the hands of the newspapers.

The object of this meeting he said, was to endeavor to interest college men in future public and political service. He dwelt on the necessity for greater activity in local politics by college graduates. Then warming to his subject, remarked that perhaps the best way to explain how this might be done was to outline his own early experiences in ward politics in lower New York, fighting Tammany [Hall]. This he did in much fascinating detail, finally bringing his story up to his present position as president. Here he paused, and looking around the room, again reminded us of our pledge of secrecy saying that he wished to tell us something of the present condition of the country. Quite suddenly, as well as I can now recall, he said, "Certain big business people and certain big politicians have come to consider themselves more powerful than the government of the United States. I shall shortly start to fight this menace without gloves—there will be a great storm over this country before I am done, but my successor in office will calm the rough seas created by the impetuous Roosevelt. I am now, as shown by the election results, a popular president. When my term expires—mark my words—I shall leave the White House the most, certainly one of the most, unpopular presidents ever to leave office—however, young men, we shall have a better country."

I am so sure the above quotation, even after the passage of so many years, quite accurately describes the substance of what he said. Anyone familiar with the history of his subsequent years as president can readily see how closely he followed this prediction. He drove the then powerful Senator [Joseph] Foraker [of Ohio], if my memory is correct, and certain other politicians out of public life; the 1907 panic was caused by his successful attack on a then too rampant big business fraternity, and he did leave the presidency bitterly unpopular in the eyes of a substantial group of Americans. These subsequent events, so perfectly following his purpose as expressed in December 1905, created an admiration for him on my part never, in spite of some perfectly human failings, to diminish during his entire life.

I regret being uncertain when I next saw Colonel Roosevelt. I believe it was in 1915; in any case, in January 1916, I called on him to ask him to speak at the Carnegie Hall and Century theatre preparedness meetings, referred to in a previous chapter. I remember telling him on that occasion of my memory of the White House meeting in 1905. I was to see him more frequently thereafter in 1916 and early 1917. The few letters from him in the scrap books are amazingly characteristic, and from that standpoint are of very real interest.

I received a phone call one day from the Colonel's secretary, asking if I could come up to his office (then with the *Metropolitan* magazine) at 4 o'clock. I went and found Julian Street, the writer, at a desk correcting a long printer's proof sheet with blue pencil. Mr. Robert Bacon was sitting by the window reading another copy. The Colonel came through the door and handed me a third copy of these sheets, asking me to read, correct and make any suggestions regarding an article he had written against the hyphenated German American. The proposed article opened with flattering references to the fine service in this country of many Germans from Von Steuben in the Revolution to Carl Schurz in the Civil War. It then proceeded to condemn the hyphenated German American's attitude against helping the Allies in the Great War. It was dreadfully long, too long to possibly get front page newspaper space. I read it through but did not touch the proof. After some time, the Colonel returned, taking Street's much marked copy; asking Mr. Bacon what he thought of it, he received a complementary reply. He then turned to me. With some hesitation I finally said it was too long to gain a front page, and that I thought the country would expect him to deliver such a message in person to these German Americans in their own bailiwick. "Your friends, Colonel," I said, "would expect you to go to these people and hit out at them face to face; a speech in Cincinnati or Milwaukee would be first page material all over the country."

He hesitated a moment and then shouted for his secretary. "Find out what Saturdays I have free," he said, "I am going West to tell these people what I think as Mr. Behr suggests." Subsequently he did so and made a great speech which reverberated throughout the country. Thereafter I lunched with him at the Harvard Club once in a while when he had something upon which he apparently wanted a younger viewpoint.

As I shall describe in the following chapter, at my request he spoke at the large Madison Square Garden meeting on one of the last evenings of John Puroy Mitchel's mayoralty election campaign, and also reviewed the torchlight parades on that evening. As Grand Marshall of these parades, I was riding with him in a touring car into Madison Square. It was dark, around 9:30 at night. Two policemen were standing on each running board of the car. The Colonel suddenly leaned over the side, looking carefully at one of these men. Then hitting the man on the back, shouted "Sergeant Levy, why didn't you speak to me—didn't I make you a sergeant?" The poor man turned, much flustered, and said "Colonel Roosevelt, sir, I never thought you would remember me." This is just one of innumerable examples of his remarkable memory. It seems that Levy had, when Colonel Roosevelt was Police Commissioner years before, made a daring rescue at a tenement fire and had been promptly rewarded by him with a sergeantcy.

Another charming incident comes to mind which occurred in the early summer of 1916. The Colonel had asked me to lunch with him at Oyster Bay on a Saturday. We were spending the summer at Greenwich, Connecticut, so Helen and I came across the ferry from Greenwich to Long Island in the Ford. After leaving me at Sagamore Hill, Helen went off to lunch with a friend at Glen Cove. After lunch, time flew rapidly, and I regret I cannot recall what was discussed. Finally, I looked at my watch and told the Colonel my car must be waiting outside. He got up and walked to the porch steps. Looking for the car, he saw white dresses behind a bush on the circular drive. Helen and Bee Cook had hid the Ford behind the bush. He turned to me with simulated anger and asked, "Is Mrs. Behr in that car?" On my admitting she was, he started down the steps shouting, "Mrs. Behr, get right out of that car! Get out of that car! I insist!" Much awed and excited, Helen and Bee Cook followed the Colonel into his large living room. Here for over an hour he showed these two young girls his prize possessions and utterly charmed them.

In this, the last Roosevelt experience I shall mention, I am disclosing an incident which I have never discussed before, although it might have been of history making proportion. To properly describe this incident, it is necessary to realize that by the time we entered the First World War, Colonel Roosevelt had developed a dislike and contempt for President Wilson. After the Colonel's bitter "Shadow Lawn" speech, caused by Wilson's continued appeasement after the sinking of the *S. S. Lusitania*, his dislike was fully reciprocated by the president. The Colonel and all those so ardently involved in the fight for preparedness also never could forgive the administration's neglect to prepare for a war which we were certain to enter so shortly. The hypocrisy of Wilson's campaign slogan in 1916, "He kept us out of war," was shocking to all of us. So much as necessary background to any understanding of what I am hereafter writing.

A short time after our entry into the war in the Spring of 1917, Herman Behr & Co's exclusive Russian sale agent, who also represented another American company, Mr. Victor de Heintz arrived from Russia. The Kerensky government had just recently come into power and our press had announced the appointment by President Wilson of a commission under the leadership of [former Secretary of State] Elihu Root, which was to go to Russia to advise with this new government. The general purpose of this commission was to ascertain how the United States might most effectively aid Russia. However, its primary and underlying objective was to do everything possible to keep the Russian armies in the field. A collapse of the vast Eastern Front, enabling large German forces to be moved against the front in France, would, in the opinion of the best military experts, probably lose the war.

When Mr. de Heintz first called on us, I took him into a private office, telling him I was at the moment not interested in discussing business. After we were alone, I asked him to give me his opinion of the Kerensky government, and more particularly what chance it had of keeping Russian armies in the field. He knew Kerensky and many of his compatriots in the new government and expressed little confidence in their staying long in power or upon their ability to keep Russia at war. Upon my asking him what good might be effected by the recently appointed Elihu Root commission, he replied, "I have no hope of this commission accomplishing anything. You see, Mr. Behr," he said, "Your commission is composed of eminent intellectuals. They will meet almost entirely with uneducated men who have not the required capacity to understand or cooperate with your commission. I am sorry I can give you no more reassuring answer. The Russian Army is tired and sick of war. Its only interest now is to go home and commence to enjoy the new freedom finally attained by the revolution. The Army's leadership now is largely in the hands of peasant minded soldier committees. The sole enthusiasm left is a deep love for and desire to establish democracy in Russia."

I cannot recall just why my mind suddenly turned to Colonel Roosevelt; in any case I asked him if he thought a personality like Roosevelt's would have a better chance of accomplishing the main task assigned to the Root commission. The quiet atmosphere of our talk changed abruptly. Mr. de Heintz rose excitedly from his chair and, with great earnestness said, "If Colonel Roosevelt were sent to Russia, I believe he alone might keep Russia in the war. You may be surprised to know that to the Russian laborer and peasant he has been an idol—a symbol of democracy for years past. His picture has been on the walls of thousands of peasant hovels. They believe in him. If Col. Roosevelt could tour the front in an automobile and speak to the troops, even through an interpreter, urging them not to desert their democratic allies, and offer them his leadership, I am certain hundreds of thousands would follow him—Mr. Behr, if this could be done, it might well save the war."

I was amazed at his confidence in what might be accomplished by Colonel Roosevelt in Russia. I have not attempted to cover all the detail of this conversation but when Mr. de Heintz left, I pondered over what he said, and the more I thought the more I also became convinced that he might be right. After lunch I phoned to the Colonel's office and arranged to meet him at five o'clock in the apartment of one of his friends (which he was using for some meetings) on the southeast corner of Fifth Avenue and 56th Street. When I arrived, he was alone. Sitting on a sofa with him, he at once plunged into matters regarding the volunteer division he hoped to lead to France. It was some minutes before I was able to speak of what I had in mind. Knowing his anxiety to get to France, I commenced by discussing the strategic position of the war, and got from him the admission that the war might well be lost if the Russian front collapsed. Only then did I repeat my morning's conversation with Mr. de Heintz. The Colonel patiently heard me through. When I had finished, however, he got to his feet and, with his usual intensity said, "I am not going to Russia—I am going to France to fight, and you are going with me!" When he had reseated himself, I said, "Colonel, of all your many qualities, the purest of all is your patriotism. You are a soldier. No matter how sincerely you desire to go to France, if you agree with me that there is a chance, even a slight one, of your being able to hold the Russians in the trenches, I have no doubt of your answer." He looked at me and shaking his head said, "Even if I agreed with you, that man in Washington would never send me to Russia."

I had aroused his interest, and knew also that he saw the deadly danger of a Russian collapse. I got up and said, "Colonel, I want your permission to explore this matter through Colonel [Edward M.] House, [President's Wilson's closest advisor]." He walked to the door, putting a hand on my shoulder, "Karl," he said, "you may survey the situation, but I'll not promise now to go. In any case, you must not imply that I am seeking any such assignment, and if Wilson should, by any possible chance offer me such a mission, I must have plenipotentiary powers." I had made better progress with him than I dared hope. Assuring him that I would handle my inquiry with Colonel House so as not to embarrass him, I left with a light heart.

The Root commission, from the best information I could obtain, was likely to sail within a week. If it once left, I was sure there would be little chance of President Wilson sending Colonel Roosevelt to Russia. I called on Gordon Auchincloss (Colonel House's son-in-law) the morning following my talk with Colonel Roosevelt. I told him in detail of my conversation with Mr. de Heintz, emphasized the latter's business standing and ability, and offered to bring him to Colonel House so he could give his viewpoint first hand. Regarding Colonel Roosevelt, I told him only that in light of the vital importance of keeping Russia in the war, I was certain that if the president gave him such a mission, with necessary plenipotentiary authority, Colonel Roosevelt could not refuse, in spite of his desire to go to France.

When I had finished, I asked Auchincloss whether he agreed that this was a matter worth of serious consideration by the president, and whether he would discuss it at once with his father-in-law. Without hesitation he said he thought it very important, with much merit and promised that evening to give Colonel House a careful resume of what I had said. As I left, he referred to the antipathy to each other—of Wilson and Roosevelt—and expressed doubt of any successful outcome, although he felt the idea might intrigue his father-in-law. He promised to press the matter and appeared genuinely interested.

Three days passed before I received a phone call from Auchincloss asking me to come to his office. When I was seated in his office, he said he wished to talk freely, and asked that I keep what he had to tell me in confidence, which I promised to do. He then said that Colonel House's interest had been aroused; that he had spoken to President Wilson on the matter and had been turned down. Frankly, he said, I believe the president's refusal to send Colonel Roosevelt to Russia was not entirely based on personal dislike, but more on his doubt of being able to control the Colonel if he were given a mission at such a distance with plenipotentiary powers. So ended this prospective mission. To this day I feel that failure to send Colonel Roosevelt to Russia may have caused thousands of soldier lives. We almost lost the war in the great German offensive of March 1918, made possible by transfer of hundreds of thousands of German troops from the Russian front after its collapse, which the Colonel might well at least partially have prevented.

In the Spring of 1916, while I was busy helping to organize the great preparedness parade, my friends Guy Emerson and naval engineer Thomas C. Desmond organized the Roosevelt Non-Partisan League. I took no active part early in this work yet Emerson and I frequently talked together evenings. We hoped to arouse enough enthusiasm to help influence the

Republican politicians to come out for Roosevelt in advance of the Republican Convention. We all felt the danger of impending war, and no other national leader compared to Roosevelt in our minds.

They obtained the use of a vacant store on Vanderbilt Avenue, opposite the Grand Central [Station], and put a large sign in the window urging all who felt that Colonel Roosevelt should be our next president to come in and sign up with the League. It is astonishing to record that well over a hundred thousand who passed this store signed their names in a few months' time. The country, I believe, in 1916 would have overwhelmingly elected Roosevelt over Wilson had he been nominated by the Republicans. One evening late in the Spring of 1916, Emerson and Desmond told me that the Colonel had no engagements for a Saturday two weeks hence; they wished to know if I had any ideas for this vacant day which, if not filled, meant no Roosevelt publicity in the newspapers on the following Sunday. After a day or two, I thought of the idea of having a pilgrimage to Oyster Bay by men from all parts of the country to ask him to run for the presidency.

After exploring this idea with Emerson and Desmond, it was decided that we had too little time. I then proposed such a pilgrimage of men from around New York. I told them I would guarantee to fill as many special trains as could be obtained from the Long Island Railroad. It was a month or so after the great preparedness parade and I had no worry about producing the men. Desmond contacted the railroad and could obtain only three special trains of ten or twelve cars each. We figured these could carry about 3,500 and made plans accordingly. I drafted a postcard, a copy of which I unfortunately have lost, but I remember its substance. We selected a group of prominent friends of the Colonel, whose names were to be printed as a committee on the bottom of this postcard. The card contained an invitation to join the undersigned committee in a pilgrimage to Oyster Bay to personally meet Colonel Roosevelt in his home and urge him to run for the presidency. We mailed a proof of this card to each proposed member of this committee, obtaining their approval to the use of their names. The card then was mailed to some thousands of selected preparedness parade groups. The postcard advised the receiver to board the special trains at the Long Island Depot at 2 p.m. on the specified Saturday; that no railroad tickets need be purchased in advance and that everyone had better come early as we could not assure adequate room for all on the trains.

Emerson, Desmond and I were to each take charge of a train. I reached the station about 1:45 p.m. and found it so crowded I could not get anywhere near the train gates. I went down a back way, climbed over some tracks and got on one of the special trains. They all were soon crowded, men standing in the aisles, some 500 or more being left behind at the station.

Arriving at Oyster Bay, with the Seventh Regiment Band at our head, in columns of four, our three thousand or more men marched to Sagamore Hill. I have some good photographs of this affair in the scrap book. The Colonel was waiting for us, much elated when he saw such an unexpectedly large crowd. He urged everyone to gather up close to the porch before starting to speak, suggesting that some might hear better if they came up on the porch. His invitation was accepted by too many, resulting in part of the porch collapsing.

The Colonel made one of his rousing speeches, amid wild enthusiasm. When he had finished, he asked everyone to form in single file and go through the house to the rear living room where he proposed to meet every man. He did so. It took over an hour and a half for him to shake every man by the hand. His recognition of innumerable men by name was startling to me as I sat on a sofa behind him. This small affair accomplished the national publicity result we desired and was well worth the effort. It is sad to relate, however, that Hughes was nominated after all by the Republican Convention which followed some weeks later.

CHAPTER 13

When Trumpets Call: Stanley M. Isaacs

Fig. 13.1 Photo portrait of Stanley M. Isaacs (1922). Edith S. Isaacs, *Love Affair with a City*

Theodore Roosevelt heard a "trumpet" call him to public service, according to social activist Jacob Riis.¹ So, too, did his disciples. It beckoned them to crusade for good government, conservation, direct democracy, labor rights, and public health. Historian Patricia O'Toole chose to call her biography of Theodore Roosevelt *When Trumpets Call* because "in the reminiscences of those who fell under his spell the trumpet is a recurring image."² Roosevelt urged Americans to decline "ignoble ease" and pursue a strenuous life defined by enthusiastic civic duty. That doctrine inspired countless followers, and the reminiscences of Stanley Isaacs offer evidence of the power of Roosevelt's appeal. Those who harkened to Roosevelt's call for strenuous living often subscribed to Roosevelt's core beliefs and remained dedicated to him throughout their life. Isaacs provides a case in point.

Born in Manhattan, like Roosevelt, Isaacs lived in New York City all his life. From a prominent Jewish family, his father published a weekly newspaper that, during the antebellum years, supported the abolition of slavery and naturally aligned the family with the Republican Party. Isaacs joined the Republicans as a young boy and gravitated to Roosevelt first through his father's connections, and then as an adult who campaigned for the McKinley-Roosevelt ticket in 1900. When Roosevelt founded the Progressive Party in 1912, Isaacs followed; he then gravitated back to the Republican Party as Roosevelt did in 1916.

When Roosevelt died in 1919, Isaacs persisted in his emulation. He campaigned for social justice, most notably for settlement housing. He joined United Neighborhood Houses and campaigned for reforms in social services for low-income New Yorkers. He became a leading figure in the city's Welfare Council, the Federation of Jewish Philanthropic Societies, the American Jewish Committee, and the Education Alliance. The rise of fascism in Europe prompted Isaacs to join the National Refugee Service to assist those fleeing Nazi persecution and, when Hitler invaded the Soviet Union, Isaacs signed up to the American Committee for Russian War Relief. Impending war with the Axis Powers fueled Isaacs's political vocation. Mayor Fiorello La Guardia appointed him Manhattan Borough president in 1938 and when his four-year term ended, Isaacs ran for City Council and remained on that legislative body until his death in 1962. During his time on the City Council, he continued his reputation as a progressive Republican, sponsoring legislation that outlawed racial discrimination in housing and working with La Guardia to permanently defeat the Tammany Hall political machine. A relatively unsung hero of social reform, Isaacs drew his inspiration from New York's favorite son. In his testimony to Mary Hagedorn, he details how Roosevelt imparted that enthusiasm.

The Hagedorns transcribed their recordings, and Isaacs confirmed their accuracy. That transcript appears here without some questions posed by the interviewers. Otherwise, it is unchanged.

* * *

My first memories of Mr. Roosevelt are based on my father's relationship with him. My father knew him very well when he was Police Commissioner of New York. He was a very good friend of Jacob Riis and was very much interested in the cleaning up of conditions on the lower East Side—and the three of them worked together. He had great respect for Theodore Roosevelt. He was active in the Republican Party, had been a candidate for Justice of the Supreme Court at one time, and was deeply involved in efforts looking toward sound an honest government in New York City. Because of this acquaintanceship, of course, I too was interested in Theodore Roosevelt when he became Police Commissioner of New York. I don't think I knew anything about him before then.

It was exciting, because the papers were full of him. He was absolutely straight, absolutely honest from my point of view, a very effective person and, I think, a very important person in the city. He was my boyhood hero; that about sums it up. I read all about him, I saw the cartoons in the papers and enjoyed them, I liked his personality. I must have seen him from time to time but I have no recollection of meeting him until he ran for governor in 1898; then I know I met him because my father was speaking in the campaign for him. He spoke on the same platform. I was introduced to him after my father finished speaking. He came in to speak at some lower East Side meeting—I don't remember where. My father introduced me to him and he banged me on the back and said, "I hope you'll grow up to be a good Republican like your father." A man doesn't forget that sort of thing. That was the first time I met him.

He had battles when he was Police Commissioner. The law provided, for example, that there couldn't be liquor sold on Sunday. He didn't have strong views about the sale of liquor on Sundays; but if it was prohibited by law, he made up his mind that law would be enforced. His theory was that if there was a law on the statute books it had to be lived up to. If you didn't like it, you'd have to try to have it repealed, but as long as it was there the Police Commissioner of the City had no choice but to enforce it. As a matter of fact, my father ran for judge in 1895 and it was the reaction against Sunday closing which Roosevelt enforced that probably caused the reaction against the [Republican Mayor William L.] Strong administration and brought about the defeat of those who ran that year.

There was a parade—I'm sure you know about it—of the brewers and those interested in brewing, to protest against Sunday closing. And Roosevelt proceeded to sit in the grandstand and review the parade! It was just further evidence that he was perfectly fearless, perfectly courageous.

Then he was called to Washington to be assistant secretary of the Navy and I read about him then, and of course when he organized the Rough Riders. When the Spanish War came on, I was 16 and deeply interested in it. I followed everything about the Spanish-American War, I knew all the war vessels by name and by sight on the Hudson River. I followed Roosevelt's career very closely and was delighted when he ran for governor after the war.

As to further contacts—I was quite active in politics; I was 21 in 1903, but in 1897 I worked in what was the first Fusion campaign, when Greater New York was established. I was working with the Citizens Union as a sort of assistant-assistant-assistant captain for Seth Low, who was the candidate of the Citizens Union and the Good Government Clubs at that time. And I worked at the polls and certainly attended meetings in 1900 when McKinley and Roosevelt ran for president. I didn't vote in those days but I know I attended meetings and I worked in my own district.

I didn't meet Roosevelt again until I did casually in 1906. That year we had our first Assembly District Republican Club ball and Theodore Roosevelt honored us by coming in just for a moment or two and showing himself there. He was buffeted around by the people surging around him. I saw him at a distance; I didn't have a chance to talk to him.

I joined the Progressive Party in 1912 and was made leader of my own district. I organized the Progressive Club of that district in 1912 and went down to see Roosevelt with a delegation of six or seven people to ask him if he would come to our meeting. Somehow or other he called me by name. Now I hadn't seen him between 1898 and then so that he could recognize me—that was 14 years. I'm sure that he had a list of people who were coming, but he picked me out from the group, just the same. I was very much excited by that.

I told that to Mrs. [Corinne Roosevelt] Robinson one time. She said that she was always amazed at his ability, somehow or other, to recollect people no matter how long ago he had seen them. She told me the story—I don't know whether this is part of your biographical literature or not—of the day that her daughter graduated from school. She asked Theodore Roosevelt to be the commencement speaker, which he was. After the ceremonies were over, he stood there while all the girls of the graduating class filed past him, were introduced to him and shook hands with him.

One girl said to him, "I've met you before Mr. Roosevelt, but you won't remember it."

"Wait a minute," he said—this is Mrs. Robinson's story as she told it to me—"Wait a minute—" and he put up his hand to his eyes, closed his eyes and said, "Yes, I remember you. You were in a rodeo in Denver two years ago and you were riding on a calico pony."

This girl just couldn't believe it because at that rodeo he had probably seen several thousand people and, of course, thousands and thousands before and after. Mrs. Robinson, she said she remarked to her brother that night, "Theodore, how could you possibly have remembered that girl?"

He replied, "I don't know, but when I put my hand to my face and closed my eyes, I saw her riding in front of me on a pony." It was quite extraordinary. He had an amazing ability to remember names and to recognize people. It was a great asset politically ...

Then, for those four years I worked very closely with him. There were dinners given, Progressive dinners which I helped to organize; I was vice chairman of the Progressive county committee—New York County—Francis Bird was chairman; I was leader of my own district and worked every year for the Progressive Party. I presided over a meeting at a hall at 67th Street where Theodore Roosevelt spoke in 1914, still have the tickets for the meeting, and some sheets from his speech. Ethel and Richard Derby [TR's daughter and son-in-law] were guests of honor at that meeting. I met Mr. Roosevelt from time to time, during that period, and always found him immeasurably inspiring. As I say, he was my boyhood hero and that was that. I was impregnated with the idea that he was the kind of man I wanted to follow if I ever had the opportunity.

I still regard him as the greatest preacher of his age. People said that he used clichés and platitudes and that he repeated things that everybody else had said—which was true, but he gave it emphasis and direction and made it stick. And he lived himself. You felt that there was complete sincerity in everything he said and did. It was exciting just to have known him.

Without the slightest question, contact with him in my own case left an absolutely indelible mark on me. I don't want to be smug—but I couldn't do anything wrong, thinking of him. I couldn't go back on the kind of thing that he stood for and said he did. That's the kind of life that I want to live all my life. I was in politics for 50 years, but I didn't hold office until I could be completely independent. He had that advantage when he was young, because he had enough money to live on without having to worry whether he won or lost an election from the point of view of sending his children to college or taking care of his family. I wanted to be in that position and I didn't reach that position until my children were married. Then I was reasonably independent; then I held office for the first time. But I made up my mind that I was going to hold office and follow his standards—which I honestly think I have done. It may sound conceited, but I really think so ... I have very loyal friends, and people are backing me who would not have backed me if they didn't have respect for my own character. I mentioned Learned Hand because I showed you a letter from him, written to me in 1912 when I was district leader of the district in which he lived. At that time, he praised my leadership of the district and was quite startled that the Republican Party in my district was put into third place, with the Progressives second even if they couldn't come first; because it was a rock-ribbed, old-fashioned, conservative Republican district. He and I have been friends ever since and he has given me magnificent support when I had some problems to face. Many others—I won't go through a list of names—who may have disagreed with what I've done from time to time, give me credit for being honest and sincere, doing what I think right.

In the political field, there are a great many office-holders who think that the right thing for them to do is to find out what their constituents want and do it—that's their duty. I mean that a man who is a legislator and represents a district thinks that that's his job. My own feeling is that that's all wrong, and for two reasons: in the first place, you can never find out what your constituents want. You can find out what the noisy and active or organized ones have in mind, but those who differ quietly don't say a word and you never know really what the majority of the people want. Secondly, your job is to do what you think right. If your constituents don't like it, they have the remedy of throwing you out of office, of refusing to re-elect you. But I don't believe that a man who holds office has a right to go against his own convictions even if he thinks his constituents would like it.

We have the same thing now. There's an effort to put fluoride in the New York City water supply so as to improve teeth conditions so far as young children are concerned. It's the one automatic way of stopping tooth decay or checking and reducing tooth decay among children from, roughly, 3-years old up to 15 years old if the water carries it. The use of fluoride has no harmful effect whatsoever—at least that's the consensus of opinion among those well informed among the medical associations of stature and among the doctors and dentists. The Health Department is for it and the Board of Health is for it. On the other hand, there has been a tremendous organized movement against it, mostly led by cranks of one kind or another—the same kind of people who are against vivisection and who would fight that in the legislature, the same kind of people who would be against vaccination if that were a new problem coming up.

Well, at any rate, this fluoride process I'm sure is sound, and, although I get a lot of letters opposing it, I write to each one that I intend to support it. I think that's a sounder thing to do that just not answering those letters or to say, "Thanks for your letter, I'll give it further thought—" which is the easiest thing to write and which a lot of people do. I think Roosevelt—Theodore Roosevelt—handled things with complete directness. Then there is another quality he had that I try to have, though I can't say I have succeeded. He acted automatically on a moral issue. He didn't have to think and debate and worry what he should do when such an issue came along, because he followed his instinct; and his instinct was to do the right thing that he believed in. If an issue comes along where there may be political advantage in taking one side or the other and you try to debate it, it's awfully hard to think clearly because you have to weigh the political phase as well as the moral phase as well as the intellectual phase. But if you just make up your mind right away what to do, then your response can be automatic—and it's apt to be far sounder than if you try to give it too much thought; I mean, if it involves a moral issue. I don't mean this to apply if it's a decision that has to be made weighing various technical questions.

The game that Mr. Roosevelt played was to make up his mind and stick to it. People thought very often that he was hasty in decision. He was quick, decided, because he was *prepared* for a decision: and that's another thing I've learned from Roosevelt. When he expected to face an issue, very often he had made out his notes and had his answers, or even a formal statement, all ready—which sometimes he never even used—because he wanted to be prepared. I have found that a very useful thing to do: If you know that something's coming up, sit down and write out your own ideas carefully, in advance when you have plenty of time; then when the issue arises you don't have to give it much thought for you've already analyzed your own ideas and are prepared to answer the question when it comes.

There are lots of minor ways in which what I've learned about Roosevelt's techniques and tactics have helped me, but the main thing is that Roosevelt's soul has inspired me. It really has ... you can reason more clearly if you don't try to analyze all the petty phases of a proposition but settle it on the basis of the main issue—if it involves a moral issue. Then you don't have to worry any more. That's what Theodore Roosevelt did—I know he did. Time and again he says in his autobiography that he wasn't sure, when he decided something, but that it would end his career or that it would be fatal or arouse unlimited opposition—but he did it anyway. And it never did end his career, because I think people wanted a man who was ready to face issues and decide on their merits.

I think the same thing is true today, as a matter of fact. I think the people of this country are looking for a man who has the courage to do what he believes right and pays no attention to anything else. I wish we had leadership of that sort ... It's perfectly right to compromise on issues that aren't moral issues. Take these very minor things in the [New York] City Council. Something comes up, somebody wants to pass a resolution or something. You know the resolution means nothing; it isn't a law or anything else but just an expression of opinion in the Council. If it's not important you can go along with it because it means nothing. But if there's a decision you have to make where, for example, the Council is asked to pass a resolution with which it has no real concern, I apply this principle: I won't vote for or against a resolution, whether I like it or don't like it, if it's a resolution I don't think it's proper for the Council to enact. I record myself as not voting.

Because of local pressures, the Council people will propose a resolution urging Congress to do something that may or may not be for the good of the country. Even if I approved what the resolution contained, I would be recorded as not voting because it isn't our business to tell Congress what to do. It's our business to act on matters concerning the City of New York. If the problem concerns the city, we can properly pass a resolution: for example, asking Congress to pass a bill which would provide additional funds for housing of which we would get the benefit in New York. But if they ask me to vote on a resolution that says that this country should send arms to Israel, I would not vote for it, whether I believed in it; or if I were against it, I would be recorded as not voting because it isn't something that we have a right to express our opinion on.

I had great admiration for Mr. Roosevelt for inviting Mr. Booker T. Washington to dinner at a time when that just "wasn't done" in Washington, especially.

But he didn't invite him, I gather, to challenge the stupidity of those who were prejudiced against Negros. He invited him there because he was a great man, well informed, and he wanted to sit down at table with him and learn from him ... It was just an unconscious evidence on Roosevelt's part that he himself had no prejudices but he was interested in any man of stature, anxious to learn from him, associate with him and be with him—and of course, he paid no attention to his race or his creed or his color.

And—another thing that he always showed all his life—he wanted to help other people, especially the obscure and insignificant, the poet who didn't have recognition yet—Edwin Arlington Robinson was one and I think Arthur Guiterman was another. Arthur Guiterman never forgot those contacts, because it involved appreciation of his poetry; and the same thing, of course, was true of Robinson. I think that what you develop when you're young in the way of recognition of the traits and character of some men whom you'd like to imitate stays with you all your life. If you have the opportunity to carry on along those lines, you do it.

By and large you admired everything he did; because even when you disagreed you knew that what he did was a matter of sincere conviction on his part, and whether you agreed with him or not you respected his decisions. You never had the feeling that he consciously did something that he thought wasn't right. It doesn't make any difference to me what a man does if he accepts and lives up to really high standards. The fact that you may think he might have done something differently is less important than your recognition that he did what he was convinced was right. And Roosevelt was that kind of a person.

You were at the Republican convention in 1912, weren't you, Mr. Isaacs?

No. I was a Republican in 1912 and I was acting president of my club in my district; I followed the Republican convention with great interest; I was undecided at that time as to what I would do. The way the convention acted and, in my opinion, stole the nomination for Taft from Roosevelt convinced me that those in charge of the party were not acting honestly. Then I had friends who had already joined the Progressive Party, two young friends whom I liked very much. One was Lyndon Bates, who died on the *Lusitania*; and the other was Francis Bird, son of Charles Sumner Bird, who was very active in the progressive movement. They had both helped to organize the Progressive Party.

I had a letter from Francis Bird telling me of his talk with Roosevelt when he himself made up his mind to join the Progressive Party. He wrote me that he wanted to talk things over with me when I could see him in New York. It was in August of 1912, as I recall it that I finally decided to join the Progressive Party. I resigned from the Republican Club in my district and went into it. I did not go out to the convention in 1912, but I was a delegate to the Progressive National Convention in 1916. I was a delegate to the State convention in 1912 that nominated Oscar Straus for governor. That was a very exciting affair because there were two rival candidates. On was Mr. [William H.] Hotchkiss—I'm speaking only from memory—and one was Mr. [William Ambrose] Prendergast. Both wanted to be candidate for governor and the party was pretty well divided between them. At the convention some delegates became very excited and began to talk about Oscar Straus urging his nomination; then the convention got into line and nominated Oscar Straus, taking the control away from their leaders. Straus became the candidate and, I think, a very worthy candidate of the party. I had known him for years; he and my father had been very good friends.

From that time on I was active in the Progressive Party, but it was the bad handling and the unfair tactics in 1912, I think, that swayed me most. I felt that there had been direct primaries in many states—there were no such things as direct presidential primaries in New York—but state after state went for Roosevelt against Taft, so far as the Republicans were concerned, with a Republican popular majority of 2-1, 3-1, and 4-1. And even in those states anti-Roosevelt delegates were counted in as official delegates to the convention. Of course, the southern delegates were counted for Taft in the main, were corralled for Taft. There was practically no Republican vote down South. They represented nothing but the organized Republican machine. I am sure that if there had been any *popular* test in 1912 before the Republican convention, Roosevelt would have shown himself stronger than Taft overwhelmingly; I mean by a vote of 3 or 4 to 1. That was made clear on Election Day. When the election took place, Taft was a poor third. Roosevelt came in second, but Wilson of course, won ...

I did not go to Theodore Roosevelt's funeral at Oyster Bay when he died in 1919. I have always regretted it, but I felt that there would be such a mob there that I thought I would not join that crowd. But I did become a part of what was called the "Roosevelt Pilgrimage" that visited Roosevelt's grave annually on the anniversary of his death, until Mrs. [Edith] Roosevelt became so old that she could not act as hostess any longer. Those were most inspiring trips to me. The group that went there were almost the same, year after year, and included many of Roosevelt's closest friends. They'd take the train together, drive up from the station, go first to the Theodore Roosevelt grave where there would be a brief ceremony, a wreath placed on the grave, and then proceed to the home of Theodore Roosevelt at Sagamore Hill. Then they would gather in the trophy room, where someone would talk about his connections with Roosevelt and tell interesting and inspiring details. Usually, Mrs. Roosevelt would bring out some letter or some memorandum or tell some story that was usually off the record and quite secret but illustrated the kind of man that Theodore Roosevelt was. That, and just walking around the room, seeing the trophies and the books that belonged to him and all that sort of thing was tremendously inspiring. To hear those who had been closely associated with him, especially from the time he was president was very exciting to me. To meet with them year after year was to renew recollections and renew that very inspiration. It meant a great deal to me to be able to go down there.

I should think that, in the Centennial year [of Roosevelt's birth, 1957–1958], it might be a good idea to have a pilgrimage to the grave, on January 6 [the day he died].

I think it would be very sound. And I'm sure that not only all those who formally gathered together and went would go again, if they're still here, but a good many others would want to make that trip with them. It would be a very wonderful visit and wonderful parade of devotees and would constitute renewed inspiration. I should think that would be true.

PART IV

Brothers in Arms

CHAPTER 14

Roosevelt's Enduring Legacy: Frederick Trubee Davison

Fig. 14.1 Photo of Frederick Trubee Davison at Bolling Air Field (1926), Library of Congress

Theodore Roosevelt left an enduring legacy for the American armed services. His charge up San Juan Heights ranks as one of the most heroic episodes in U.S. military history. His children and grandchildren led their country throughout the "American Century." His eldest son earned the Medal of Honor storming the beaches at Normandy on D-Day. Two of his grandchildren led CIA interventions in the Middle East during the Cold War.[1] Successive generations of Roosevelts have served in the military or as cabinet secretaries, soldiers, and intelligence officers. Those who fought with TR, or his progeny, have often related an affection for that Rooseveltian idea of strenuous living and an adherence to American values. As fuzzy as these ideas might be, a set of devotees in the armed forces found meaning and guidance in Roosevelt's legacy. Frederick Trubee Davison was one such disciple.

Davison's upbringing closely mirrors that of Roosevelt's children. Born three months earlier than TR's youngest son, Quentin, and into an enormously wealthy and philanthropic New York family, Davison came from the same blue blood class. His father, Henry Pomeroy Davison led many of New York's largest banks and chaired the international League of Red Cross Societies. The family settled in Long Island, not far from the Roosevelt estate at Oyster Bay. Frederick Trubee Davison and Quentin became friends before they attended the Groton School for Boys. They both graduated in 1914. Quentin enrolled at Harvard; Davison enrolled at Yale, and as students they prepared for the coming war. Quentin went to Plattsburg, New York, where his father's friend Major General Leonard Wood had organized a summer training facility for war preparedness. Davison helped to organize the Yale Naval Aviation Unit to monitor and protect the Atlantic coastline.

Quentin and Davison's seemingly parallel lives deviated during the war. In the summer of 1917, Davison crashed his airplane in a training session and broke his back. After a long stint in the hospital, he returned to Yale and graduated in 1919. Quentin served with the U.S. Air Service in France, until 10 July 1918 when a German fighter shot down his plane and killed the young man. He was buried where his plane crashed. Quentin's death devastated those who knew him and Davison shares some memories of his friend in the oral history testimony.

Theodore Roosevelt died less than six months after Quentin, and Davison lost his childhood friend and lifelong mentor in those months. The Roosevelts had left an enduring impression, and after the war Davison sought to follow in their footsteps. Like TR, he attended Columbia Law School and served as a New York State assemblyman before joining the cabinet of presidents Calvin Coolidge and Herbert Hoover as Assistant Secretary of War. As a lifelong Republican, his political career came to an end in 1932 when the Great Depression spurred a backlash against Republicans and a wave of Democratic victories. When Davison ran for lieutenant governor of New York that year, he was roundly defeated, and never again campaigned for elected office. Instead, he took a philanthropic position as president of the American Museum of Natural History and, like Theodore Roosevelt, traveled to Africa on a scientific field trip as a salve to his political wounds. Davison's experience with military logistics and knowledge of aviation did not go untapped, however. After the attack on Pearl Harbor, he served as a special assistant to Hawaii's military governor and returned to Washington in 1943 to oversee the Army's aviation division. He retired as a brigadier general, the same rank as Theodore Roosevelt, Jr. and, after the war, Davison advocated for continued military preparedness, and specifically American superiority in air power. He joined the Central Intelligence Agency as its head of personnel before retiring permanently. Davison died 14 November 1974, less than a mile from Sagamore Hill.

Davison provides only a short reminiscence. Nevertheless, it gives a profound impression of TR's enduring legacy. Davison recalls a meeting with Secretary of War Henry Stimson, a leading figure in Franklin Roosevelt's cabinet. Stimson, a life-long Republican and proponent of American intervention on the side of the Allies, owed much to TR who appointed him Attorney General for the Southern District of New York and gave him a start in politics. Stimson went on to serve President William Howard Taft as secretary of War (1909–1913) and President Herbert Hoover as secretary of State (1929–1933). He joined FDR's cabinet in 1940, after the Nazis defeated France, in a political reshuffle that put the government on a nonpartisan war footing. As a late septuagenarian during World War II, Stimson was the oldest cabinet secretary and the one responsible for managing the greatest war effort of a generation, including oversight of the Manhattan Project. The war had taken a toll on Stimson, and he retired two weeks after the second bomb fell on Nagasaki. His career spanned two world wars, and provides a key link between the "Square Deal" of Theodore Roosevelt's administration to the "New Deal" of Franklin's. Davison remembers a meeting that Stimson called in 1945, attended by the nation's leading generals and civilian administrators of the war. At it, Stimson invokes the legacy of Theodore Roosevelt as inspiration for the war effort. It illustrates his deep affection for the former president and how that fondness was passed down from one generation to the next.

Harlan "Bud" Phillips interviewed Davison in 1951. The interview formed part of Phillips's work toward his doctorate, and this interview predates the Hagedorns' involvement. The content of the interview was relayed to the Hagedorns who reinterviewed Davison in 1955 exclusively on his memories of Theodore Roosevelt.

* * *

Could you please tell me about the meeting which Secretary of War Stimson held during the latter part of World War II, when he read aloud to the military and other leaders who were in Washington a speech about Theodore Roosevelt?

It was in January of 1945—which, of course, was at the height of the war, a few months before the defeat of Germany. I received instructions to be at the secretary of War's office at 12 noon. I couldn't imagine what that was all about, and when I arrived there, I found that there was a very distinguished group present. The ones whom I can remember definitely were [Chief of Staff of the U.S. Army] General [George] Marshall, [Commanding General of the U.S. Air Force Henry "Hap"] Arnold, [Commanding General of the Army Service Forces Brehon] Somervell, [Deputy Chief of Staff of the U.S. Army] General [Thomas] Handy, I think—I'm not sure about Handy. Then, on the civilian side, were [Under Secretary of War] Bob Patterson, [Assistant Secretary of War] Jack McCloy, [Assistant Secretary of War] Robert Lovett, [Special Assistant to the Secretary of War] Harvey Bundy, [Special Assistant to the Secretary of War] George Harrison and perhaps three or four more. I'm not absolutely certain that that is a complete list, but I'm certain that all those I mentioned were there—except, as I say, I have some doubt about General Handy.

Shortly after we arrived, Mr. Stimson came in—everybody stood up, of course—and still, as far as I know, nobody realized what this meeting was all about. Mr. Stimson then said, in effect, this: that today, that day, was the 25th anniversary of the death of Theodore Roosevelt, that Roosevelt was a very great man and Mr. Stimson thought it was a fine thing to stop and ponder on great men from time to time. He said that he couldn't hope to explain or describe Roosevelt to us but that he proposed to read a speech which was given in 1919 by [former Secretary of State] Elihu Root at the Century Club. [Stimson] then reminisced about Roosevelt at some length, read the speech and then reminisced some more. He talked particularly about his break with Roosevelt, how that was one of the saddest experiences of his life and how happy he was at the eventual reconciliation.

It was a most impressive thing to have done, and I think everybody who was present felt that way about it. In General Marshall and the civilian members of the War Department you had just about the busiest men in the world, and at Mr. Stimson's suggestion they took an hour out in the middle of the day to think about Theodore Roosevelt and his greatness.

Could you tell about the reactions of any of the men following it? I don't remember the speech that was read—Elihu Root's speech—but did it have a bearing on the wartime policy of that time in World War II?

I don't recall anything like that in Mr. Root's speech. It was an attempt by Mr. Root to describe Roosevelt as an individual—and it was a wonderful job. That speech, of course, you can acquire. That's on the record. One thing I should say, and that is that Mr. Stimson was one year off in his calculations. It should have been 1944. That was the 25th anniversary. I found out later that the reason for that was that he had thought about it before the end of the year and so was thinking about it in terms of the year that had gone by. But that didn't have any bearing, of course, on the moving quality of the meeting itself.

Did you feel that that meeting was definitely appreciated by all those men?

Oh, absolutely. I never talked with any of the military men about [the speech], but I talked with McCloy, Lovett, and George Harrison, and they all felt as strongly about it as I did. It was quite an emotional experience.

I understand you have a story in connection with Quentin Roosevelt's death?

It must have been in July of 1918. A Japanese Red Cross delegation was staying with my father, who at the time headed the American Red Cross. He wanted to take them over to Sagamore [Hill] to meet the Colonel. It was at the time that Quentin was reported lost, but nobody knew whether he had been killed, was a prisoner, or what had happened to him. I think it was in that morning's papers, or a day or two before, that General Pershing had reported that somebody thought they had seen Quentin level off, and that was the latest news that we had had in regard to Quentin.

So, we went over to Sagamore Hill—I went with this Japanese delegation and with Father. Alice Longworth was there. The ex-president greeted us, took us around the Trophy Room, explained some of the trophies and then made a very thoughtful speech to the Japanese. It wasn't simply a routine speech about "how nice it was to have you around," and things like that, but it was a speech that required thought, concentration, memory for dates and other things that meant he had to be thinking about what he was saying.

I had known Quentin and been a good friend of his. As I went out the door I said to the Colonel, "What hope have you for Quentin?"

He said, "Trubee, just 20 minutes before you arrived, I received this telegram from President Wilson." Then he showed me the telegram from Wilson that told of Quentin's death. It was one of the most extraordinary exhibitions of control and courage that I have ever seen.

Was there any evidence of a break in his armor of control after he showed you the telegram?

Well, he of course looked very tense, but he didn't break down. It must have been a very difficult experience for him to go through, with these foreigners arriving and having to entertain them in the way that he did. Mrs. Roosevelt was there but she never came down.

How did Mrs. Longworth seem? Because she evidently had had the news at that point.

She wasn't gay, but she was perfectly controlled and very gracious and acted as a wonderful hostess to us.

You mentioned knowing Quentin before. Did you have any other stories about him?

Well, there was an amusing little story about him that I happened to remember the other day. It was told to me by the late Judge William E. Luyster of Glen Cove, many years ago. This incident must have occurred around 1916, when Judge Luyster was a justice of the peace in the township of Oyster Bay, before Glen Cove became a city. I don't know why I remembered it as clearly as I do, but it was just one of those stories that you do remember.

Quentin had what we now call a "hot-rod car." He had rebuilt it to look like a racing car, had taken the muffler off so that it made a lot of noise, and one day was arrested for speeding—brought up before Judge Luyster. Judge Luyster said, "Young man, does your father know about this?" Quentin said, "Yes, sir, he does. And he told me that I was a disgrace to the family, that the Roosevelts were all law-abiding citizens and here I had gone and broken the law. He hoped that I'd be fined a 100 dollars and, if I was, I'd have to pay it myself."

CHAPTER 15

The Last Rough Rider: Jesse Langdon

Fig. 15.1 Photo of Colonel Roosevelt and the Rough Riders atop San Juan Hill (1898), Library of Congress

On 10 July 1970, Douglas Scott from Columbia University's Oral History Research Office interviewed Jesse Langdon in the subject's house in Westchester County, just north of New York City. As one of the last surviving members of the First United States Volunteer Cavalry regiment (better known as the Rough Riders), Langdon won glory in the Spanish-American War for his part in the charge up San Juan Heights. Theodore Roosevelt commanded the regiment, first as lieutenant colonel, then as colonel. The war took the United States from being a continental hegemon to a world power and, for Roosevelt, transformed his reputation as a New York aristocrat to a household name revered for bravery and leadership. He dubbed the charge up San Juan Heights his "crowded hour," and the battle was immortalized as one of the war's defining moments. Roosevelt received much of the credit, not least because he published a memoir of his time in Cuba. After the war, the Republican Party of New York enlisted Roosevelt to run for governor in a year when it seemed destined to lose. Roosevelt's name reversed the party's fortunes and he won the governorship. That brief military adventure in 1898 propelled a long political career, and Roosevelt remained forever grateful to the men of the Rough Riders as he ascended to high office.

Jesse Langdon, born in 1881, first met Roosevelt as a young boy in the Dakota Badlands, well before he struck national fame. Roosevelt had taken up ranching, and Langdon's father did veterinary work. The two would meet again in 1898 when Roosevelt put out a nationwide call for cavalry recruits to fight against Spain. Langdon answered the call and served as Roosevelt's orderly, putting them side-by-side during the invasion of Cuba and the charge up San Juan Heights. Langdon, only 16 when he enlisted, lied about his age and directly petitioned Roosevelt for a place in the regiment. Once on the front lines, Langdon witnessed numerous events later commemorated in Roosevelt's war memoirs. He tells of the charge up Kettle Hill and the death of Captain Bucky O'Neill, the Arizona sheriff who Roosevelt revered for "his wild and gallant soul."[1] Langdon's recollection of the sights and smells of war, the transport across the Caribbean, and the poor provisions of the regiment offer a vivid image of a volunteer army.

While much of Langdon's testimony about Roosevelt recalls the 1890s when the Rough Riders became heroes, he also regales the interviewer with stories of a colorful life beyond the war. Langdon joined Buffalo Bill's legendary Wild West Show in 1899. The show toured the world as a troupe of reenactors who staged scenes from the American frontier, including battles with Native Americans and rodeo feats of strength and skill. Langdon also enlisted in the U.S. Army to fight in the Philippine Islands. Despite his enthusiasm for an adventure in the Pacific, Langdon saw little fighting due to ill health and was decommissioned after a long recovery. Upon returning to the United States, he took up veterinary surgery, a profession his father had trained him for long before the Army or Buffalo Bill came along. Langdon spent two decades as a veterinarian, until his father died, and then gave up the family business and turned his hand to design and invention. He filed patents for a variety of commercial products, and used the proceeds to found a charity. He outlived all his fellow Rough Riders, passing away in 1975 at the age of 94.

Langdon's age and the many decades between his recollections were recorded raise questions about his reliability. In some cases, Langdon retrieves memories from 80 years prior. Journalist Clay Risen levels some doubt about Langdon's reminiscences, believing that it ranged from "an equal mix of reliable fact, truth-tweaking, misremembering, and flat-out fabrication."[2] Risen takes particular umbrage with Langdon's recollection of Bucky O'Neill's death, a supposed knife fight on board a transport ship, and his tale of boxing the British heavyweight champion in 1901. Yet, Risen uses many other parts of Langdon's testimony, in part because the authenticity of these stories has been verified by the accounts of other Rough Riders and, to some extent, Roosevelt's memoirs.[3] Exaggeration certainly has crept into these yarns and Langdon may have developed and evolved these tales at the annual Rough Rider reunions, where veterans retold their stories like fishermen tell about the one that got away. But Langdon's memories remain consistent over time—as do those of Arthur Tuttle, Frank Brito, and George Hamner, the three next-last surviving Rough Riders who Langdon outlived.[4] Their stories provide great color to the dry historical facts, a sensory perception to the "Age of Roosevelt." We can almost smell the odors of the bygone Wild West from Langdon's account.

This is the last collected testimony of the oral history project, coming almost 15 years after the first interviews with Roosevelt's contemporaries. And it differs somewhat. Instead of an interview with Hermann and Mary Hagedorn, Langdon met with a Columbia oral historian. Also, Langdon never read and edited the transcript to verify his remarks. Scott transcribed Langdon's statement from the recording, but did not share it with the subject to verify the accuracy. As a consequence, Langdon's transcript remains in his vernacular. The transcript has been edited somewhat to remove repetitive statements, digressions, in some cases the interviewer's questions, and the details of Langdon's time in the UK and his charitable foundation. Where the dialogue becomes conversational and inconsequential, edits have been made to retain focus. Contemporary syntax edits and paragraph breaks have also been added where his testimony naturally breaks. This makes the text more readable.

* * *

Mr. Langdon, I'd like to ask you how did you come to hear about the recruitment for the United States Cavalry Division [also known as the Rough Riders] which was forming?

The way I came to hear about it, I knew the war was impending with Spain and I asked my father if I couldn't enlist, that I wanted to help fight the war and he said no, that I was too young—about 16 years old at that time. So, I ran away from home and went to Minneapolis, Minnesota and enlisted in the Thirteenth Minnesota Infantry by lying about my age. I told them I was 19 and I was a big boy and I passed for it. Just after I left the recruiting office, they had an Extra on the street—an Extra newspaper, and they announced that Theodore Roosevelt was recruiting a regiment to go to Cuba. And I said, "Well, that's my regiment." So, I went back and told them I was only 16 and the Thirteenth took me off the roster and I proceeded to beat my way to Washington, D.C. That's where I first heard about it, in Minneapolis, Minnesota an Extra paper that stated that Theodore Roosevelt was recruiting a regiment.

Were you living in North Dakota at the time?

I was born and raised in Fargo, North Dakota, born at Fargo, North Dakota, May 11, 1881. I lived there all my life up until that time. I had finished my primary schooling and I had at that time one year in the North Dakota Agricultural College where my father was Professor of Veterinary Science. Of course, I ran away to enlist.

Were you thinking of becoming a veterinarian or running a farm?

I was raised in medicine. When I was seven years old, I could name every bone in the human body and when I was nine years old, I performed a neurectomy on a horse, which is quite a difficult operation. I was also trained in human anatomy and medicine and I practiced both in later years, after I got out of the army.

How long did it take you to make your way from Minneapolis to Washington, D.C.?

Well, I think it took me about a week. When I left Minneapolis, I left in a car loaded with shirts and of course it was very cold in that country in early April. That was just about the first of April—last of March, first of April. And I buried myself in the shirts thinking that I would get warm. But the shirts had been thoroughly cooled and it almost froze me to death. So, I got out of the shirts and commenced tramping around and whipping my arms around to keep warm and I had to do that all night. By golly, I couldn't stay still at all, because it was almost zero weather.

When I arrived in Chicago, I inquired the way to the Union Station. The fellow that I inquired of was in the yards in Chicago and he said, "Well you better—you'll be arrested," he says, "if you're caught here in the yards, if I were you, I'd get out of the yards. So, I said, "Well, where is it?" And he showed me and I stayed in the yards and went up there and there was a B & O train that I found that was a through train to Washington, D.C. I decided that that was my transportation to Washington. So, I climbed up on top of what they call the accordion—the hobos used to call it that—that's the vestibule between the two passenger cars and I hid up there until they got started. I rode that to the first division. I've forgotten the name of the first division. Of course, they located me up there and I was chased by the police and the yard men and the train crew and everybody else. But I managed to dodge around and climb onto the rods underneath the passenger coach. Incidentally, the rods are provided with trusses and the trusses have turnbuckles, they have two turnbuckles about three feet apart and a two inch by four, a two-by-four plank is through the turnbuckles to keep them from turning and I climbed up on top of those planks and that's where I rode [to] the next division. They didn't find me there. So, I changed from riding the rods and got on top and lay down on the top and had my fingers through the ventilator opening. They started to close the ventilator on my fingers and I was afraid I'd fall off. So, I had to climb clear up on the top and take a hold of each side of the ventilator section in order to stay on while it was moving. Then I rode what they call the blind baggage, the baggage car next to the engine tender. It has no door in it. I had heard that that was a good place for a hobo to ride so I decided I'd try that. So, I rode there, and I even went so far as to get into the water tank of the engine and I had there. Then I was afraid that they'd bring more water in on top of me so I climbed out of there.

I finally landed up on the division into Harper's Ferry, Maryland. I had climbed onto the cowcatcher of the engine—that cowcatcher was made of wooden slats and there was a hole in the top of it. I climbed down through that hole and sat on the cross chains that braced the inside of the cowcatcher. That's the way I came into Harper's Ferry. The engineer came down to inspect the bearing journals underneath the front of the engine and he spied me sitting there and he said, "Why, you darn fool," he says—only he used more violent language—"you'll fall off from there and get ground to mincemeat."

I said, "Well, I already rode the whole division here."

He said, "You get off or I'll call a cop."

So, I got off and ran into the weeds and hid. They unhooked the engine and took it to the roundhouse. A new engine came out and hooked on. In those days they always made a lot of fuss getting started. They would choo-choo and the wheels would turn and finally they'd get enough sand on the rails so the wheels took hold. I made a run and climbed on to that cowcatcher. That cowcatcher was made of steel and had a solid steel deck and there wasn't any place to hide. So, I was marooned right up there in front of the engine where everybody could see me as I went through the different stations. I decided that if I pulled into Washington exposed like that I'd land in jail instead of with the Rough Riders. When I pulled into the yards at Washington, D.C. the train slowed up and I waited until I thought it would slow up more, but it started to speed up, so I decided to jump while I had a chance. So, I jumped off and I lit on my hands and knees and turned a somersault and scraped the side of my face in cinders, and tore my overalls open over my knees. I was a sight to be seen. I had a black eye. But I walked into Washington.

Now, incidentally, two years before that I had been to Washington with my father and spent the winter there while he was preparing to become a Professor Veterinary Science at North Dakota Agricultural College. So I knew my way about. I had sent myself five dollars ahead and also my best suit of clothes had been sent by prepaid expense. I went down to pick up my clothes and they wouldn't let me have them without identification. So, I went to pick up my money order for my money and they wouldn't let me have it without identification because of course I was a horrid looking sight. So, I happened to remember a Negro barber up near the Pension Department, northwest there in Washington—near East Street N.W., that's where we lived while we were in Washington—when I walked into the shop he said, "Why, Langdon," he said, "what happened to you?" And I told him my story. So, he had me get in the bathtub and gave my clothes to his wife. She patched my overalls up and I got cleaned up. He took me down and identified me and I got my five dollars and my clothes.

I got dressed up and decided I would go down to the House of Representatives which was in session at the time. M[artin]. N. Johnson was our Congressman at the time and I knew him, he was a personal friend of the family. So, I sent my card in with a page boy and told him it was an emergency and I would like to see him. He came right out and he said, "What happened to you?"

I told him my story and said, "I wanted to enlist in Roosevelt's Rough Riders and they were recruiting here in Washington, D.C. and I wanted a letter of introduction to him, because it was hard to get into that regiment, or so I understand."

So, he says, "No, I can't do a thing for you until I hear from your father. Now, here's a book of franks. Take this book of franks and send a telegram to your father and leave enough franks with the telegraph office to pay for the answer and when I get his consent, I'll give the recommendation."

So, I went out into the street and here was an [newsboy] on the street [with the headline]: "Rough Riders Eastern Contingent in Washington, D.C. are leaving for San Antonio, Texas Four o'clock this afternoon."

"Oh, my golly," I said to myself, "I won't have a chance, what am I going to do?" I gave the address of the recruiting office there on E Street, next to the Navy Department and I went over there and started up the steps, and who should I meet coming down the steps but Teddy Roosevelt himself.

I walked up to him and I says, "Are you Mr. Roosevelt?"

He says, "Yes, Sir!"

"Well," I said, "my name is Langdon," and I told him my whole story, how I beat my way and the whole business and how I got there and darned if he didn't listen to me for five or ten minutes, because I gave him the whole story.

And he says, "Eh! Well," he says, "can you ride a horse?"

I says, "I can ride anything that wears hair."

"Well," he says, "go on upstairs and tell them I sent you." That's the way I enlisted in the Rough Riders.

That afternoon we loaded up to go to Texas and Roosevelt came down to the station to see us off. But they didn't swear me in. I didn't know that all they did was put you on the roster and it bothered me. And I was a callow country kid of course, so I went up and I said, "Mr. Roosevelt, they didn't swear me in."

"Well," he says, "Langdon, I'll tell you what to do. You go down to San Antonio and when I get there you come to my headquarters and I will swear you in personally."

And so, I waited, and so after we got to San Antonio I went up to the tent and knocked on the tent post in the center of the opening end of the tent. He was sitting there at a desk and he always had a bible on his desk, every time I ever saw him, he always had a bible handy. So, he says, "Yessir, Langdon! What can I do for you?"

"Well," I said, "you promised to swear me in when you got to San Antonio."

He said, "So I did, so I did!" That's the way he talked, you know. So, he picks the bible up and walks over and he says, "Come on around behind the tent, between the tent and the highboard fence here." They were in the fairgrounds of San Antonio and they had a highboard fence behind the tent. So, we went in between there and he had me put my hand on the bible and the other hand up, the left on the bible and the right in the air and he swore me in. I saw that he was having a hard time to keep from laughing and of course it bothered me. I didn't see anything wrong with what was being done because I thought that was the way it ought to be done. So, a week later I tumbled to the fact that it was fun for him because they called the whole regiment together and swore them all in at once. Nobody was sworn in, they were only put on a roster until we got to San Antonio and they swore us all at once. He just did that for fun, you know. But at that, I was the first Rough Rider sworn in.

Incidentally, after service in Cuba I was the last one sworn out, the last one discharged, because I was furloughed home from Montauk Point where we landed when we came home due to the fact that I had malaria. They forgot about me and I wasn't discharged. So, Woodbury Kane, my captain, wrote me a letter and said that the regiment had been discharged at Montauk Point and that I had better get in touch with the War Department and get my discharge. So, I wrote the War Department and they ordered me to North Dakota, or Dakota, it wasn't North Dakota at that time and I was discharged on December 7, 1898. So, I was in the Rough Riders three months longer than anybody else. I was the first one to enlist and the last one discharged. And that's a fact.

Do you remember what the trip from Washington to San Antonio was like on the train?

Well, it was just a dusty, hot trip, that's all I can tell you about that. The New York contingent was in K Troop and I was in K Troop because I enlisted in Washington, D.C. I was the boy that was sort of roustabout for them. I was full of energy and I was willing to help everybody. They would send me out to buy food at the stops and all that sort of thing. Outside of that there was no adventure on the trip, except plenty of dust and heat. That's all the recollections I have for it. When we got to San Antonio, they bedded us down in the Exhibition Building and the Exhibition was infested with tarantulas and scorpions and all sorts of wildlife. Frankly, I was scared but those fellows out west, they didn't pay any attention to them. But I couldn't sleep at first because I was real nervous about those scorpions and tarantulas and I couldn't get used he them.

Anyhow, horses were delivered to us at San Antonio and when the horses were shipped in, they notified the boys about it. I could outrun most anybody and I was the first man in the picket line. I looked them over quick and I saw [one] with a black mane and tail and I decided that was my horse. So, I ran in and unhooked a halter from the picket line and brought him out and jumped aboard and he commenced bucking with me. I was right in front of Teddy Roosevelt's tent. Well, I was never separated from a horse in my life except twice against my will and in both cases the saddle came off with me. And I rode to a finish bareback right in front of [Roosevelt's] tent. We drilled there for a couple of weeks. Of course, we all had wild horses—the horses would buck and everything else.

When we were ordered to Cuba, or ordered to go East, we loaded up … It took us three days to go to Tampa, Florida. On my way to Tampa, I happened to be a guard in the hospital section of the train. We allotted a double seat to each man who was really sick. On the end double seat at one end of the car there was a fellow who was quite sick. He was laying there with his feet across on both sides of the seat to add a little comfort. A fellow came in and grabbed his feet and threw them down off the seat and gave him a cussin' about why he was hogging the whole thing and all this sort of thing. This character was a man by the name of San Antone. He'd killed two or three fellows; he was a notorious desperado—we had quite a number of them with us—and he was a great man with a knife. Well, I had my carbine and I walked up and threw the carbine down on him, after he started to pull his knife, and I chased him out of the car. The next day I was off on guard and in the morning, I wanted to wash my hands and face. We were parked on a high grade next to a sluice and I took a basin and went down to the sluice and got a basin of water and set it on the steps of the car and started to wash myself. And this San Antone came up and kicked me in the face and knocked me down the embankment.

Well, I came out of that sluice punchin' mad and I just went up over those steps and when he tried to kick me, I pulled him on his rear and jumped up the steps and picked him up and I shoved his head through the window of the car and, of course, it cut his neck. A fellow by the name of Arizona Billy Smith came in and he was going to put a knife into me for picking on a man smaller than I was. [Henry] Hayward, who was the New York policeman, happened to be there and I guess that's all that saved me from getting carved up. So that's the way the incident ended. But this fellow lost his priority to go to Cuba. He never got there because these fellows that were too bad, they were left behind. That was my experience getting to Tampa, Florida.

When you were training in San Antonio do you remember any Indians [Native Americans] who were a part of the Cavalry Division?

Oh, a lot of Indians in our outfit. Yes, we had one in particular I should mention—Tom [Thomas Jefferson] Isbell. He was in L Troop. He was a man of indomitable courage. He was wounded seven times at Las Guasimas. Incidentally, the conditions under which he was wounded should be mentioned because it involves one of the bravest and finest men I ever knew and that was Captain [Allyn] Capron of L Troop.

When we were deployed at Las Guasimas, we were deployed to the right-hand side of the trail coming up a ridge from a place called Siboney. Out of the middle of a valley bordering to our right as we came up there was a projection, a precipice like projection, into a closed valley. On the top of that projection there was a blockhouse and on each side of the blockhouse there were trenches. The Ninth Cavalry came up that ravine, that closed valley and they had some pretty serious losses coming up there. But we of course came up the ridge and we outflanked the Spaniards. At this time, incidentally, [Colonel Leonard] Wood was in charge of our tactics. He and Teddy stayed pretty close together. He worked out this scheme of outflanking them and coming up on the ridge where they didn't expect anybody to be because we had a pretty stiff climb coming up out of Siboney. They wouldn't look forward to anybody coming up the bluff that we climbed in order to get there, so they weren't looking for us on what would be their right flank. We put them on the run and Ninth Cavalry and another Negro regiment, the Tenth, and I think the Thirty-Sixth white cavalry came up the ravine or valley and they went around the blockhouse to the right which they couldn't have done if we hadn't chased the Spaniards out of their trenches and blockhouse. So that is a brief description of the battle of Las Guasimas.

Getting back to the subject of Captain Capron and Tom Isbell: Captain Capron wanted to charge the trenches and the blockhouse to the right and he found a trail that went through an opening in the fence that led to the blockhouse. When he got to the opening Tom Isbell said, "Cap," he says, "you better not go through there, because they've got the range on this and they're going to pour it into it."

Captain Capron says, "Follow me," and he steps through and he took it right through the chest and was killed then and there. It made Isbell sore so he went through anyhow and he took seven bullets. But he stood up and the rest of them went through there. They lost about a third of L Troop there. Outside of that we didn't have any casualties to speak of.

K Troop, our right flank was exposed to the right flank of the Spaniards and we were ordered to advance to the right toward the blockhouse. We got into a jungle there, Spanish [bayonet plants] and thorns so thick nobody could get through and we didn't have any machetes, so we just had to sit there. We picked off a few of them while we were sitting there. But the main battle was fought by L Troop. The diversion made by the colored troops no doubt saved a lot of casualties, and no doubt we saved them a good many casualties by putting those Spaniards on the run. So, it was a 50-50 proposition.

How often did you see Teddy Roosevelt while you were at San Antonio?

Every day.

Can you remember any incidents of his partaking with you in the training?

Well, he gave his commands. He was a lieutenant colonel at the time. He shoved himself in everywhere he could to learn all he could. You know he was an active man. He was the greatest bundle of energy the Lord ever made. He got so that he could handle us in great shape. [Colonel] Wood, of course, was a trained regular army officer and he had a good pupil in Teddy. Teddy was looking for knowledge, he was that kind of a man. And he was the kind of a man who would listen to the most lowly person, because as he used to say, "You can get wisdom from the mouths of babes, as the bible says." He said that very thing. And he said, "I found that it pays to listen to anybody and if anybody tells you anything that you already know, just let them believe that they told it to you for the first time and figure that they're going to tell you something new. Because they might do it."

You got the horses at San Antonio. What other kinds of equipment did you get?

Well, we had the McClelland saddles, the regular cavalry equipment. Of course, none of the boys liked the McClelland saddles and some of them put their own saddles right on them, the regular cowboy saddles ... When we got to Tampa from San Antonio, we had to leave our horses behind in order to leave. And of course, Teddy was busy planning away to get us to Cuba, because he wanted to be number one getting there. So, he led us onto a coal train and ran us down to the harbor on the Gulf. There was a ship there called the *Yucatan*. It had been assigned to the Third Cavalry. But the Third Cavalry wasn't there and he just loaded us onto the *Yucatan* and when the Third Cavalry got there, there wasn't any room for them. Of course, that got the regulars kind of sore at us because he got away with murder. He didn't let any grass grow under his feet getting us there first.

How old were the people in K Troop? You were 16 ...

I was 17. I enlisted on the seventh of April—I went on the roster on the seventh of April and I was 17 [on] 11 May 1898. I was the youngest man in the regiment. We had men up to 60 years old in our regiment. They allowed them to enlist because they were notorious policemen and notorious sheriffs and notorious gunmen of all kinds and they didn't need any commanders to fight. They knew how to take care of themselves. And I'll say this: our whole regiment fought that way. And Roosevelt never undertook the usual methods of command. He just told us where to go and left the rest to us, because he knew that we'd take care of ourselves.

I was raised ... with a gun in my hand, too. I shot my first rifle when I was five years old and I could use any kind of firearms sufficiently by the time I was ten or eleven years old. Of course, I was raised in the wild west, too. Incidentally, my father was chief state veterinarian for the territories of both North and South Dakota and Roosevelt had bought some Texas cattle for his ranch up at Medora, North Dakota. His cattle were dying and Roosevelt came from the east and they called my father up there and that's where I first saw Theodore Roosevelt. I went to sleep next to a corral, I can still remember it. And when I woke up ... Dad picked me up and took me over and laid me on a dugout with a dirt roof and I went to sleep again there. The reason he always took me everywhere was I was the apple of his eye and he wanted to show me off. So, he got Teddy over and he shook me awake and he told me who this was. He said, "This is the Commissioner of New York your father used to talk about and you heard your mother talk about." And Roosevelt picked me up like this [gestures] and he wore glasses with extremely heavy lenses. And when you looked at him from your side it was like looking through the wrong end of a telescope. His eyes were about half their normal size. Well, naturally that's what I saw when I looked through there and it didn't make a very good impression and I said, "You let me down, you let me down," I said, "I'm no baby." My father used to repeat that often afterwards. So, he let me down. But that's the first time I ever saw Teddy Roosevelt. That was some experience. The next time I saw him, actually, you can believe it, I recognized him from that memory ... even though I was only five years old when I first saw him. That was about 1886. That was I think about the last time he went out [to North Dakota]. He lost his shirt on that farm.

The people in the regiment were very varied. You've mentioned gamblers and you've mentioned cowboys. A lot of your group, you said, came from the east, from Washington and New York.

Yes. They were prominent New Yorkers and every one of them had an athletic record of some kind. For instance, [Charles] Knoblauch was a champion swimmer. Knoblauch was from Yale University and he rescued, incidentally, two Negros from drowning when they were making a landing at Daiquiri. He also dove in and retrieved their rifles. In real rough breakers. He was quite a guy. There was always a little feeling there, because in this New York contingent, most of them were millionaires it showed what kind of men they were to take a chance with their lives in the front lines. They were the real thing and they would have made first class westerners. But westerners never did fully accept them. Because they picked out good, husky fellows out of the westerners and mixed them in the K Troop. Ultimately, it resulted in us westerners doing most of the hard work, the guard duty. I don't' know whether I should tell that or not, but it's a fact. But I don't take anything away from them.

Woodbury Kane was at that time the President of the American Tobacco Company, a multi-millionaire. He was our captain at the time we went into the fight at San Juan Hill. On the way through the cane breaks, prior to the time we got to San Juan Hill, he was carrying with him a sabre that kept getting between his legs so he took the belt and put it around his neck and hung his sabre over his shoulder. He said, "I'll tie this thing up so it won't get between my damn legs anymore," and he said, say, "Boys,

I'll tell you the truth, I'm scared as hell, but I've got to be a good captain and I'm going to be one." And he did, and boy, he was right at the head of the band all the way through clear to the top of the hill. No question about it, he had what it takes, if you know what I mean. It doesn't matter what your classification is, millionaire or pauper, if you've got what it takes, you've got the same status as a good patriotic citizen.

How was the crossing at Tampa, when you got on the boat? What was it like on the boat as you moved out?

The accommodations were very poor. They didn't' make up any bunks and we had to sleep in hammocks and, of course, the first night the men were tumbling out of hammocks all over the place, because they never slept in one. You never heard such cussin' in your life as those cowboys did after laying in a hammock. Then they didn't have any food and all we had was tomatoes and hardtack. And so help me, the hardtack had dates on it—1868! That's a fact, left over from the Civil War. And it was so hard you couldn't chew it at all. It needed a hammer to bust it up and it was hard to break it with your fingers. We used to put it in water to try and soften it up and it wouldn't even soak the water up. So, we had to chew and chew and chew.

But in a hurry, they loaded on about 20 quarters of beef that were embalmed by a special process that wouldn't poison a person. And we hung them all over the deck of the ship and we hung them in the saloon and everywhere else. Well, it was real hot weather and when we got out at sea, they commenced to swell up and they all exploded and we had meat all over the decks, and down to the saloon and everything else. I was cleaning meat up on my hands and knees in the saloon and Teddy Roosevelt come along and says, what are you doing down here? We've got deck hands to do this work. Well, I said, I thought I'd help clean up. He says, the deck hands will take care of that. He wouldn't let the Rough Riders clean up the mess. He made the deck hands do it. He thought it was their prerogative.

[The crossing from Tampa to Cuba] was just a long, hard trip on a starvation diet of unedible hardtack and tomatoes. That's all I can say about it. A lot of seasickness. These cowboys weren't used to the ocean. They didn't have a chance to hold much down on the trip. When we got there, they filled up on mangoes and all kinds of wild food in Cuba and that gave them all diarrhea. It was a pretty tough proposition.

What was the landing like? Where did you actually land?

The Spaniards had taken all of the planking off of the docks. All that was left on the docks at Daiquiri were the strainers. The surf was very rough indeed. We had loaded a few horses on for the officers. I've forgotten how many, I think five or six or seven. Only one horse was landed. The rest of them swam out into the sea, because when they saw the breakers why, they wouldn't go on in. It was only the fact that I had a fellow in a boat lead one that we got any horses there at all. This horse that was led in was ridden by Teddy Roosevelt up Kettle Hill as far as—well, it wasn't a blockhouse—it was an old hacienda, about half way up Kettle Hill.

Kettle Hill was a part of San Juan Hill and led into San Juan Hill. We either killed or captured all the Spaniards in there as we went up. They were the only Spaniards that had a chance to shoot at us, because Captain [John W.] Parker of the Twenty-Sixth United States Infantry was in charge of three Gatling guns. He had a squad, I think, of sixteen men with those Gatling guns. Well, the night before we went up to San Juan, why Billy McGinty and myself and some of the other Rough Riders took our pack horses that we had for some machine guns that we were going to use and we rode the pack horses on the pack saddles and used the pack ropes and we hauled the Gatling guns up to within range of San Juan Hill from the left-hand side of San Juan River so they could [reach] the trenches. Well, of course the next day when we came across the cane breaks, we had to cross San Juan River. Incidentally, in getting to San Juan River the regulars had put up a reconnaissance balloon and it made a beautiful target for the Spaniards and we lost quite a few men because they had to march under that to get into the river. But they finally shot the balloon down. When they got into the river and crossed the river and went up through the cane breaks toward San Juan Hill, the first man killed on the way to San Juan after we left the river was Haywood. This is the man that kept me from being stabbed aboard the train. Just as I came out from the river, he was ahead of me maybe 50 feet and when he was hit it sounded like you hit your fist in a pillow. He fell down and put his hand on his abdomen and he said, "I'm hit boys. Now, go ahead and leave me alone. I don't want anybody to stay here with me." So, we went ahead. He died later. Anyhow, we went on ahead and left him laying there.

The cane breaks had grown up to quite a bit of jungle, too. Occasionally, [we marched through] Spanish [bayonet], that's [a] sort of a cactus with sharp thorns on it. That wasn't nice to get through. We had to go about a mile through that cane break and we were under fire all the time. When we got to San Juan Hill there was a pond at the foot of the hill. It was at the confluence of San Juan Hill proper where it started and the foot of Kettle Hill. Intervening between the foot of Kettle Hill and the foot of the original San Juan Hill was a jungle growth, I'd say maybe about one hundred yards wide. A few of our boys went up the hill on the left-hand side of that growth and the rest of us of course went up Kettle Hill with Teddy on the right-hand side. Well, there was always more or less contention among the Rough Riders because those that were on the left side said Teddy never rode a horse at all and those that were on the right side saw him ride the horse. The fellows on the left side were wrong, but nevertheless he had dismounted when they first saw him because they didn't contact Teddy until they got up on the San Juan Hill. But that used to be a bone of contention among us at our various reunions.

Instead of giving orders, [Roosevelt] set an example. "Come on boys," and when we went up San Juan Hill, he was way ahead of us because he was on a horse, naturally, he got to the hacienda first and left him maybe 50 yards ahead of us and he went right on up the hill and he kept going and he crossed the trenches and I think he was on his way to Santiago. Three or four boys followed him and he finally stopped and looked around and found out he was alone and he came back to us. That's the way we went up San Juan Hill and that's the kind of command he used, "Come on boys, follow me," because he knew that was it for the kind of fellows that he had to lead, because he couldn't tell them much.

How long did it take you to get up the Hill with Roosevelt?

Well, I would say 20 minutes. Some of the colored troops were with us. They had I think maybe twenty-five or thirty cavalry mixed up with us and they also had a few of the Sixth white cavalry and a few of the Third that were mixed up with us. We didn't go up the Hill in any kind of alignment at all. We went up there like a mob, but none of our boys needed any kind of commands. They were out to kill; they were out to do business and that was it. They didn't need anybody's help and an ordinary command would have been resented and Teddy knew it. You know what I mean, they weren't the kind of fellows that you could kick around. We had a man in our regiment by the name of [Thomas] Hall. He was a young adjutant general. He was cashiered. Roosevelt said that he resigned from the regiment under section so-and-so. He didn't tell that he was cashiered, because the boys, a half a dozen of them, threatened to kill him when they got to Cuba and they would have, too. Don't think they wouldn't. He was afraid to come to the front and he ran to the rear and he stayed there. And he was cashiered for cowardice.

What were the Spaniards like?

Really, I'm ashamed to tell you. When we arrived at those trenches the Gatling guns had shot most of the Spaniards through the head. Some of them had two or three bullet holes through their heads and were laying there, and so help me God, they looked like kids about twelve years old. All of us boys kind of felt ashamed of ourselves, we really did. Because those poor kids had those jeans uniforms, blue and white striped uniforms made out of jean cloth, and they had rope soled shoes way too big for them tied on their feet and the ends of the toes were turned clear up because the shoes were so big for them, and those poor kids, several hundred of them, lay there dead. I don't know of a single man that was killed by a Spanish bullet going up San Juan Hill with the exception of "Bucky" O'Neill, Captain [William O.] "Bucky" O'Neill, from Arizona, and he was killed by a Spanish bullet because he stood up and the boys hollered at him, we all hollered at him, "Get down, get down!" That was after we got to the top. He said, "A Spanish bullet was never mortared to kill me," and he no more than gotten the words out of his mouth when he got a Spanish bullet through the mouth, came out the back of his neck, killed him dead, right on the spot. But that's the only man that I could swear I know was killed by a Spanish bullet. The rest of them suffered casualties due to the Seventy-First New York Infantry who were behind us and shot us up from behind. They thought that we were Spaniards running away and they didn't know that we didn't have uniforms. Some of them explained that they saw the bright orange capes pinned back on the shoulders of some of the regulars going up, the regular cavalry, and they thought they were the Spanish officers and they took particular aim at them and they killed several of those fellows going up there and a lot of our fellows. But the Spaniards had no chance because those Gatling guns invaded those trenches. Why, before we started our charge, we hollered to each other, "The gats, the gats, come on boys," and that's the way we started up the hill after Teddy.

The division that was behind you, shooting up the Hill at you ...

Yes, that was the Seventy-First [New York Infantry]. I think that Roosevelt didn't mention that [in his book] because he used to be a member of that militia. He let them occupy the blockhouse on the top of San Juan Hill when they got there. In his book [*The Rough Riders*] he tells the truth, that they occupied it. They occupied it. But he was a first-class politician, but he was sincere and he wasn't afraid of the devil himself, and he had what it takes.

Then we all dug trenches and [the Seventy-First] occupied trenches alongside of us. We occupied trenches immediately up on San Juan Hill above Kettle Hill. We dug a zig-zag trench out to a sharp-shooters' trench about 50, 75 feet long. Lieutenant [William] Tiffany, the son of William Tiffany, the owner of the Tiffany jewelry company, a millionaire, was in charge of the sharpshooters. He was a very fine shot himself. I happened to be a good shot and I was in the sharpshooters' trench. He called on us each individually to take a shot whenever we saw a movement over there so we had the individual pride in knowing who we hit and who did the shooting. Incidentally, he said, "Langdon, it's your turn." And they were leaving the guard about 700 yards away and I could see the tin cans bouncing on their backsides because they had their cooking kits fastened to [the] back of their belts and those Spaniards went across an opening there, they had to get into the blockhouse, and I can see them bouncing yet. But I come up there with my gun and I lay there for a little bit and pulled the trigger and nothing happened. I forgot to unlock my piece. So, I banged my head and unlocked my piece and a bullet went through my hat and shaved the hair on the back of my head. I only escaped because I forgot to unlock my piece. If I hadn't left my piece locked, I would have been shot through the head, you see. But Tiffany was right there and he exposed himself more than anybody in those trenches. He was a brave man, I'm telling you. There was nothing wrong with those New Yorkers, except they liked to see the other fellow do the work.

What was Roosevelt doing all this time?

Well, any orders that were given he gave us: to stay there, or to come, or so on. But as far as troop orders or open formation or anything like that was concerned, he left that up to the boys because they wouldn't have paid any attention to him anyhow. He knew his men, because he had a wild bunch, you know. You can't command the kind of people he had. They'd be insulted because they knew they could take care of themselves. You understand? You get to understand the disposition of that kind of people, you know.

Incidentally, they had issued shoes to us made out of cow hide and of course they got wet and then they got dry and they actually chafed us clear to our tendons. Half of us had to cut our blankets up and use them for shoes. When I went up San Juan Hill my shoes were hung around my neck by the shoelaces and I went up there with blankets on my feet. A lot of the boys did. That's something that isn't mentioned, but that's the truth. Oh, it was terrible. You could practically see my tendons through the skin. It was a terrible torture. I would say that a third of us had to do it. The rest of them had their own boots and shoes. They allowed you to do that and I was sorry that I didn't keep mine. The only part of a uniform we had, they issued us a double breasted, one hundred percent wool blue shirt, with the temperature at 115°. A lot of them had their shirts off and were stripped and had the sleeves of their shirts tied around their necks. Now, if they had a true picture of the Rough Riders going up there—they had one made by [Frederic] Remington. It shows Woodbury Kane in practically his right position. Relatively, it shows the position of everybody, including Teddy at the head. That's in Roosevelt's book. But that was a drawing made by Remington. But as a matter of fact, we were rags in tatters. We were a horrid looking bunch, I'll tell you that and we weren't very graceful walkers, because most of our men never did a step of walking in their lives unless they had to.

After a two week stay in the trenches, you said you moved to El Caney?

El Caney, yes. Well, that's where we were when Santiago surrendered. And that's where I stayed. I took yellow fever there and then on top of that they quarantined me and I was under quarantine for a couple of weeks. We lay on the ground. That was our couch. Then they brought me back to camp after I got out of the hospital. Then I was afflicted with malaria. Then they wanted us to occupy Cuba. Teddy wouldn't stand for it. He made the War Department order us home. You'll see an account of all that in his book. Lucky he did. There wouldn't have been any of us left. We lost more men from fever than died in combat. So, he got a hold of the ship the *Miami*. The ballast in the *Miami* had shifted and all the way across back to the United States it had a list of I'd say, 10 or 15 degrees. When it was rough you could hardly walk on the deck. When they got to Montauk Point, I was very sick and I think they really thought I was going to die. I didn't stay there. I was furloughed home. But they followed me home and they asked me if I thought I was going to be able to get there and I said, you bet. I had picked up a Krag[-Jørgensen rifle] out of the battlefield that I didn't turn in. And I kept that and took it home with me ... I took that back to Fargo with me and hunted with it for years.

Do you remember anyone else aside from Maverick who was in the hospital with you?

Let me see. No, I tell you, I don't. I wasn't really myself. I'll tell you one thing though. Teddy Roosevelt came in and the sweat on his brow, and his face was as red as fire, and me with yellow fever. And he came into the hospital tent and he says, "Langdon—I was temporarily in my right mind—how are you getting along?" Now, they never quarantined him for coming in there. I've always thought about that. But he did actually come into the tent while I was down and in and out of consciousness with yellow fever. He was that kind of guy. He wasn't afraid of anything. And his men came first. And he knew how to handle them and he knew how to pick them. Don't think he didn't.

What was the countryside like at the time in Santiago? How were the Cubans living?

Well, the Cubans were camping out in the jungle. They had dilapidated rifles. They were ragamuffins and they were conspicuous by their absence when the fighting came up. They never did help us a bit. They were on the run. They came up after the battle was won.

What were the living conditions like? It's been reported in history books that it was terrible squalor, poverty and these kinds of things.

Oh, yes. They were eating snake meat and the beef that we got in cans, we could hardly eat it. It wasn't beef, it was canned horse. We traded that canned horse when we got any and we thought we were getting chicken. Instead of that we found out that we were getting boa constrictor. It was delicious. Nice white meat and it tasted like chicken. I know some of the boys would rather starve on the canned horse. It was really funny when they found that they were eating snake meat.

Roosevelt claims in his book that we were taken care of, but we were, to the best of his ability. But I tell you right now, it was a pretty slim fare and everybody down with dysentery and malaria. The living conditions were something terrible.

So how long were you in Santiago before you were shipped out?

I wasn't in Santiago at all. I stayed in El Caney at the hospital [for several] weeks, two or three weeks.

I boarded the ship *Miami*. I went through Santiago to get to the ship. It's where we got on the ship [to go home]. Incidentally, Roosevelt loaded a couple of those bronze cannons from Santiago on there and had them melted up into medals. I've got one of the medals, I can show you. He sent me a medal in December; it's engraved on the back here.

Once back in the United States, where did you go?

I went to Montauk Point. I didn't stay there. I was furloughed home. I don't know anything about anything that happened there because I left the same day we got there.

My trip home was sort of a dream. I wasn't halfway in my right mind and I was nauseated. I had malaria with all the usual chills and fever and nausea and of course I had that on the train coming home. I couldn't tell you much about the trip outside of that because it was one of more or less suffering. You know you don't have any recollections when you are as sick as I was.[5]

When you arrived home in North Dakota, what was your father's first reaction?

My father's first reaction? Well, he was pretty proud of me. That was his first reaction. That's all I can say about it. He never quit bragging about it, my being a Rough Rider. Oh, incidentally, just before we left Washington, D.C.—I'm harking back now—a telegram came from my father to Theodore Roosevelt and he read it to all of us when he gave us our departing speech in his office in the Navy Department. He read my father's letter and he was proud to have me in his regiment. And it had his full consent. Sixteen years old. Well, I was 17 when I returned home. We were only in about 90 days—that is in active service. Of course, I was in three months extra as I explained to you.

Upon your return home what did you do then? What kind of job did you get?

Well, I went back to the Agricultural College, but I never did graduate. It wasn't necessary. I took over my father's practice. He got sick and I took over his veterinary practice and also practiced as a physician wherever it was necessary. Then I moved to Omaha, Nebraska. I practiced as a veterinary surgeon and physician in Nebraska. Then I moved to Washington and did the same thing later on. All together, I practiced 18 years as a physician and veterinary surgeon. I used to perform all the usual surgery only known in the book. I used to love surgery, because I could handle anything.

After being a veterinarian, what did you do, after practicing?

Well, as long as my father was alive, I remained a veterinary surgeon and physician, because Dad always said, "The reason I made a veterinary surgeon and physician out of you is so you could always make a living." He said, "Your so-and-so grandfather on your mother's side was nothing but an inventor and he was drunk most of his life," and he said, "I want to make something out of you so that you can make a living." Well, as soon as my father died, then I quit the veterinary business and entered into invention as a profession. And I have 189 United States patents. And I have sold and marketed sixty-two of them, which is a world's record. The United States Patent Office statistics show that only one patent out of one thousand is ever commercialized. I commercialized sixty-two out of 189 and I gave to this Foundation $417,000 in cold cash.

What type of things were you inventing?

Well, I invented in all different categories. Mostly valves because that's where I made the most money. But I've invented anything and everything that you can think of, from special shoes and shoe attachments for people, to hair curlers, and anything you can think of. Where I thought I could make something a little better, I invented it. I'll give you a list. That's the easiest way to tell you. I've got a list here and I can give it to you.

Did you serve in the First World War?

No sir, I didn't. In the first place, I couldn't have enlisted if I had wanted to, because I lost my right lung in the Philippines. I re-enlisted later and went to the Philippines. Before I entered in this veterinary practice. Right after I was a Rough Rider. First thing I did was to go with a wild west show.

Well, the wild west show came to Fargo after I'd come back from the west recovering from my malaria and all that. I had met the advance man, Burke, before the show got there and I said, "I would like to enter the wild west show when it gets here, how about a recommendation?" He said, "I'll tell them to hire you." So, when the show got there I went down and Johnny Baker was in charge of the show at that time. Buffalo Bill, of course, was manager and with them, owner of the show. Johnny Baker said, "Well I tell you, we have a horse here called Blue Dog. If you can stay with Blue Dog to the end of the arena, why, you've got the job." Billy McGinty, my sidekick in the Rough Riders—he was in K Troop, and of course I've mentioned him—afterward, he was closest to me of anybody. So, he bet with the rest of the Rough Riders that I couldn't stay with the horse. Well, of course Billy knew I could stay with anything. So he got $125 up among the rest of the Rough Riders. There were 13 Rough Riders with [the Wild West Show] at the time that I applied for the job. So, I got on the horse and he started bucking at the front end of the arena and when he came back to the back end, why of course the guy ropes while the bucking is going on ... so that if the horse bucks into the inside ... they can let go of them and they won't get in trouble. I noticed that Tom Isbell, who was an expert with a rope—he could do all kinds of fancy rope work—he could jump a horse or a man through a rope or jump through himself, or he could catch anything on the run, and all that—and by golly, my horse was going right for his rope and he was looping it this way and I said, I'll never get off this horse against my will and have to like it if I get looped by him. So, I'm going to dismount. So, I reached down and got the horse by the head and jerked his head around and threw him and lit a-running on my feet. I threw the horse; the horse didn't throw me. And Billy McGinty won his money.

When did you go back to the Philippines?

I went immediately after the wild west show. I rode the train. [The wild west show] used to winter in Massachusetts at that time. And they used to [go] through New York City. So, when I got my final payment, instead of leaving the train I got back on the show train and I took the show train clear through to New York. Incidentally, on the way to New York I had quite an adventure. I had to get off the train to get something to eat. So, all I could find was pie. The train was stopped there only 20 minutes and I went into a place and I bought an apple pie, one of the best I ever ate. And I gave the woman a bill and among the change she gave me a quarter that didn't look right. After I got on the train and looked at it, I saw it was dated 1925. So, I put that quarter in a pocket that I never used, because there was a hole through it and I had put a patch on the other side of the pocket and of course there was a space between the patch and the pocket and I put the quarter in there and forgot about it. When I got to New York of course I wanted adventure and I heard that the surest way to get adventure was to show your roll in one of those New York dives down on the Bowery. So, I made for the Bowery. I wanted adventure and I didn't care how it came. I went into a basement saloon and there was a man sitting at a table with a woman. I went over the table and said, "Do you mind if I sit down here?"

And he said, "No of course not."

"Will you have a drink with me," I said.

"Oh, have one with us."

"Oh, no, I'll pay for it," I said, and of course I had a big bunch of ones and twos—twos were popular in those days—but on the outside of it I had a 20. I only had $150. I pulled the roll so they could see it.

He said "Bring him a good one."

"Well," I said, "I'm just drinking beer."

"Well, that's all right, we've got special beer."

So, they brought the beer and instead of sipping it I put it down the hatch like that and in two seconds, that's all I remember until the next morning. Mickey Finn. I woke up in an alley—no shoes, everything gone except my pants. In November. Well, I was almost close to death and I had vomited and I was laying in it. I was between two buildings that looked a mile high and they weren't over that far apart. I was out in this alley, they threw me out there and by golly, I got up and staggered around a while and felt my pockets. There I was. I went out on the street and I thought everybody would be looking at me and by Jove, I felt that quarter down in my pocket. I pulled that out and I said, "By golly, that's an heirloom." I saw three bells hanging out in front of a place and I went in there and I said, "I've got an old heirloom here and it's worth $100."

He said, "I'm not interested."

"Oh, yes," I said, "it's a 1925 quarter," and I showed it to him, the Jew who was running the place.

"Oh, that," he said, "I'll give you 50 cents."

I never will forget that. "Oh well," I said, "forget it." And I started to put it back in my pocket and I bargained with him and he finally offered me five dollars for that quarter.

So, I went into a Turkish bath and to a Negro there I said, "Look, here's five dollars." I gave him my five dollars and I said, "when I was on the street, I noticed shoes there with elastic in the side for a dollar and a quarter a pair. And I noticed underwear for 25 or 30 cents apiece." In those days, those were the prices. "You go out and buy that for me and" I said, "you have enough money left, I'd like to have a little left, why, maybe you can pick me up a secondhand coat or something and a shirt." And by golly, if he didn't come back and give me a dollar and 75 cents and everything I asked for. So, I got dressed up and I made for the nearest recruiting station and I enlisted to go to the Philippines.

Then I happened to think about Captain Woodbury Kane. He said "If ever you're in New York, I live at the Knickerbocker Club. You call me up." So, I called him up at the Knickerbocker Club. He was there and he said, "Oh, Langdon, come on down and have supper with me. Be sure and come. I'll have some of the other boys in New York here that you know. Come over here and we'll have a visit." So, I went up to the Knickerbocker Club and I was never in a place like that before in my life. We spent a very pleasant evening. He said, "I'm taking a cruise to India on my yacht and I want to hire you as a steward, that is, ostensibly." He said "You won't be a steward; you'll be with us in the first cabin. But I presume you'd like to have some wages and I'll pay you as a steward."

I said, "Listen. I've already reenlisted to go to the Philippines and I want to see a part of that fracas."

"Well," he said, "I'll buy you out. Give me the phone," he says, "and I'll call them up and buy him out."

I said, "No, I won't be bought out. I want to see service in the Philippines." So that's when I started for the Philippines, after I left him. I went to the Presidio. And, incidentally, the drill sergeant at the Presidio—I got a little absent-minded and I didn't hear what he said and I was marching right off alone. A fellow come and grabbed me by the arm and he said, "What in the hell is the matter with you?" "Oh," he said, "for so-and-so's sake, if it ain't Jesse Langdon. Don't you know me?"

I said, "Sergeant [Frederick K.] Lie [of K Troop]." He was back in the army. And by golly I met Lie there in Presidio. He said "I'm going to be with the Third Cavalry in the Philippines and he said if you can get a transfer back to the Third Cavalry, why, I'll probably be a sergeant in the Third Cavalry, and I'll meet you in the Philippines." So, I started for the Philippines.

Notes

Chapter 1: Introduction

1. Michael Patrick Cullinane, *Theodore Roosevelt's Ghost: The History and Memory of an American Icon* (Baton Rouge: LSU Press, 2017), 127–8. For further examples of Hagedorn's role in shaping TR's legacy see pp. 22–6, 64–71, 135–69.
2. Paul Thompson, *The Voice of the Past: Oral History* (Oxford: Oxford University Press, 2000), 3.
3. Theodore Roosevelt Association Executive Committee Minutes, 6 May 1919 in Theodore Roosevelt Association Papers, Houghton Library, Harvard University.
4. *Throughout Roosevelt Country with Roosevelt's Friends*, directed by Hermann Hagedorn (1919), Theodore Roosevelt Digital Library, Dickinson State University (http://www.theodorerooseveltcenter.org).
5. Jerrold Hirsch, "Before Columbia: The FWP and American Oral History Research," *The Oral History Review* 34, no. 2 (Autumn 2007): 1–16.
6. Allan Nevins, *The Gateway to History* (New York: D. Appleton, 1938), iv.
7. Rebecca Sharpless, "The History of Oral History" in Thomas L. Charlton, Lois E. Myers, and Rebecca Sharpless, *Thinking about Oral History: Theories and Applications* (New York: Altamira Press, 2008), 10–11.
8. Allan Nevins to Hermann Hagedorn, 5 February 1943, Hermann Hagedorn Papers, Box 10, Folder: Nevins, Yale University.
9. Nevins and the Columbia Oral History Center collected the memoirs of Karl H. Behr (unpublished 1945), an interview with Murray T. Quigg (1950), and an interview with Frederick Truebee Davison (1951). Davison

mentions Theodore Roosevelt briefly in his interview with Columbia's Oral History Center, and Hagedorn reinterviewed him in 1955. Mary Hagedorn to Louis M. Starr, 22 June 1958 in Theodore Roosevelt in Theodore Roosevelt Centennial Commission Papers, Box 44, Folder 44, Sagamore Hill NPS Archives.

10. The Theodore Roosevelt Memorial Association saw the partnership with the Columbia Oral History Center as a natural extension of its work to revive Roosevelt in the public imagination. Assistant Director of the Theodore Roosevelt Centennial Commissions said that "it requires where we work with organizations" like the Center, "that the material provided be related to their own programs." Sidney Wallach to Theodore Roosevelt Memorial Association, 15 January 1957 in Executive Committee Minutes, Theodore Roosevelt Association Papers, Houghton Library, Harvard University.
11. Harlan Phillips conducted several interviews and served as Nevins's lieutenant until 1965. He published the reminiscences of Supreme Court Justice Felix Frankfurter in 1960. Louis Starr later became the "patriarch of oral history" as one friend called him. Starr succeeded Nevins as director of the Columbia Center until his death in 1980. *Felix Frankfurter Reminisces: Recorded in Talks with Harlan B. Phillips* (New York: Doubleday, 1960); "Louis Starr: A Remembrance," *The Oral History Review* 8 (1980): 93–7.
12. Alice Roosevelt Longworth, recording 4153–side 2, Theodore Roosevelt Birthplace, New York.
13. Ibid.
14. Alice Roosevelt Longworth, recording 4153–side 1, Theodore Roosevelt Birthplace, New York.
15. Ibid.
16. The files were digitized by Marc Hess at Dataworks in New York City. I am most grateful to Marc and NPS curator Daniel Prebutt who coordinated efforts to modernize the recordings.
17. Cullinane, *Theodore Roosevelt's Ghost*, 80–135.
18. Theodore Roosevelt Association Executive Committee Minutes, 27 October 1945, 17 September 1946, 27 October 1947, and 16 March 1948 in Theodore Roosevelt Association Papers, Houghton Library, Harvard University; Elting E. Morison (ed.) et al, *The Letters of Theodore Roosevelt*, 8 vols. (Cambridge, MA: Harvard University Press, 1951–1954).
19. Kathleen Dalton, "Theodore Roosevelt and the Progressive Era" in Christopher M. Nichols and Nancy Unger, *A Companion to the Gilded Age and Progressive Era* (Malden, MA: John Wiley and Sons, 2017), 289–9.
20. Cullinane, *Theodore Roosevelt's Ghost*, 131.

21. Theodore Roosevelt Association Executive Committee Minutes, 23 December 1947 and 16 March 1949 in Theodore Roosevelt Association Papers, Houghton Library, Harvard University; Carleton Putnam, *Theodore Roosevelt: The Formative Years, 1858–1886* (New York: Charles Scribner's Sons, 1948). Incidentally, Mary Hagedorn worked on both projects. Her father promoted her to the team of academics gathering correspondence for the eight volumes of letters and to O'Laughlin who hired her as a research assistant. The jobs made Mary a TR expert in her own right. Mary Hagedorn to Hermann and Dorothy Hagedorn, 17 February 1948, 13 October 1948, and 3 December 1948 in Hermann Hagedorn Papers, Box 5, Folder: Hagedorn, Mary, Yale University.
22. U.S. Senate, Doc. no. 36, Final Report of the Theodore Roosevelt Centennial Commission, 86th Cong., 1st sess. (1959), 7.
23. John Higham, "The Cult of the American Consensus: Homogenizing Our History," *Commentary*, February 1, 1959.
24. Cullinane, *Theodore Roosevelt's Ghost*, 130–5.
25. Frederick Trubee Davison, transcript, Columbia University Center for Oral History.
26. Howard K. Beale, *Theodore Roosevelt and the Rise of America to World Power* (Baltimore: Johns Hopkins Press, 1956), vii–viii, xi.
27. William Savacool, transcript, Columbia University Center for Oral History.
28. Bertrand Russell in John Herman Randall and Horace Holley (eds.) *World Unity: Interpreting the Spirit of the New Age* (1931), 190.
29. For a considered analysis on oral history and memory, see Sandy Polishuk, "Secrets, Lies, and Misremembering: The Perils of Oral History Interviewing," *Frontiers: A Journal of Women Studies* 19, no. 3 (1998): 14–23; Sandy Polishuk, "Secrets, Lies, and Misremembering: Take II," *Oral History Review* 32, no. 2 (2005): 51–8. For a critical analysis of individual perception, see Eric Schwitzgebel, *Perplexities of Consciousness* (Cambridge, MA: MIT Press, 2011).
30. Ezra P. Prentice, recording 4154–side 1, Theodore Roosevelt Birthplace, New York.
31. Samuel McCune Lindsay, transcript, Columbia University, New York.
32. Geoffrey C. Ward, *A First Class Temperament: The Emergence of Franklin Roosevelt* (New York: Harper Perennial, 1989), 247.
33. William J. Mann, *The Wars of the Roosevelts: The Ruthless Rise of America's Greatest Political Family* (New York: Harper Perennial, 2016), 147. At no point does Mann mention Elliott's illness or Tadd's visits with family members.
34. Mrs. Longworth jokes with Mary Hagedorn that she would like to do an indiscreet interview, telling family secrets. One can only imagine what it might sound like given the volume of indiscretions she mentions.

35. Alice Roosevelt Longworth, recording 4153–side 2, Theodore Roosevelt Birthplace, New York.
36. Alice Roosevelt Longworth, 4152–side 1, Theodore Roosevelt Birthplace, New York.
37. August Munn Tilney, transcript, Sagamore Hill NPS Archives, New York.
38. Ibid.
39. Marian Knight Garrison, transcript, Sagamore Hill NPS Archives, New York.
40. Three recordings do not appear in the book: Mary Bissell's, Helen Sargant Hitchcock's, and Judge Philip J. McCook's. Bissell's and Hitchcock's are similar in many ways to Georgiana Far Sibley who also lived next door to Corinne Roosevelt Robinson. The outlier is the recording of Judge Philip J. McCook. The 33-minute tape recording was spliced over two reels, making the procession of the interview unclear. The Judge refers to TR's inauguration, but otherwise makes similar observations to other participants.
41. Morison et al, *Letters*, vol. 1 (1951), xv.
42. Hermann Hagedorn to William Sheffield Cowles and Margaret Krech Cowles, recording 4150–side 1, Theodore Roosevelt Birthplace, New York.
43. Betty Boyd Caroli, *The Roosevelt Women* (New York: Basic Books, 1998), 17.
44. "Hermann Hagedorn, Biographer of Theodore Roosevelt, Is Dead," *New York Times*, 28 July 1964.
45. U.S. Senate, Doc. no. 36, Final Report of the Theodore Roosevelt Centennial Commission, 86th Cong., 1st session (1959), 7, 13–46.
46. Mary Hagedorn to Corinne Robinson Alsop, 22 March 1955 in Theodore Roosevelt Association Records, Box 88, Sagamore Hill NPS Archives.
47. Mary Hagedorn to Mrs. Marie Bissell, 20 June 1955 in Theodore Roosevelt Association Records, Box 88, Sagamore Hill NPS Archives.
48. The book works off Donald Ritchie's maxim that "cutting away tangential material [is] appropriate so long as the original meaning is retained. The goal is to sharpen the focus without putting words in the interviewee's mouth or altering the essence of what was said." Donald A. Ritchie, *Doing Oral History* (Oxford: Oxford University Press, 2014), 129–30.

Chapter 2: The Other Washington Monument: Alice Roosevelt Longworth

1. Owen Wister, *Theodore Roosevelt: The Story of a Friendship, 1880–1919* (New York: Macmillan, 1930), 87.

2. Stacy Cordery, *Alice: Alice Roosevelt Longworth, from White House Princess to Washington Power Broker* (New York: Viking, 2007), 374–5.
3. Ibid., viii.
4. Daniel Prebutt to Michael Patrick Cullinane, 2 May 2019 (email).
5. Alice Roosevelt Longworth, *Crowded Hours: Reminiscences of Alice Roosevelt Longworth* (New York: Charles Scribner's Sons, 1933).
6. Cordery, *Alice*, 287, 310–11.
7. Michael Teague, *Mrs. L: Conversations with Alice Roosevelt Longworth* (New York: Doubleday, 1981), viii–ix.
8. Ibid., ix.
9. Ibid., xv.
10. Mrs. Cowles's letter to Theodore Roosevelt includes the story of Elliott's decline and, since 2019, can be found at Harvard University's Houghton Library in the Anna Roosevelt Cowles Papers. Despite recent claims that these letters have gone unseen until sold to Harvard and republished in the *TRA Journal*, Carlton Putnam and Edmund Morris (among others) have used the letters in their books about Roosevelt's childhood. Elliott's "condition" remains vague, yet what emerges (as Mrs. Longworth confirms here) is a sense that TR's brother had a disorder of some magnitude that required medical attention, but went untreated. See Gregory A. Wynn, "A Remarkable Cache of Newly Discovered TR Letters," *TRA Journal* 40, no. 1, 2, & 3 (Winter-Spring-Summer 2019): 7–10.

Chapter 3: From Hyde Park to Oyster Bay: Helen Roosevelt Robinson

1. Caroli, *Roosevelt Women*, 2.
2. Ibid., 67–182. See also, Peter Collier with David Horowitz, *The Roosevelts: An American Saga* (London: Andre Deutsch, 1994), 32–45, 74–97, 111–20.
3. Caroli, *Roosevelt Women*, 389.
4. Clarence Martin, "The Southern Heritage of Theodore Roosevelt" in Natalie Naylor, Douglas Brinkley, and John Allen Gable (eds.), *Theodore Roosevelt: Many-Sided American* (Interlaken, NY: Heart of the Lake Publishing, 1992), 35–44.
5. Helen Roosevelt Robinson to Mary Hagedorn, 11 December 1954, Theodore Roosevelt Association Records, 1979, Box 88, Sagamore Hill NPS.
6. When TR visited England in 1910, he asked if a politician would take him on a bird walk. Edward Grey, an avid ornithologist, obliged and the men struck up a keen friendship. In 2010, UK ornithologists commemorated

the meeting with a trail that takes walkers through the same forested area. "When Roosevelt and Earl Grey Paid a Visit on the Birds of England," *Literary Digest*, 8 May 1920; "Walking in the Footsteps of Former President," [Bournemouth] *Daily Echo*, 11 June 2010.
7. Mrs. Cowles was actually 45.
8. Biographers, including Hermann Hagedorn, have explained how Edith Roosevelt "hardened herself to the injuries the children sustained on their adventures with Father." On one occasion, she found Theodore bleeding from a head wound and told him to go bleed in the bathroom. See Hermann Hagedorn, *The Roosevelt Family of Sagamore Hill* (New York: Macmillan, 1954), 37–8; Kathleen Dalton, *Theodore Roosevelt: The Strenuous Life* (New York: Vintage, 2002), 134–5.

CHAPTER 4: THE NEXT GENERATION: WILLIAM AND MARGARET COWLES AND CORINNE ALSOP COLE

1. For the historical treatment of TR, FDR, Eleanor, and the wider family see James MacGregor Burns and Susan Dunn, *The Three Roosevelts: The Leaders who Transformed America* (London: Atlantic Books, 2001).
2. Marc Peyser and Timothy Dwyer, *Hissing Cousins: The Untold Story of Eleanor Roosevelt and Alice Roosevelt Longworth* (New York: Doubleday, 2015), 198.
3. Interestingly, Shef gets a phone call while interviewing with the Hagedorns in which it sounds as though he has been informed about his election as speaker.
4. Corinne Robinson Alsop Cole says nine or ten months old.
5. It is likely this is a different set to those mentioned in Chap. 1 regarding Elliott's illness. These letters likely refer to those in Eleanor's possession regarding the time Elliott was in Paris.
6. Martha Bulloch Roosevelt's mother's maiden name was Martha Stewart. According to a letter written by Anna Roosevelt Cowles, at 16, Martha Stewart married Georgia Senator John Elliott. When he died (1827), she later married her stepson-in-law James Bulloch, Sr.
7. Howard K. Beale, "Theodore Roosevelt's Ancestry: A Study in Heredity," New York Genealogical and Biographical Record 85, no. 4 (October 1954): 196–205.

Chapter 5: First Lady of the World: Anna Eleanor Roosevelt

1. On these and other accomplishments, see Hazel Rowley, *Franklin and Eleanor: An Extraordinary Marriage* (New York: Farrar, Straus, and Giroux, 2010); Doris Kearns Goodwin, *No Ordinary Time: Franklin and Eleanor Roosevelt: The Home Front in World War II* (New York: Simon and Schuster, 1994); Mary Ann Glendon, *A World Made New: Eleanor Roosevelt and the Universal Declaration of Human Rights* (New York: Random House, 2002).
2. Eleanor Roosevelt, *Tomorrow Is Now* (New York: Harper & Row, 1963), 134.
3. FDR biographer Geoffrey Ward has explored other traumas, including emotional and sexual abuse. Geoffrey C. Ward, *Before the Trumpet: Franklin Roosevelt* (New York: Konecky & Konecky, 1985), 291–2. See also, Dalton, *Theodore Roosevelt*, 140–2, 560n; Blanche Wiesen Cook, *Eleanor Roosevelt: The Early Years, 1884–1933* (New York: Penguin, 1993), 56–78.
4. Joseph P. Lash, *Eleanor and Franklin* (New York: W. W. Norton, 1971), 59, 61.
5. Cullinane, *Theodore Roosevelt's Ghost*, 84–7.
6. Wiesen Cook, *Eleanor Roosevelt*, 38–78; Caroli, *Roosevelt Women*, 233–90; Hagedorn, *Roosevelt Family of Sagamore Hill*, 27, 30–3, 40.

Chapter 6: The Scions of Sagamore Hill: Ethel Roosevelt Derby and Eleanor Butler Roosevelt

1. Hagedorn, *Roosevelt Family of Sagamore Hill*, 424.

Chapter 7: A Grande Dame: Georgiana Farr Sibley

1. "Grande Dames Who Grace America," *LIFE*, 26 January 1968.

Chapter 8: The Worst Friend of the Worst Boy: Barclay H. Farr

1. Sidney Milkis, "Theodore Roosevelt: Family Life," *Miller Center, University of Virginia* (https://millercenter.org).
2. For examples of this see Kay Redfield Jamison, *Exuberance: The Passion for Life* (New York: Vintage Books, 2004), 3–21; John Milton Cooper, *The Warrior and the Priest: Woodrow Wilson and Theodore Roosevelt* (Cambridge, MA: Belknap Press, 1983).

3. Ryan Swanson, *The Strenuous Life: Theodore Roosevelt and the Making of the American Athlete* (New York: Diversion Books, 2019), 81–2.

Chapter 9: The Political Backroom: William M. Chadbourne

1. For and excellent treatment of New York politics and the machines, see Terry Golway, *Machine Made: Tammany Hall and the Creation of Modern American Politics* (New York: W. W. Norton, 2014).
2. Nicolas Lemann, "Hating on Herbert Hoover," *New Yorker*, 16 October 2017.

Chapter 10: That Tammany Boy: Henry Root Stern, Sr.

1. Golway, *Machine Made*, 10–37, 132–77.

Chapter 11: Secondhand Memories: Murray T. Quigg

1. Edmund Morris, *The Rise of Theodore Roosevelt* (New York: Random House, 2010), 487.
2. Ibid., 730.
3. Quigg and Roosevelt had a falling out in 1885 or 1886 when Roosevelt sought to close public houses on Sundays to comply with city statutes. Quigg disagreed and believed the row had ended his friendship with Roosevelt. That proved untrue. Ibid., 529.

Chapter 12: The Account of a College Man: Karl H. Behr

1. "Clemenceau Pleads for Col. Roosevelt," *New York Times*, May 28, 1917; Michael Patrick Cullinane, "Theodore Roosevelt in the Eyes of the Allies," *Journal of the Gilded Age and Progressive Era* 15, no. 1 (January 2016): 85–6.
2. The full unpublished autobiography of Behr is available at the International Tennis Hall of Fame in Newport, Rhode Island.
3. Behr refers to Booth as a senator, but he was mayor of South Pasadena.

Chapter 13: When Trumpets Call: Stanley M. Isaacs

1. Jacob A. Riis, *Theodore Roosevelt, the Citizen* (New York: Macmillan, 1904), 96.
2. Patricia O'Toole, *When Trumpets Call: Theodore Roosevelt After the White House* (New York: Simon and Schuster, 2005), 2.

Chapter 14: Roosevelt's Enduring Legacy: Frederick Trubee Davison

1. Collier, *Roosevelts*, 341–482; Hugh Wilford, *America's Great Game: The CIA's Secret Arabists and the Shaping of the Modern Middle East* (New York: Basic Books, 2017), 17–30.

Chapter 15: The Last Rough Rider: Jesse Langdon

1. Theodore Roosevelt, *The Rough Riders* (New York: G. P. Putnam's Sons, 1900), 136.
2. Clay Risen, *The Crowded Hour: Theodore Roosevelt, the Rough Riders, and the Dawn of the American Century* (New York: Simon and Schuster, 2019), 289.
3. One of Langdon's recollections about Roosevelt's glasses being shot off by Spanish troops does not appear in Roosevelt's memoirs, and one would think such a tale of heroism would have appeared in his retelling. Other recollections bear similarity with Roosevelt's account. Roosevelt's book *The Rough Riders* has received substantial review and scrutiny. While critics might class the book as a political memoir or grossly egotistical, critics have not challenged the facts as Roosevelt depicts them.
4. "Last of the Rough Riders," *Ogdensburg Journal*, 3 June 1971.
5. Roosevelt's memoirs account for the trip home and the treatment his regiment received at Montauk. Roosevelt, *Rough Riders*, 235–44.

Works Consulted

Manuscript Collections

Allan Nevins Papers, Columbia University.
Anna Roosevelt Cowles Papers, Houghton Library, Harvard University.
Hermann Hagedorn Papers, Beinecke Library, Yale University.
Hermann Hagedorn Papers, Houghton Library, Harvard University.
Theodore Roosevelt Association Oral History Project, Columbia University.
Theodore Roosevelt Association Oral History Project, Sagamore Hill NPS, Oyster Bay, New York.
Theodore Roosevelt Association Oral History Project, Theodore Roosevelt Birthplace NPS, New York, New York.
Theodore Roosevelt Association Papers, Houghton Library, Harvard University.

Books and Articles

Beale, Howard. *Theodore Roosevelt and the Rise of America to World Power*. Baltimore: Johns Hopkins Press, 1956.
Beale, Howard K. "Theodore Roosevelt's Ancestry: A Study in Heredity." *New York Genealogical and Biographical Record* 85 (1954): 196–205.
Bishop, Chip. *Quentin and Flora: A Roosevelt and a Vanderbilt in Love during the Great War*. CreateSpace, Independent Publishing Platform, 2014.
Brady, Tim. *His Father's Son: The Life of General Ted Roosevelt, Jr*. New York: Penguin Books, 2017.
Brough, James. *Princess Alice: A Biography of Alice Roosevelt Longworth*. Boston: Little Brown, 1975.

Burns, Eric. *The Golden Lad: The Haunting Story of Quentin and Theodore Roosevelt*. New York: Pegasus Books, 2017.
Burns, James MacGregor, and Susan Dunn. *The Three Roosevelts: The Leaders Who Transformed America*. London: Atlantic, 2001.
Caroli, Betty. *The Roosevelt Women*. New York: Basic Books, 1998.
Charlton, Thomas L., Lois E. Myers, and Rebecca Sharpless. *Thinking About Oral History: Theories and Applications*. Lanham, MD: AltaMira Press, 2008.
Collier, Peter, and David Horowitz. *The Roosevelts: An American Saga*. New York: Simon & Schuster, 1994.
Cook, Blanche Wiesen. *Eleanor Roosevelt: The Early Years, 1884–1933*. New York: Penguin, 1993.
Cooper, John. *The Warrior and the Priest: Woodrow Wilson and Theodore Roosevelt*. Cambridge, MA: Belknap Press of Harvard University Press, 1983.
Cordery, Stacy A. *Alice: Alice Roosevelt Longworth, from White House Princess to Washington Power Broker*. New York: Penguin, 2008.
Cullinane, Michael Patrick. "Theodore Roosevelt in the Eyes of the Allies." *The Journal of the Gilded Age and Progressive Era* 15 (1): (2016): 80–101.
———. *Theodore Roosevelt's Ghost: The History and Memory of an American Icon*. Baton Rouge, LA: LSU Press, 2017.
Dalton, Kathleen. *Theodore Roosevelt: A Strenuous Life*. New York: Vintage, 2004.
Glendon, Mary Ann. *A World Made New: Eleanor Roosevelt and the Universal Declaration of Human Rights*. New York: Random House, 2003.
Golway, Terry. *Machine Made: Tammany Hall and the Creation of Modern American Politics*. New York: W. W. Norton & Company, 2014.
Goodwin, Doris Kearns. *No Ordinary Time: Franklin & Eleanor Roosevelt: The Home Front in World War II*. London: Touchstone, 1996.
Hagedorn, Hermann. *Roosevelt in the Bad Lands*. Boston: Houghton Mifflin Company, 1921.
———. *The Roosevelt Family of Sagamore Hill*. New York: Macmillan, 1954.
Hagedorn, Hermann, and Gary G. Roth. *Sagamore Hill: A Historical Guide*. Oyster Bay, NY: Theodore Roosevelt Association, 1977.
Higham, John. 1959. The Cult of the American Consensus: Homogenizing Our History. *Commentary*, February 1, 1959.
Hirsch, Jerrold. "Before Columbia: The FWP and American Oral History Research." *The Oral History Review* 34, no. 2 (2007): 1–16.
Jeffers, H. Paul. *In the Rough Rider's Shadow: The Story of a War Hero—Theodore Roosevelt Jr*. New York: Ballantine Books, 2003.
Kohn, Edward P. *Heir to the Empire City: New York and the Making of Theodore Roosevelt*. New York: Basic Books, 2014.
———. *A Most Glorious Ride: The Diaries of Theodore Roosevelt, 1877–1886*. New York: Excelsior Editions, 2015.

Lash, Joseph P. *Eleanor and Franklin: The Story of Their Relationship.* New York: W.W. Norton & Co., 1971.
Lemanski, William E. *Lost in the Shadow of Fame: The Neglected Story of Kermit Roosevelt.* Mechanicsburg, PA: Sunbury Press, 2012.
Longworth, Alice Roosevelt. *Crowded Hours: Reminiscences of Alice Roosevelt Longworth.* New York: Charles Scribner's Sons, 1933.
Longworth, Alice Roosevelt, and Michael Teague. *Mrs. L.: Conversations with Alice Roosevelt Longworth.* Garden City, NY: Doubleday, 1981.
"Louis Starr: A Remembrance." 1980. *The Oral History Review* 8: 93–97.
Mann, William J. *The Wars of the Roosevelts: The Ruthless Rise of America's Greatest Political Family.* New York: Harper Perennial, 2018.
McCullough, David. *Mornings on Horseback.* New York: Simon and Schuster, 1981.
Morgan, Ted. *FDR: A Biography.* New York: Simon and Schuster, 1985.
Morris, Edmund. *The Rise of Theodore Roosevelt.* New York: Random House, 1979.
———. *Colonel Roosevelt.* New York: Random House, 2010.
Morris, Sylvia. *Edith Kermit Roosevelt: Portrait of a First Lady.* New York: Coward McCann & Geoghegan, 1980.
Naylor, Natalie A., Douglas Brinkley, and John A. Gable, eds. *Theodore Roosevelt Many-Sided American.* Interlaken, NY: Heart of the Lakes Publishers, 1992.
Nevins, Allan. *The Gateway to History.* New York: Appleton-Century, 1938.
Nichols, Christopher McKnight, and Nancy C. Unger. *A Companion to the Gilded Age and Progressive Era.* Malden, MA: Wiley, 2017.
O'Toole, Patricia. *When Trumpets Call: Theodore Roosevelt after the White House.* New York: Simon & Schuster, 2005.
Oyos, Matthew. *In Command: Theodore Roosevelt and the American Military.* Lincoln, NE: Potomac Books, 2018.
Peyser, Marc N., and Timothy Dwyer. *Hissing Cousins: The Untold Story of Eleanor Roosevelt and Alice Roosevelt Longworth.* New York: Doubleday, 2015.
Polishuk, Sandy. "Secrets, Lies, and Misremembering: The Perils of Oral History Interviewing." *Frontiers: A Journal of Women Studies* 19, no. 3 (1998): 14–23.
Putnam, Carleton. *Theodore Roosevelt: The Formative Years, 1858–1886.* New York: Charles Scribner's Sons, 1958.
Riis, Jacob. *Theodore Roosevelt, The Citizen.* New York: The Outlook Company, 1904.
Risen, Clay. *Crowded Hour: Theodore Roosevelt, the Rough Riders, and the Dawn of the American Century.* New York: Scribner, 2019.
Ritchie, Donald A. *Doing Oral History.* Oxford: Oxford University Press, 2015.
Robinson, Corinne Roosevelt. *My Brother, Theodore Roosevelt.* New York: Charles Scribner's Sons, 1921.
Roosevelt, Archie. *For Lust of Knowing: Memoirs of an Intelligence Officer.* Boston: Little Brown & Co, 1988.
Roosevelt, Eleanor. *Tomorrow Is Now.* New York: Harper and Row, 1964.

Roosevelt, Eleanor Butler. *Day Before Yesterday: The Reminiscences of Mrs. Theodore Roosevelt, Jr.* Garden City, NY: Doubleday, 1959.

Roosevelt, Theodore. 1951–1954. *The Letters of Theodore Roosevelt.* Edited by Elting E. Morison, John Blum, Hope W. Wigglesworth, and Sylvia Rice. Cambridge, MA: Harvard University Press.

———. *The Free Citizen: A Summons to Service of the Democratic Ideal.* Edited by Hermann Hagedorn. New York: Macmillan, 1956.

———. *Theodore Roosevelt on Race, Riots, Reds, Crime.* Edited by Archibald B. Roosevelt. Metairie, LA: Sons of Liberty, 1968.

———. *The Rough Riders, an Autobiography.* New York: Library of America, 2004.

Rowley, Hazel. *Franklin and Eleanor: An Extraordinary Marriage.* New York: Picador, 2011.

Schwitzgebel, Eric. *Perplexities of Consciousness.* Cambridge, MA: MIT Press, 2013.

Swanson, Ryan. *The Strenuous Life: Teddy Roosevelt and the Making of the American Athlete.* New York: Diversion Books, 2019.

Thompson, Paul Richard. *The Voice of the Past.* Oxford: Oxford University Press, 2009.

Ward, Geoffrey C. *Before the Trumpet: Young Franklin Roosevelt, 1882–1905.* New York: Harper & Row, 1986.

———. *A First-Class Temperament: The Emergence of Franklin Roosevelt.* New York: Harper & Row, 1989.

Wilford, Hugh. *America's Great Game: The CIA's Secret Arabists and the Shaping of the Modern Middle East.* New York: Basic Books, 2016.

Wister, Owen. *Theodore Roosevelt: The Story of a Friendship, 1880–1919.* London: Macmillan, 1930.

Acknowledgments

The oral history project owes its existence to Hermann Hagedorn, the unsung champion of Theodore Roosevelt's legacy and a tireless collector of Rooseveltiana. His daughter Mary also deserves credit for her attentiveness and professionalism. Together the Hagedorns have left this remarkable collection to posterity.

The current keepers of the collection deserve our thanks, too, especially NPS curator Daniel Prebutt who made it possible to digitize the recordings. Daniel carefully transported the magnetic reels to Marc Hess's office at Dataworks, some ten blocks from the Roosevelt Birthplace archive in Manhattan. Daniel loves the Birthplace and goes out of his way to share that affection. Other NPS staff were indispensable. Susan Sarna, NPS curator at Sagamore Hill, located files that had been moved from the Birthplace to Roosevelt's Long Island home, and Laura Dabrowski Cinturati, the Sagamore Hill Museum technician, managed to deal with my endless requests for archival resources. The NPS is a national treasure and people like Daniel, Susan, and Laura make it possible for us to better understand the past and how it matters for the future. Columbia University curator for oral history Kimberley Springer also facilitated the digitization of collections stored in the Butler Library and helped with copyright clearance.

The inspiration for the book originated with Ted Kohn's publication of Roosevelt's diaries, and other reference books like Elting Morison's *Letters* project, Hart's *Cyclopedia*, or Heather Cole's *Descriptive Bibliography*. I pick up these books more often than I do biographies and scholarly monographs, perhaps because I feel they bring me closer to the past. That is my hope for this volume. If it brings us closer to TR and the Roosevelt family, I will count it as a great success. My contribution to these reminiscences has been influenced and supported by a vast community of TR scholars and stakeholders, including the Theodore Roosevelt Association, the NPS "Friends" (of Theodore Roosevelt Island, Sagamore Hill, and the Birthplace), the Theodore Roosevelt Legacy Partnership on Long Island, the Theodore Roosevelt Center at Dickinson State University, the National Park Service and its many volunteers. There are too many people to name individually, but I must add particular thanks to Stacy Cordery who took the time to read through the manuscript with a keen eye that has made it clearer and more accurate.

Finally, it is the great patience of my wife and two boys that I owe infinite thanks. Without their support, so little is possible, or worth it.

Index[1]

A
Abbott, Lawrence, 213
Acheson, Dean, 47, 187
Adirondacks, 81
Albany, 53, 56, 139, 178–181, 204
Allds, Jotham P., 179, 180
Allenswood Academy, 77, 110
Alsop, Corinne Robinson, 11, 14–17, 36, 40, 50–52, 76–78, 88–89, 110–121, 125, 151, 276n4
Alsop, Elizabeth, 39
Alsop, Ian, 39
Alsop, John deKoven, 117
Alsop, Joseph Wright, IV, 92, 127
Alsop, Joseph Wright, V, 97
Alsop, Patricia Barnard Hankey, 39
Alsop, Stewart, 28, 39, 40
America First Committee, 27
American Committee for Russian War Relief, 226
American Jewish Committee, 226
Amos, James, 139, 164, 165
Anderson, Larz, 63
Arnold, Henry "Hap," 242
Auchincloss, Gordon, 221

B
Bacon, Robert, 213, 217
Badlands, *see* North Dakota
Baker, Johnny, 266, 267
Baker, Newton, 190
Barnes, William, 182
Batt, Meta, 136
Bayard, Mary Clymer, 63, 64
Bayard, Thomas F., 63
Behr, Helen Newsom, 212, 218
Behr, Karl Howell, 9, 16, 211–223, 271n9, 278n3
Behr, Sally, 16, 213
Bidwell, George, 207, 208
Bird, Charles Sumner, 234

---

[1] Note: Page numbers followed by 'n' refer to notes.

288 INDEX

Bird, Francis, 229, 234
Bissell, Mary Truesdale, 9, 12, 15, 16, 274n40, 274n47
Bombard, Owen, 20, 205
Bonnet, George, 41
Bonnet, Odette Pelletan, 41
Booth, Charles Beach, 213, 278n3
Borah, William, 11, 26–28, 78, 102, 107, 214
Boston, 54, 70, 83, 176
Brito, Frank, 247
Brown, Franklin Q., 213
Brown, Lathrop, 113
Bryce, James, 177
Buffalo Bill Wild West Show, 246, 247, 266
Bullitt, William Christian, 40
Bull Moose Party, *see* Progressive Party
Bulloch, Irvine Stephens, 115
Bulloch, James Dunwoody, 115
Bundy, Harvey, 242
Burgess, John, 195

C
California, 95, 153, 176, 177, 183, 213
Campobello, 59, 110
Canada, 37, 189
Cannon, Joseph, 35
Capron, Allyn, 254, 255
Carnegie Hall, 214, 216
Carow, Charles, 31
Central Intelligence Agency (CIA), 240, 241
Century Opera House, 214
Chadbourne, William Merriam, 17, 173–191
Chapman, John Jay, 191
Chicago, 3, 54, 95, 96, 249
China, 28, 48, 176
Ciechanowski, Jan, 28, 41
Cincinnati, 41, 217

Citizens Union, 228
Civil Service Commission, 206
Civil War (U.S.), 3, 37, 91, 217, 258
Clark, E. H., 213
Clemenceau, Georges, 212
Cobb, George H., 180
Cocks, William M., 179, 186
Cold War, 7–9, 27, 29, 44, 48, 49, 240
Columbia University, 3, 5, 6, 177, 194, 195, 215, 240, 247
Columbia University Oral History Project, 3, 4, 15–21, 30, 126, 157, 205, 213, 246, 271n9, 272n10–11
Connecticut, 16, 17, 36, 77, 218
Cook, Bee, 218
Cook, Helen, 218
Coolidge, Calvin, 26, 61, 241
Coudert, Frederick, 213
Cowles, Anna Roosevelt, 13, 16, 28–37, 49–52, 61–73, 76–94, 98–101, 104–105, 109–112, 124–131, 147, 275n10, 276n6
Cowles, Margaret Krech, 16, 17, 34, 75–121, 129, 131, 276
Cowles, William Sheffield, Jr., 16, 17, 34, 75–121, 125, 129, 131, 276n3
Cowles, William Sheffield, Sr., 34, 36, 64, 65, 67
Crocker, William Henry, 183
Cuba, 204, 206, 246, 248, 252–254, 256, 258, 261, 263
Cutting, Olivia Murray, 127
Cutting, Robert Bayard, 177
Cutting, Robert Fulton, 177, 191

D
Dark Harbor, 114
Daughters of the American Revolution, 61

INDEX   289

Davenport, Frederick N., 182
Davis, Helen Brooks, 41
Davison, Frederick Trubee, 7, 8, 18, 239–244
Davis, Pauline Sabin, 28, 41
Davis, Richard Harding, 38
Delcassé, Théophile, 196
Democratic Party, 14, 62, 76, 156, 174, 181, 186, 191, 194, 196, 197, 199, 213, 241
Derby, Ethel Roosevelt, 6, 13, 18, 20, 21, 56, 80, 99, 133–140, 144, 151, 152, 157, 164, 199, 229
Derby, Richard, 229
Desmond, Thomas C., 221–223
Dewey, Thomas, 26
Dix, John A., 181
Drum, Hugh, 175, 189
Duff, James A., 168
Duff, Joseph, 168
Dulles, John Foster, 47

E
Education Alliance, 226
Edward VII, King, 86
Eisenhower, Dwight D., 7, 14, 27, 43, 44
Elkhorn ranch, 2
Ellis, Betsy, 31
Ellis, Ralph, 31
Emerson, Guy, 214, 221–223
England, 9, 37, 47, 62–64, 66, 84, 111, 128, 275–276n6

F
Fargo, 248, 264, 266
Farmington, 16, 17, 36, 69, 77, 88
Farr, Barclay Harding, 3, 4, 12, 18, 144, 151, 155–170
Federalist Party, 194
Federal Writers' Project, 3

Ferguson, Homer, 108
Ferguson, Isabella, 130
Ferguson, Robert, 64
Fisher, Fred, 43
Florida, 10, 83, 253, 254
Foraker, Joseph, 196, 216
Formosa, 47, 48, 187
France, 29, 48, 184, 190, 196, 219–221, 240, 241

G
Gardner, Augustus Peabody, 35
Gardner, William Amory, 93, 165
Garrison, Marian Knight, 12, 18, 21
Germany, 47, 57, 187, 189, 212, 219, 221, 241, 242
Girl Scouts, 61
Glaser, Leo, 177
Goddard, Norton, 177
Good Government Clubs, 195, 197, 199, 228
Gracie, Anna Bulloch, 72, 89–91
Gracie, James King, 90
Graham, Katherine, 42
Grant, Ulysses S., 37
Great White Fleet, 57, 167
Grey, Edward, 66, 187, 275n6
Griscom, Lloyd C., 176, 180, 185
Groton School, 93, 103, 104, 156–158, 160, 163, 165, 240
Gruber, Abe, 180
Guiterman, Arthur, 233

H
Hadley, Herbert S., 181
Hagedorn, Hermann, 1–21, 27–30, 61–62, 77–78, 104, 109, 112, 115, 125–126, 134–135, 145, 157, 176, 195, 205, 213, 227, 242, 247

Hagedorn, Mary, 4–6, 8–11, 14–21, 27–30, 61–62, 77–78, 125–126, 134–135, 145, 174, 176, 205, 213, 227, 242, 247
Hall, Frank, 135
Halpin, William, 178
Hamilton, Alexander, 194
Hamner, George, 247
Handy, Thomas, 242
Hanna, Marcus A., 30
Harding, Warren G., 26, 95, 96, 186
Harrison, George, 242, 243
Harvard University, 77, 103, 146, 272n10, 275n10
Hawaii, 241
Hayward, Henry, 254
Hearst, William Randolph, 178, 213
Heintz, Victor de, 218–221
Hibben, John Grier, 168
Hinman, Harvey D., 179
Hitchcock, Helen Sargant, 12, 18, 50, 274n40
Hollister, John, 41
Hoover, Herbert, 241
Hope, Bob, 42
Hopkins, Harry, 119, 120
Hopkinson, 36, 94
Hotchkiss, William H., 234
House, Edward M., 188–190, 212, 220, 221
Howe, Louis, 119
Hughes, Charles Evans, 10, 174, 178–183, 186, 223
Hyde Park, 10, 11, 59–73, 76, 85, 86, 88, 104, 114, 275–276

I
India, 39, 101, 176, 269
Intercollegiate Civic League, 177
Isaacs, Stanley Myer, 19, 225–235, 279
Isbell, Thomas Jefferson, 254, 255

J
Jackson, Andrew, 194
Japan, 57, 120, 121, 176, 243
Java, 176
Jefferson, Thomas, 7, 254
Johnson, Hiram, 95, 183
Johnson, Martin N., 251
Jusserand, Jean Jules, 177

K
Kane, Woodbury, 252, 257, 263, 269
Kean, John, 12
Kennedy, John F., 27
Kennedy, Robert F., 27
Kent, Frank, 40, 41
Kerensky, Alexander, 45, 212, 218, 219
Kerr, Jean, 43
Kipling, Rudyard, 170
Knoblauch, Charles, 257
Kodak, 144

L
La Farge, Florence Lockwood, 177
LaGuardia, Fiorello, 17, 174
Lambert, Alexander, 160
Landon, Agnes, 162
Landon, Cornelia, 162
Landon, Henry Hutton, Jr., 162
Langdon, Jesse, 19, 245–269, 279
League of Nations, 26, 45, 46, 77, 107, 190
League of Women Voters, 149
Lea, Homer, 213
Lewis, John L., 102, 106, 108
Lichnowsky, Karl Max, Prince, 187
Lie, Frederick K., 269
Lincoln, Abraham, 7, 37, 215
Lindsay, Samuel McCune, 9, 10, 19
Lodge, Henry Cabot, 107, 150, 153
Loeb, William, 178, 179, 208

INDEX   291

Longworth, Alice Roosevelt, 4, 5,
    9–12, 15–16, 19, 25–57, 61, 69,
    76–78, 101, 107, 125, 135, 137,
    139, 145, 151, 163, 243, 244,
    273n34, 274–275
Longworth, Nicolas, 26, 27, 41, 53,
    106, 107
Lovett, Robert, 242, 243
Lowden, Frank, 95
Lowell, Abbott Lawrence, 180
Ludlow, Genevieve, 63
Ludlow, William, 63
Lusitania, S.S., 218, 234
Luyster, William E., 244

M
MacArthur, Douglas, 175, 184
Madison Square Garden, 183, 217
Makin, Alice, 41
Makin, Roger, 41
Marshall, George, 242, 243
Martin, Joseph W., 108
Maryland, 249
Massachusetts, 267
McCarthy, Joseph, 29, 41–44
McCloy, Jack, 242, 243
McCook, Philip J., 19, 274n40
McCoy, Frank Ross, 184
McGinty, Billy, 259, 267
McKenna, Mary, 135
McKenna, Rose, 135, 139
McKinley, William, 204, 207,
    226, 228
McLoughlin, Maurice, 212
McMillan, Grace Roosevelt, 137
Menken, S. Stanwood, 213
Messinger, Sadie, 82
Mexico, 183, 184, 188, 189
Milwaukee, 183, 217
Minnesota, 248
Mitchel, John Purroy, 175, 183, 217
Moore, John Bassett, 195

Morison, Elting E., 272n18
Morocco, 196
Mount Rushmore, 1
Munn, Anne Elder, 148
Munn, Charles Allen, 50, 148
Murdock, Victor, 35

N
National Guard, 183, 188, 189, 213
National Park Service (NPS), 5, 6,
    133, 134, 272n16
National Security League, 213
Nevins, Allan, 3, 4, 15, 157, 272n11
New Jersey, 18, 21, 77, 144, 145,
    156, 168, 170
New York, 3, 9, 10, 12, 14, 42, 54,
    60–62, 69, 76, 77, 81, 83, 92,
    97, 104, 110, 124, 125,
    135–137, 144, 151, 162, 168,
    174–180, 183, 185, 186, 188,
    191, 194, 197, 199, 204,
    206–209, 213, 214, 216, 222,
    226–229, 231, 232, 234, 240,
    241, 246, 252, 254, 257,
    267–269, 272n16
Nichols, Courty, 151
Nixon, Richard M., 27, 29
Nixon, Thelma "Pat," 41
North Dakota, 2, 248, 252, 256,
    257, 265

O
Odell, Benjamin, 177, 178, 206
Ohio, 26, 53, 96, 196, 216
O'Laughlin, John Callan, 7, 273n21
Oldgate, *see* Farmington
Old Orchard, 134
O'Neill, William O. "Bucky," 246,
    247, 261
Orange, New Jersey, 18, 21, 77, 103,
    144, 145

O'Rourke, Annie, 135, 136, 139
Oyster Bay, 2, 4, 8, 10, 11, 31, 36,
    59–73, 76, 77, 90, 124, 134,
    137, 139, 151, 156, 158, 164,
    180, 186, 207, 209, 218, 222,
    223, 234, 240, 244

P
Panama, 167
Parker, Alton B., 213
Parker, John W., 259
Paris, 76, 80, 99, 100, 104, 111, 175,
    189, 276n5
Parker, Wayne, 166
Parsons, Herbert, 177, 178, 185,
    208, 215
Patterson, Robert, 242
Peabody, Endicott, 103, 104
Pearl Harbor, 241
Penrose, Boies, 196
Pepper, George Wharton, 213
Pershing, John J., 190,
    191, 243
Persia, 176
Philippines, 176, 266, 267, 269
Phillips, Caroline Drayton, 114
Phillips, Harlan "Bud," 3, 4, 18, 157,
    242, 272n11
Phillips, William, 176
Platt, Thomas Collier, 10, 178,
    191, 206
Plattsburg Camps, 189
Porcellian Club, 118
Potter, Grace, 159, 160
Prendergast, William A., 234
Prentice, Ezra Parmalee, 9, 13, 20
Princeton University, 156, 158, 168
Progressive Party, 8, 21, 70, 71, 77,
    174, 182, 183, 226, 228, 229,
    233, 234
Putnam, Carleton, 7, 275n10

Q
Quigg, Lemuel E., 177, 178,
    203–205, 208
Quigg, Murray T., 20, 203–209,
    271n9, 278

R
Radford, Miriam Ham, 34
Reading, Lord Rufus Isaacs, 191
Reagan, Ronald, 27
Red Cross, 61, 134, 243
Remington, Fredric, 263
Republican Party, 10, 26, 27, 35, 76,
    77, 180, 181, 185, 186, 191,
    194, 196, 199, 204, 206, 208,
    226, 227, 230, 246
Riaño y Gayangos, Juan, 49
Riis, Jacob, 176, 226, 227, 279n1
Rinehart, James Bryce Gordon, 176
Robinson, Corinne Roosevelt, 13–15,
    18, 21, 28, 31, 33, 34, 51, 52,
    61, 68, 76–80, 90–93, 95–96,
    109, 112, 115–117, 126–130,
    144, 145, 148, 151, 154,
    229, 274n40
Robinson, Edwin Arlington, 233
Robinson, Helen Roosevelt, 10, 20,
    34, 59–73, 81, 86, 103, 110, 150
Robinson, Monroe Douglas, 52, 117,
    148, 154
Robinson, Theodore Douglas, 11, 33,
    60, 61, 83, 117
Rochester, 144, 151
Roosevelt, Alice Hathaway Lee, 28, 33
Roosevelt, Anna Curtenius, 60
Roosevelt, Anna Eleanor, 6, 10–13,
    20, 26, 34, 53, 60, 76, 77, 81,
    86, 99, 103, 109, 110, 113,
    123–131, 134, 135, 138, 139,
    144, 150, 152, 158, 159, 164,
    167, 168, 184, 208, 235, 244

Roosevelt, Anna Hall, 124
Roosevelt, Archibald, 60, 99, 137, 138, 160, 163
Roosevelt, Belle Willard, 99
Roosevelt, Dorothy Quincy, 114
Roosevelt, Edith Carow, 2, 11, 28, 31, 62, 69, 73, 77, 98, 109, 126, 129, 130, 134, 137, 138, 152, 158, 161, 164, 235, 276n8
Roosevelt, Eleanor Butler, 6, 18, 20, 133–140, 277
Roosevelt, Elizabeth Riley, 84
Roosevelt, Elliott Bulloch, 10, 12, 38, 39, 62, 78, 99, 100, 115, 124, 275n10
Roosevelt, Emlen, 136
Roosevelt, Franklin Delano, 6, 8, 11, 20, 26, 34, 47, 53, 60, 62, 76, 77, 86, 93, 99, 103, 104, 107–109, 112–115, 118–121, 124, 131, 134, 188, 241
Roosevelt, Gracie Hall, 99, 110, 112
Roosevelt, Helen Astor, 62, 84
Roosevelt, James Roosevelt "Rosy," 60–62, 76, 78, 81, 82, 84–87
Roosevelt, James Roosevelt "Tadd," 10, 78, 81, 82, 87, 88
Roosevelt, Kermit, 3, 4, 56, 60, 93, 99–101, 144, 151, 155–158, 160–165, 167
Roosevelt, Martha Bulloch, 32, 62, 72, 88, 276n6
Roosevelt, Philip James, 161
Roosevelt, Quentin, 137, 152, 163, 240, 243, 244
Roosevelt, Robert Barnhill, 115
Roosevelt, Theodore (president), 1–4, 6–16, 25, 27, 34, 35, 37, 47, 57, 60–62, 65, 70, 76–79, 87, 100, 115, 119, 124, 126, 130, 131, 134–138, 140, 144, 145, 149, 151, 152, 154, 156, 157, 160, 161, 163, 166–170, 174–177, 179–181, 185, 186, 188–190, 194, 195, 204–209, 212–216, 218, 219, 221, 222, 226–229, 231–235, 239–244, 246–248, 251, 253, 256, 257, 260–265, 272n9, 272n10, 275n10, 276n6, 278n3, 279n3, 279n5
Roosevelt, Theodore, Jr., 60, 136, 158, 241
Roosevelt, Theodore, Sr., 32, 60, 71, 79, 89, 91
Roosevelt, Sara Delano, 13, 76, 77, 85, 104, 114
Roosevelt Non-Partisan League, 16, 221
Root, Elihu, 10, 175, 182, 184, 185, 190, 200, 219, 242, 243
Rough Riders, 14, 19, 64, 149, 204, 206, 228, 245–269
Rush, Tom, 197
Russia, 8, 44, 45, 48, 176, 184, 189, 212, 218–221, 226
Russian revolution, 212
Russo-Japanese War, 176

S

Sagamore Hill, 2–4, 6, 13, 30, 31, 56, 133–140, 151, 152, 156–158, 163, 166, 180, 181, 184, 218, 223, 235, 241, 243
St. Louis, 54
San Antonio, 251–256
San Francisco, 138, 168, 176
San Juan Heights, Cuba, 14, 240, 246
Sanders, Archie, 178–180, 182
Savacool, William, 8, 9, 13, 21, 57
Scarth, Helen, 93, 94
Schurz, Carl, 217
Scotland, 64
Scott, Douglas, 19, 246, 247

Selmes, Martha "Patty," 130
Sherman, James S., 180
Sibley, Georgiana Farr, 12, 21, 143–154, 274n40, 277
Sibley, Harper, 144, 151
Simonds, Frank H., 178, 179, 182
Simpson, Wallis, 34
Smith, Alfred E., 188, 194
Somervell, Brehon, 242
South Dakota, 177, 256
Souvestre, Marie, 80, 111
Soviet Union, 27, 226
Spaak, Paul Henri, 187
Spanish-American War, 190, 228, 246
Spencer, Earl Winfield, 34
Starr, Elizabeth Parrish, 117
Starr, Louis M., 4, 21, 195, 272n9, 272n11
Stern, Henry Root, 21, 193–201, 278
Stevens, Frederick C., 182, 186
Stevens, F. W., 178
Stimson, Henry L., 8, 181, 213, 241–243
Storer, Bellamy, 53
Straus, Oscar, 234
Street, Julian, 217
Strong, William L., 206, 228
Sturm, Paulina Longworth, 51
Sullivan, Mark, 180–182
Sweeny, Mary, 136

T
Taft, Helen "Nellie," 35
Taft, Martha Bowers, 102
Taft, Robert A., 187
Taft, William Howard, 10, 35, 36, 57, 168, 174, 175, 179–182, 185–188, 190, 233, 234, 241
Tammany Hall, 174, 194, 197, 226, 278n1
Tardieu, Andre, 191

Tennessee Coal and Iron, Co., 188
Theodore Roosevelt Association, 15
Theodore Roosevelt Birthplace, 6, 16–21, 272n12, 272n14, 273n30, 274n35, 274n36, 274n42
Tiffany, William, 262
Tilden, Samuel, 194
Tilney, Augusta Munn, 12, 18, 21
Titanic, HMS, 212
Truman, Harry S., 124, 187
Tubridy, Bridget, 136
Tuttle, Arthur, 247

U
United Nations, 44–46, 126, 190
U.S. Steel, 188

V
Vatican II Council, 144
Versailles, Treaty of, 26, 27, 76
Vietnam, 29, 44, 48
Villard, Oswald Garrison, 175, 178, 185, 191
Von Steuben, Freidrich, 217

W
Wadsworth, James W. Jr., 178
Wagner, Charles, 111
Wallach, Sidney, 272n10
Ward, Mary Augusta, 111
Washington, Booker T., 71, 233
Washington, DC, 12, 26, 30, 32, 36, 50, 53, 55, 71, 102, 105–108, 126, 128, 134, 137–139, 151, 163, 164, 168, 174, 177, 178, 184, 195, 207, 208, 214, 215, 220, 228, 233, 241, 242, 248–253, 257, 265, 266

Washington, George, 215
Watergate, 27
Welch, Joseph, 43
Welling, Richard, 199
Wells, David, 63
Wheeler, Benjamin Ide, 138
White House, 4, 26, 27, 34, 35, 43, 53, 76, 81, 120, 124, 126, 129, 130, 134, 139, 151, 156, 163, 164, 166, 167, 174, 179, 181, 195, 208, 212, 215, 216
Whitney, George, 118
Wilcox, William R., 183
Wilhelm II, Kaiser, 9, 186, 187, 196, 200
Willard, Erskine, 151
Wilson, Woodrow, 8, 9, 26, 45–47, 107, 156, 168–170, 175, 184–186, 188–190, 212, 214, 215, 218–222, 234, 244
Wimbledon, 212
Wood, Henry Wise, 213
Wood, Leonard, 61, 95, 184, 190, 214, 240, 254
World War I, 9, 14, 57, 76, 103, 104, 106, 107, 118, 175, 183, 187, 188, 194, 212, 213, 218, 266
World War II, 7–9, 27, 57, 76, 144, 174, 188, 241–243

X

Xerox, 144

Y

Yale University, 77, 194, 212, 257
Yat-Sen, Sun, 213

GPSR Compliance

The European Union's (EU) General Product Safety Regulation (GPSR) is a set of rules that requires consumer products to be safe and our obligations to ensure this.

If you have any concerns about our products, you can contact us on

ProductSafety@springernature.com

In case Publisher is established outside the EU, the EU authorized representative is:

Springer Nature Customer Service Center GmbH
Europaplatz 3
69115 Heidelberg, Germany

www.ingramcontent.com/pod-product-compliance
Lightning Source LLC
LaVergne TN
LVHW020341260326
834688LV00045B/1473

GPSR Compliance
The European Union's (EU) General Product Safety Regulation (GPSR) is a set of rules that requires consumer products to be safe and our obligations to ensure this.

If you have any concerns about our products, you can contact us on

ProductSafety@springernature.com

In case Publisher is established outside the EU, the EU authorized representative is:

Springer Nature Customer Service Center GmbH
Europaplatz 3
69115 Heidelberg, Germany

www.ingramcontent.com/pod-product-compliance
Lightning Source LLC
LaVergne TN
LVHW020326260326
834688LV00037B/885